I0029744

The Geo-Politics of the City

Edited by Stephen Barber

((forumpress

Forum Press
The Global Policy Institute
London Metropolitan University
31 Jewry Street
London, EC3N 2EY

www.global-policy.com

First published 2007

ISBN: 978-0-9554975-2-0   (paperback)

Contents

Foreword   v
Peter Jay

Contributors   xi

Acknowledgments   xvii

About the Global Policy Institute   xviii

1   **The Geo-Political Economy of the City**   1
    Stephen Barber

2   **City of London – Global Village: Understanding the**   19
    Square Mile in a Post-industrial World Economy
    Kathy Pain

3   **The City and the End of Geographical Proximity**   39
    David Lascelles

4   **London as a Global City**   55
    Sam Whimster

iii

5 Geo-Politics, the 'War on Terror' and the   93
   Competitiveness of the City of London
   Richard Woodward

6 European Supra-National Bonds: What (Political)   123
   Risks Lie Ahead?
   Lauren Phillips

7 Managing Chaos: An Examination of FX Policy   143
   in the UK from Bretton Woods to Tiger Woods
   Alex Brassey

8 Is the Global Economy Sustainable?   165
   Güler Aras & David Crowther

9 India and China: Emergence of the Elephant   195
   and the Dragon
   Swati Raju

10 Challenges to the City in a Globalised World   225
   Andreas Prindl

Foreword

Peter Jay

This is a most useful book. It addresses a most interesting question at a most apt moment; what can and should be the future of the City of London? It addresses it in all of its bearing, political, economic, financial, commercial, technological, ideological, security, ethical and many others. And it addresses it through the pens of scholars and thinkers whose reputations claim our respect, all brought together under the deft baton of an editor who from long experience as commentator and analyst knows his subject and knows how to tell a fascinating story.

For three hundred years at least the City of London – commonly and significantly "the City" in most mouths – has embodied, represented and transmitted the global outlook, political and commercial, which has informed British policy and performance throughout an era that in the eighteenth century began the transformation of economic growth worldwide, in the nineteenth century played hegemon to the first truly global trading and monetary system, in the twentieth century survived the direst threats yet and through it all built and then released an empire. But perpetually it has seemed under threat.

When I was a child I watched from the heights of Hampstead as the bombs fell and the City burned. Now I sit in board meetings discussing "business continuity", where ever more frightful disruptions of the capital's financial life are contemplated by solemn security experts and planned for by busy executives. As Housman did not quite write, then 'twas Hitler, now 'tis Islam (or a deformed bit of it).

Today, the threats – real or supposed – are legion; and physical ones are probably in the long run the least serious. As Richard Woodward shrewdly observes in these pages:

> A far greater danger…is posed by an overzealous reaction that appreciably raises the costs of transacting business in the City, deters skilled labour by demonising foreigners and minority groups, undermines innovation, and detracts from more pressing issues such as the dilapidated transport infrastructure.

Just as Wall Street and the US economy long ago shrugged off the slight macro-damage of 9/11, so the City as it has often done before has yet again demonstrated that physical assaults on its real estate and its personnel cannot quench the animal spirits which fuel the furnaces of such a widely needed financial centre. The threats, which could be mortal, are of quite a different character, including, as Woodward fears the self-inflicted damage of ejecting the international baby rather than the criminal bathwater.

Competitiveness is the air which the City, like all other commercial eco-systems, breathes. Its chemistry is well analysed in these pages. To compete, a financial centre must be the best place, or among the best places, to do business. Language, law, justice, communications, the right kind of man- and woman-power and the things that attract those men and women are the fundamentals. All the rest – money, technology, management, systems – you can buy.

What, for me, is not a threat at all is the rise of great economies in other parts of the world. In the 'fifties it was America and the dollar, in the 'sixties Germany, in the 'seventies Japan, in the 'eighties and 'nineties "Asia"; and now it is China and perhaps India. But for those who provide financial services competitively the growth of the GNPs of other economies' and the expansion of markets worldwide are opportunities to do more business; and, while staying competitive requires constant vigilance and improvement, it poses no threat except to those who wish to lie all day on feather beds.

The greatest potential threat to the City is always Westminster and Whitehall. Mortal damage can indeed be done there, if taxes and regulations create an environment in which the world's animal spirits no longer wish to do business. This is not a matter of the kind of specific subsidies and privileges for which special-interest lobbies campaign (farmers and film-makers spring to mind), but rather of abstaining in general from the kind of disproportionate response to the occasional scandal and excess which has saddled New York and the rest of the US with Sarbanes-Oxley.

Of course, as Güler Aras & David Crowther argue here, proper corporate social responsibility, better governance, sharper risk management and ever greater transparency are necessary and important, not only for the success, but also for public understanding and acceptance of the value and legitimacy of the business sector. But, except in Marxist ideology, the legitimacy of business does not require its extinction. Likewise, the tax system, however much it may recognise a goal of distributive justice in society, including both poverty relief and greater equality, must still allow necessary incentives to call forth the effort, enterprise and invention required for economic performance.

But there is another political threat, less direct but potentially more insidious than Westminster and Whitehall; and that is the kind of political reaction to the challenges and changes stemming from globalisation which unleashes a revived surge of protectionism, nationalism and racism such as destroyed the last great pre-1914 globalisation and visited upon mankind the worst half-century in modern history.

One does not need to suppose a return to the horrors of 1914 to 1945 (and much later for those in, for example, eastern Europe and China) in order to take seriously the possibility of a new politics based on fear of Chinese economic strength, fear of cheap imports and cheap labour for outsourced employment, fear of and hostility to migrant labour and crude appeals to national and ethnic identities which still command atavistic loyalties and still stir deep emotions. Politically weak governments, trying to guard their right flank from outright racism and their left-flank from outright protectionism, may be tempted to play up their own versions of both a protectionist and a racist strategy, i.e. some form of economic and maybe even political nationalism.

One need only scan the tabloid universe in Britain today to understand the danger. It is idle and false to pretend that globalisation – the progressive integration of mankind, his economy, his culture and society into an ever more unified community – is irreversible and proof against such reactions.

If the political will is there for such a retreat into ethnically defined nationalism, with or without quasi-Marxist interpretations of the global economy, then no amount of new technology will stop it. The technology will simply be used for that new, or resurrected, political agenda. Such a political reflex would strike at the roots of the City and, of course, at the roots of many other things even more profoundly important than the City – our freedoms, our prosperity and our humanity.

Much, indeed, will depend on Europe, both the place and the institution. In these matters Europe frequently rides two horses: a "grey" and a black.

The "grey" is international and outward-looking in spirit, inclusive in membership, liberal in trade and economic matters, collaborative in external affairs, global in consciousness, multi-cultural in character, lukewarm and relaxed about "identity". The black is the opposite, concerned to "build Europe", an embryo nation in itself, looking in to that construction more than out from it – and then in a spirit of apprehension (of China) or rivalry (against the US) rather than of global partnership – anxious to define ultimate borders and to put limits to membership, preferring "deepening" to broadening, a *pouvoir* rather than an *espace*, autarkic, protectionist and interventionist in its economic reflexes.

Much rides for the City, as well as for so much else, on the resolution of the tension between these horses. The rider may simply fall or one horse may kick over the traces and be released. The acid tests may come over agricultural protection in the Doha round, over the treatment of cheap imports from and outsourcing to Asia, over Europe's response to inward migration from the south and east, over Turkey's application for membership of the EU, over the construction of a single foreign and security policy or perhaps over the constitution.

Europe may look out in hope and compete and welcome and beckon and tolerate and collaborate on international matters when it can. Or, in fear, it may look in and withdraw and exclude and reject and condemn and forge a central command. When, for example, I hear the arguments that Turkey is not Europe and Turks are not Europeans, I hear the distant crunch of jackboots.

A Europe harnessed to the "grey" would be an immensely sustaining and liberating political and economic environment for the City; and in it the City might be expected to excel and to confer great benefits on Europe as a world class, perhaps the world class, place to do business.

Harnessed to the black horse it could be otherwise. Fortress Europe would become more important, the global horizons less. More would depend on political jockeying at the European centre, in Brussels, less on market forces and global markets. Regional prowess would outweigh global potential. Would London be officially endorsed as a "champion" and would it thrive on the forced-feeding and official favour for which it might have to compete in a political marketplace?

These are perhaps natural reasons why the City's money has for so long been on the "grey". But, however that may play out, all participants in the arguments, in Europe and beyond, will I believe find pertinent and reliable material in this excellent anthology; and I allow myself the personal dream that it may help the "grey" past the winning post, as well as reinforcing the City's other preparations for the exciting future which, as ever, confronts it.

Contributors

Güler Aras is Professor of Finance and Director of the Graduate School at the Yildiz Technical University, Istanbul. She received a PhD in Banking and Economy with high honour and previously obtained her MBA and bachelor degrees also with first rank. Güler has taught corporate finance at undergraduate, graduate and doctorate level. She serves as visiting professor at a number of universities and as adviser to a numerous government bodies. She is the recipient of best scientific work award of Association of Institutional Investors Board in Turkey and is a founder and member of various associations and research centres. She is also a member of several international editorial and advisory boards. Güler Aras is the author of 5 books and has contributed over 100 articles to academic, business and professional journals and magazines and to edited book collections. She has also spoken extensively at conferences and seminars and has acted as a consultant to a wide range of government and commercial organisations. Her research focuses on financial economy and financial markets with particular emphasis on the relationship between corporate social responsibility and a firm's financial performance.

Stephen Barber is Senior Research Fellow at the Global Policy Institute, London Metropolitan University where he is Head of the City of London and Political Economy Programme. Previously, he was Research Director of the University's European Research Forum, which he joined in 2004 upon completion of his PhD. A frequent contributor to the financial press he has spent thirteen years working in the City of London's financial industry most recently as Head of Research for the stockbroker Talos Securities. He has published two previous books: *Political Strategy: modern politics in contemporary Britain* and *The City in Europe and the World.*

Alex Brassey, who has 'led a very interesting life' according to Milton Friedman, is Managing Partner of SFI, a financial engineering consultancy, Managing Director of Liverpool Residential Ltd, Litigation Consultant to Cramer Pelmont Solicitors, Senior Partner of The Schools Enterprise Partnership and a North London School Teacher. He is formerly an Assistant Vice-President of Citibank, Director of Lehman Brothers and Head of Yen trading at Sumitomo Mitsui Banking Corporation. He is a qualified fund manager, teacher and holds an BSc (Hons) in Finance and Economics from Manchester University, an MA in Philosophy from Kings College London and is currently completing a Doctorate in Psychology at the Institute of Education. He is a husband and also a Dad of three lovely girls.

David Crowther is Professor of Corporate Social Responsibility at De Montfort University and a qualified accountant who worked as an accountant, systems specialist and general manager in local government, industry and commerce for 20 years. After a number of years in the financial services sector, including a spell in which he set up and ran a store credit card scheme, he decided to leave the business world and become an academic. In 1994 he joined Aston University as a lecturer in accounting and there obtained a PhD in 1999 for research into corporate social performance and reporting before leaving to join the University of North London. David is the author of 18 books and has also contributed several hundred articles to academic, business and professional journals and to edited book collections. He has spoken widely at conferences and seminars and acted as a consultant to a wide range of government, professional and commercial organisations. His research is into corporate social responsibility with a particular emphasis on the relationship between social, environmental and financial performance.

Peter Jay is best known as the former Ambassador to Washington and later Economics Editor at the BBC. Educated at Oxford and a veteran of the Royal Navy, Peter served for six years in the British Treasury before joining the Times as Economics Editor, during which time he also presented the television news programme *Weekend World*. After a decade at the paper, he was appointed UK Ambassador to the United States, where he served from 1977-79. Peter's book the *Wealth of Man* is an insightful, stirring account of man's pursuit of wealth from caveman to cyberspace and spans the entire globe. It has received recognition as a masterpiece of historical, economic, scientific and cultural synthesis. He is a frequent speaker at summits and conferences around the world.

David Lascelles is co-director of the Centre for the Study of Financial Innovation, an independent City of London think tank sponsored by leading banks and financial institutions to research the future of financial services. Competition among financial centres is one of his central interests. In 2004, he conducted a survey for the London Corporation on the City's competitiveness. David was previously with the *Financial Times*, where he held several key positions including Banking Editor and New York bureau chief. He is now a non-executive director of Arbuthnot Banking Group, a diversified financial services company, and the author of a recent book about the evolution of retail banking: *Other people's money*.

Kathy Pain is Research Fellow at The Young Foundation London and an Associate Research Fellow in the Globalisation and World Cities (GaWC) Study Group in the Department of Geography at Loughborough University. She is a professional Town Planner with a PhD in Geography from the University of Reading, where she investigated government urban and housing policy. She is a Corporate Member of the Royal Town Planning Institute and a Fellow of the Royal Geographical Society. She has held academic appointments at the University of Birmingham and the Open University. Her research has been widely disseminated to business and government agencies and included consultancy to the UK Treasury on 'The Euro and London-Frankfurt Relations,' February 2002, for the Government's fourth economic test for UK entry to EMU (the competitive position of the UK financial services industry and the City's wholesale markets). With an impressive publication record, Kathy has written on the subject of global city relations, the advanced service economy, sustainable development and European and UK policy.

Lauren Phillips is Research Fellow at the Overseas Development Institute in London, where she works on issues of finance for development. She received her PhD from the London School of Economics in International Political Economy. Her research explored the relationship between financial market performance and political risk in emerging market countries, and in particular in Brazil and Mexico. She received her Masters and undergraduate degrees from Stanford University. She has professional experience working in the financial sector on both Wall Street and in the City of London. Originally from the Washington DC area, Lauren currently lives in Rome with her partner.

Andreas Prindl was born in Illinois and studied modern languages at Princeton, which awarded him a BA *magna cum laude* in 1961. In 1964 he received a PhD in International Economics from the University of Kentucky and joined Morgan

Guaranty Trust Company of New York. Andy served for Morgan in New York, Frankfurt, in London as head of International Management, in Tokyo as General Manager for Japan and Korea, in London again as CEO of Saudi International Bank (a Morgan joint-venture) and Vice President of Mergers and Acquisitions. In 1984 he joined the Nomura group to set up Nomura Bank International, of which he was Managing Director and then Chairman until his retirement. He has strong interests in financial services education, and was President of the Chartered Institute of Bankers and the Association of Corporate Treasurers, first Chairman of the Banking Industry Training and Development Council, and Provost of Gresham College. He worked closely with the Know-How Fund over many years to help set up banking schools throughout the former Soviet Union. For these contributions Queen Elizabeth II appointed him CBE and City University granted him an Hon DSc. Andy has written many articles and 9 books, mostly about financial markets and ethical conflicts therein, but recently has engaged on a series of cultural anthologies about special places: *A Companion to Lucca* in 2000, *A Companion to Angouleme and the Angoumois* in 2005, and the forthcoming *Companion to Fauquier County Virginia*. His books have been translated into six languages. He is a Member of Council of Lloyds, the Master of the Worshipful Company of Musicians (the first American to be Master of a City company), a Liveryman of the Worshipful Company of World Traders, a Freeman of the Guild of International Bankers and a Governor of the Yehudi Menuhin School. Besides classical music, Andy's other interests are Asian history and art – he is an avid collector of early Chinese ceramics – and his four Cornish grandchildren. He agrees with Nietzsche that 'without music, life would be a mistake.'

Swati Raju is Lecturer in Microeconomics, Financial Economics and Monetary Economics at the University of Mumbai. While her professional career has almost entirely been spent at Mumbai, she also enjoyed a brief stint as Assistant Professor with the Indian Institute of Technology, Bombay. Her teaching and research interests focus on different aspects of the Indian economy and include issues in public finance such as sustainability of deficits, relation of fiscal deficits with macroeconomic variables, the finance-growth inter-relationship and regional disparities in India. She has published widely and delivered numerous papers on these topics including as guest lecturer for the Programme on Capital Markets at the Bombay Stock Exchange.

Sam Whimster is Reader in Sociology at London Metropolitan University and Deputy Director of the Global Policy Institute. He has taught at the University of Leipzig and held research fellowships at the universities of Heidelberg, Tübingen and Munich. He is the editor of the journal *Max Weber Studies*. He has published numerous books including *Global Finance and Urban Living*, co-edited with Leslie Budd (Routledge, 1992) and most recently, *Understanding Weber* (Routledge, 2007).

Richard Woodward is lecturer in political economy at the University of Hull. His research interests include the City of London, the Organisation for Economic Cooperation and Development (OECD), offshore financial centres, financial crime, and small island economies. He has written extensively on the OECD and European Union harmful tax competition initiatives and the governance of financial markets. His next book *OECD: The Forgotten Institution of Global Governance* will be published by Routledge in 2008.

Acknowledgements

Many people have been supportive in the process of producing this book of essays, not least the authors themselves who once again have helped to produce a diverse and thought-provoking collection. I would also like to thank Rhydian Peters of GreenEgg.net who designed the cover, Priska Preisinger, Steve Haysom, Maria Barber once again for her superb editorial assistance and Stephen Haseler, Director of the Global Policy Institute.

About the Global Policy Institute

The Global Policy Institute at London Metropolitan University was launched in 2006 and brings together academics from the social sciences and business disciplines to analyse the dynamics of globalisation and formulate policy solutions. Forum Press, created by the Institute's forerunner the European Research Forum, is the GPI's publisher. For more information about the Institute's activities, seminars, papers and publications, visit the website at: www.global-policy.com.

The City in Europe and the World (2005)

Edited by Stephen Barber

Foreword by Peter Mandelson

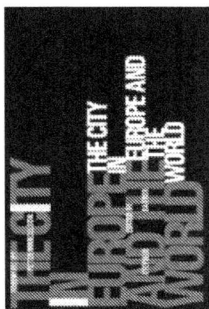

This collection of essays examines the relationship between the City of London's financial markets, politics, government, and Europe. Covering topics such as the political economy of the City, the Lisbon strategy, the Financial Services Action Plan (FSAP), the euro, relations between the City and party politics, PFI, foreign exchange, regulation, ethics, financial exclusion, European expansion, globalisation and the future of the City in Europe, the book addresses some of the major issues facing today's political economy.

Contributions from: Graham Bishop, Alex Brassey, Mario Cerrato, Patrick Diamond, Brendan Donnelly, Howard Flight, Alexandra Forter, Chris Huhne, Mario Jung, Angela Knight, Agnes Oestrich, Giancarlo Perasso, Alice Rogers, Sanjiv Sachdev, L.V. Spagnolo, Richard Woodward.

"The City was slow to wake up to the implications of the European single financial market, and even now the impact is not well understood. These essays help to describe the way the City is adapting to the sometimes conflicting pressures of globalization and the EU. It is a fascinating story."
Sir Howard Davies

"This book is a compendium of essays about the City's future by a variety of academics, analysts and politicians... Its broad theme is that the City is bigger than the EU: it taps into markets that reach far beyond the confines of Europe and the US"
David Lascelles, *Financial World*

"The City has always faced intense pressures, but the forces of globalisation and the EU are impacting it in ways not fully understood. In this book of essays, leaders in the fields of politics, economics and academia address these issues."
Securities & Investment Review

Chapter 1

The Geo-Political Economy of the City

Stephen Barber

Geo-politics of the twenty first century is characterised (or caricatured) by a shift in power away from the confined geographic states of the past. The process, which arguably the City of London led at its conception, has evolved into a global system of trade and capital flows. This globalisation has eroded the traditional power of sovereign states, replacing political power, in places, with the power of the market. Such power means that emerging economies, in China, India and elsewhere, can begin to compete with established financial centres such as the City and New York just as they can compete in manufacturing or outsourcing. But not only is the process of globalisation a long established trend, it is also less predictable in its outcomes than might be suggested by those who fear its consequences.

What we today describe as globalisation has continued a centuries old process of increasing interdependence between countries and economies. Over centuries human migration, trading routes, communication technologies, missionaries, adventurers, colonisers, tourists have all globalised the world. Only today it is happening faster than ever and, some fear, beyond our control. This raises questions about the City of London's ability, with its vast financial services industry, to continue to prosper in the new geo-political world. Some fear that neither the City nor our Western economies generally can compete adequately in the face of the new economic environment to come.

There are naturally challenges to the primacy of the City as economies in China and India move toward their potential. Swati Raju analyses the growth of these nations in chapter nine. Some in the West often appear paranoid, even xenophobic, about the menace these new emerging economies (especially China) pose to its way of life; a threat to welfare politics or an argument to adopt tax lean neo-liberal economics. They need not be. The idea that "in today's economic world a similar security risk [to the Soviet Union build-up of SS20 rockets] has developed with China's emergence as an economic power"[1] is almost unhinged paranoia. There are genuine concerns about intellectual property rights, the value of the Chinese currency and issues of child and poverty labour[2] which the international community must tackle. But some of the arguments emanating from Europe and the United States concern threats to our comfortable standard of living which might never arise and policy prescriptions which would be counterproductive.

China and India may in time develop sophisticated financial services sectors, but it is by no means inevitable. Indeed, Lyman Miller of the Hoover Institution has argued that "China is nowhere close to becoming a world financial centre, nor is the Renmimbi…likely to establish itself as the standard of foreign exchange anytime soon."[3] Nevertheless, the capitalist outpost Hong Kong has continued to prosper since British handover in 1997 and the 9% fall in the Shanghai Composite Index in February 2007 had repercussions across the world with stock markets in Europe, Japan and the USA following suit. But, while India has a developed democracy, perhaps the strongest impediment to Chinese global investment services is the Leninist authorities which remain in control of the country's every affair. Development of serious open market driven industries requires "a network of independent processes of scrutiny and accountability, undertaken by people in multiple centres of power and backed by rights and private property. A democratic election system is but the coping stone of this structure."[4]

Nevertheless, the idea that London requires tariffs and regulations to protect against this challenge represents not only near mercantile economic thinking but also a lack of appreciation for the recent history of the sector. Furthermore, despite its supposed menace to European and North American business, and, as Alex Brassey examines, financing the burgeoning US trade deficit, China has done little more than manufacture products on behalf of profitable Western companies – albeit on a huge scale. As Will Hutton has argued, "manufacturing represents only a small proportion of the value in any good – there is invention, design, financing, marketing, transporting, warehousing, advertising – and even then wage costs are not decisive. A Chinese worker may earn 4% of the wage of an American or British worker, but is only 4% as productive."[5] After all, it is innovation which fuels economic progress and transactions which feed growth. And not only does this remain the preserve of the developed economic world, but is also predominantly in the service sector of which financial services is perhaps the most significant part.

The creation of transactions is important and when one occurs – a sale of equities from one party to another as much as a sale of raw materials, energy, food or services – one party does not need to gain at the expense of the other (whichever that might be). Someone somewhere does not have to be a loser for a profit to be taken on the stockmarket; lenders and borrowers alike gain from credit deals; the provider and the recipient of a service can profit from the arrangement. Both parties can benefit from transactions and this is because the size of the world economy is not static or restricted. Economic growth allows for both parties to profit and it is the very creation of transactions which leads to growth. As Trade Commissioner, Peter Mandelson, put it, speaking at the launch of the Global Policy Institute, "China is not stealing our jobs. In fact, for every job that Europe has lost to economic change in the last two decades it has created a new one in more competitive parts of the economy thanks to growing internal and external trade...A hundred million new jobs in the developing world have not cost Europe jobs or hurt Europe economically on aggregate. In fact the opposite is true – they've made us more competitive, they've lowered our input costs and they've reduced prices for consumers. They've depressed interest rates and lowered inflation. And we are better off."[6] A view echoed by the libertarian writer Nick Gillespie who points out that not only "has the job market kept pace with massive increases in the labour supply, it has done so by creating more managerial and specialised professional jobs."[7] Mandelson and Gillespie may ignore the social cost of sustaining cheap labour (by our standards at least) to achieve some of these conditions but it stands to reason that economic growth, particularly in the financial services sector, even with the emergence of new financial centres, will benefit both these emerging world economies (including the workers within them) and the established centres of the City and New York. Indeed, if the likes of China have aspirations to develop anything close to a competitive financial services industry comparable to the City, exploiting cheap labour will never be as powerful as innovative product design and expertise.

Far from seeing China, and to a lesser extent India, as simply a threat, the City has come to view their growth as an opportunity as is made clear in a 2006 publication, *Scenarios for India and China 2015: implications for the City of London*. Hong Kong has been successful in attracting Chinese international listings but increasing numbers are now coming to London's

Alternative Investment Market (AIM). The report further identifies specific opportunities in capital markets and financing (including debt and equity, and project financing), wealth management and consultancy, advisory and regulatory services drawing upon the vast expertise available in London. And while it recognises the threat that Chinese growth might disrupt world trade, especially given fierce competition for raw materials, it foresees "ways in which the City can act as an 'honest broker' and provide informal as well as formal links across the cultural divide, to reduce the likelihood of potential disruption threatening global stability".[8] The report might be criticised for its optimism, but it is difficult to argue with its conclusion that the City must engage with these growing economies rather than shrinking from the challenge fearing global competition.

The notion that protectionism would help the City in the face of perceived competition requires addressing for it ignores both the source of business transacted in the square mile as well as the regulatory history of the financial services sector. Today, the City of London is the most international of all world financial centres. The London Stock Exchange is the most international of all bourses, with over 630 companies from at least 56 countries admitted to trading and more than 1,600 companies in the Main Market, with a value of some £4,300 billion ($7,654 billion). Since launch in 1995, The LSE's Alternative Investment Market has become a truly global market, particularly for international companies raising earlier stage capital. Some 2,300 companies have been admitted to the market, raising more than £16 billion ($28 billion), contributing to London's 40% share of the global foreign equity market. It is not only in equities that the Square Mile leads. Some 70% of all Eurobonds, 43% of over the counter derivatives and 32% of global foreign exchange turnover passes through London. The City is the largest single market for international bank lending (with a 20% share) and is the leading market for international insurance. It even dominates environmental markets, handling 80% of the $8bn EU Emissions Trading Scheme. Some 255 foreign banks are based in London and three quarters of Fortune 500 companies have offices there.[9]

In another report commissioned for the City of London in 2006, Oxford Economic Forecasting highlighted the importance of the financial services industry to the UK economy, reporting that London contributes as much as 19% of government revenues (from 12.5% of the population) and that financial and business services employ about a third of the city's workers. They continue:

> Fundamental to London's place in the UK economy, however, is maintaining the competitiveness of London in an international, rather than just a national, context. Judged in terms of success in exporting compared with other key economies, the UK's financial services industry is the most competitive part of the UK service economy...Such a positive outlook would be at risk, however, if physical constraints were to threaten the underlying competitiveness of London's internationally successful financial and business service companies.[10]

Placing barriers to participation would only harm the considerable business that has been established over the course of, not so much over the centuries since the Bank of England was formed in 1694 (to fund the Nine Years War against France) or John Castaing established the Stock Exchange at Jonathan's Coffee House in 1697 (appropriately share trading began in London to finance the Muscovy Company's attempt to reach China and the East India Company voyage to India) but rather since 'Big Bang' de-regulation in 1986.

And to understand why this is the case it must be appreciated that this is not the first time that the City has faced the threat of competition. After all, New York, now the biggest financial centre in the world,[11] was once quite subordinate to London. Throughout the eighteenth and nineteenth centuries, the City provided for the needs of what was rapidly becoming an interdependent global economy. Expanding empire, world trade and transport meant that a form of globalisation was in evidence even then. The City financed wars and was the (only) gateway to the international capital market for governments and monarchs. But it was the ravages of the Great War which saw New York supplant London as the pre-eminent world financial centre. After all, the great banks of the City had financed German and other 'enemy' countries' trade for many years in the lead up to conflict and faced devastation upon hostilities. While there were optimistic signs throughout the 1920s and 1930s, the Second World War was truly disastrous for London, wrecking commerce, infrastructure and empire and ensuring the dominance of the Dollar over the Pound as the world currency.

Indeed, it was not until the 1960s and US President J. F Kennedy's protectionist imposition of taxes on foreign borrowing in the capital market[12] that London received a much needed boost, leading to the relocation of capital and Eurobond markets to the City. But it was during the 1980s that the financial hub that so confidently strides the world market as we know it today was reborn. The 1979 abolition of exchange controls was the opening salvo[13] which led rapidly to an increase in overseas assets, a growth in international fund management, more foreign company listings, and the creation of bulldog bonds.[14] In 1983 fixed commissions and the separation between brokers and market makers were abolished together with an easing of the restrictions on ownership of member firms of the stock exchange. In 1986, Big Bang finally removed restrictive working practices and protectionism in the City. It changed the square mile from a relaxed, closed, class ridden, gentlemen's club into a vibrant, open, meritocratic market place servicing the world. At the twentieth anniversary of Big Bang, the Lord Mayor of London, David Brewer, echoed the widely held view that "without Big Bang, the City is very unlikely to have achieved today's prominent position".[15] Over the period, share trading grew by fifteen times and derivatives trading increased fifty nine fold.[16] The growth of the industry is illustrated nowhere clearer than in the FTSE 100 index of

7

leading quoted British companies by market capitalisation. When launched in January 1984 at 1000 points, the FTSE 100 was valued at £92bn. Twenty three years later, having fallen from its 1999 peak of almost 7000 points to around 6300, the top three companies in the index, Royal Dutch Shell, BP and HSBC, *each* had a market capitalisation greater than that figure.[17]

The knock-on effect of success in the City's financial services, however, was to be tougher times for the already ailing British manufacturing industry (Kathy Pain examines the post-industrialised economy in chapter two). A strong Pound on the foreign exchange markets made it harder for exporters to compete and the short-termism imposed by shareholders (predominantly fund managers and other institutional investors) has meant lower long-term investment in innovation, research and development. Even more sophisticated company analysis of recent years (which examines firms' return on investment and whether that return is sufficient to cover both the cost of providing the equity as well as its debt) seems to have had a dampening effect on the willingness of industry to take the sort of risks that have in the past produced successful business. Simon Nixon makes this point and highlights the reality that despite the ostensibly huge growth in the FTSE 100 over the two decades since Big Bang, the index has underperformed other leading indices. "Where Britain once boasted its Hansons and Whites, the real corporate buccaneers are now to be found in Germany, France, Spain, Russia and even India. As the City has become better at managing and valuing risk, it has squashed the risk-taking impulses of others".[18] But while manufacturing may have struggled to compete in the world, London's financial services have gone from strength to strength and today appear to be the dominant force in a changing, globalised, world.

The City Corporation's *Global Financial Centres Index*, has become a commonly accepted standard for evaluating and comparing what is now forty six world financial services centres. In its report published in March 2007, it ranked London as the leading financial centre in the world, just ahead of New York (and a wider margin than in the previous study), beating it in all in all five areas of competitiveness: people, business environment, market access, infrastructure and general competitiveness. It also demonstrated London and New York as being considerably ahead of their principal Asian rivals, Hong Kong and Singapore, in third and forth places respectively. Interesting from a geo-political standpoint is that while the 2005 study showed no obvious leader amongst the Asian centres, in 2007 it was clear that Hong Kong now leads the way from Singapore and that these two are well ahead of Tokyo (9th), and the two Chinese centres of Shanghai (24th) and Beijing (36th). India was ranked 39th between Rome and Warsaw.[19]

The consultancy firm McKinsey published an influential report in early 2007 which projected that the US could stand to lose up to $30bn of financial services business by 2011 given recent trends.[20] But if costs are a factor in McKinsey's analysis, they are dwarfed by the two more significant realities of conducting investment transactions in the United States: the litigious nature of modern America and once again repressive regulation most notably the Public Company Accounting Reform and Investor Protection Act of 2002, better known as Sarbanes-Oxley, introduced in the wake of high profile accounting scandals including Enron (that Güler Aras and David Crowther discuss in the context of corporate responsibility). Perhaps only the most recent incarnation of US financial services regulation, the strict rules based attitude compares unfavourably to London's principles based approach.

These are not the only factors which are undermining New York. The *Financial Times* points to "America's heavy-handed visa regime [as] an impediment. If a big Middle Eastern client cannot get a visa, why not have the meeting in London?"[21] What this tells us is that although globalisation might have increased the potential competition, the factors undermining US competitiveness are largely home grown. While other financial centres are emerging and posing a competitive threat to Wall Street, much of the business leaving the United States appears to be moving to London, hardly famed for its low salaries. But labour costs can be a misleading indicator. Financial transactions are not necessarily cheaper in low cost economies since it is sheer volume which leads to economies of scale in places such as the City. And it is difficult to compete on volumes with a centre about which such dominant statistics so easily trip off the tongue. Further, in London "high costs [are] more than offset by other factors making it a very attractive location for high value-added, internationally-traded services. Gross value added per job was 26% higher than the national average in 2005. In part, this reflects the specialisation of the London economy in a range of high productivity service sectors – most notably in financial, insurance, legal and accounting services."[22] So not only can it be cheaper, but it is in London that skilled practitioners can be found in ready supply as Andreas Prindl highlights in chapter ten, drawing on his many years in the industry. After all, the banks of the City are not simply facilitating the investment of clients' money; they are deploying their own funds for profit. Expertise makes a difference. Along with the English language, it is a major reason that neither Paris nor Frankfurt have come close to mounting a serious challenge to London, despite the location of the European Central Bank in the latter. Indeed, to the surprise of many and irritation of some, trading in the Euro is firmly centred in the City.

But something even more curious has been happening. As globalisation and technological advances make it increasingly easier to do business almost anywhere, everywhere and at any time, there is still a dichotomy between the widely held 'end of geography' arguments, discussed in this volume by David Lascelles, which contends that borders are becoming irrelevant to the market economy, and the intriguing strengthening of the established geographic centre of the City of London. At a time when it is easier and cheaper than ever before to conduct financial services business regionally and across the globe, the trend is quite the opposite. What is being witnessed is a consolidation of stock exchanges and bourses in Europe and elsewhere. The international reach of London (strengthened by its $2.19bn takeover of the Italy Borsa in June 2007) has forced the French, Dutch and Belgian stock exchange merger and the move to unite the New York Stock Exchange with Euronext. The longstanding interest NASDAQ and other international rivals have in the LSE is no coincidence. What this means is that dominant centres such as the City are actually becoming more dominant. If great swathes of business really are being lost by Wall Street, they are not being picked up by China, India or other cheaper economies. They are going to London which is seeing international new issues on its Alternative Investment Market (AIM) rapidly increase. Meanwhile the securities market can be found in economies further and wider than ever before. Given the geographic realities of physical centres, combined with the international reach of the market, not only regulation but also traditional governance is a precarious process in places such as London which have become truly global cities and is something which Sam Whimster analyses in chapter four.

This loss of business in a new global world (wherever it may be going) and the $200bn foreign exchange reserves accumulated by China each year to, as Hutton puts it, "rig its currency and keep its exports competitive"[23] might not be the only reason that New York and Washington in particular seem palpably anxious about the growth of the Chinese economy. After all it is "absurd for a poor country like China to be lending to a rich one like the US; in fact it is unsustainable, and the financial markets seem to agree."[24] There is more to it and perhaps the power the markets have assumed in the new global economy pose challenges to the geo-political order. Languishing in its position as sole superpower for almost 20 years since the end of the cold war, the United States has maintained the fiction that its global reach has been to promote democracy and freedom in the world. The reality has been a somewhat more realistic policy where the "overall strategy [is] to make the world safe for capitalism (and by extension, the USA)"[25] After all, where it is in its interests, the United States has been willing to maintain supportive relations with countries such as Saudi Arabia, Pakistan and Kuwait, hardly bastions of democratic government, while undermining legitimately elected administrations in places as far apart as the Ukraine and Venezuela. And, despite the folly of the Iraq war, America's global reach is possible because of its vast military spending which, at some $480bn, dwarfs any other nation on the planet (China spends $41bn, the EU $190bn).[26] But when China's (increasingly capitalist) economy represents around 12% of world GDP according to the IMF and the European Union edges just ahead of the USA's 17%, it is a reasonable question to ask 'whose capitalism is the United States spending $480bn to protect?'

Part of the answer must be to address the idea that the new global capitalism is not America's or Europe's or even emerging China's. Globalisation, it is said, has taken capitalism beyond the control or preserve of governments.[27] It is true that global financial markets have little respect for the machinations of politics and governments face restrictions, placed upon them by the rigidity of a global market.[28] But it would be wrong to suggest that the role of the state or political actors has become entirely marginalised. Hirst and Thompson's argument that not only does the world economy still concentrate investment and trade flows within the developed economies of the core but more fundamentally, that these global markets and trans-national capital remain within society's regulatory capacity, highlights their contention that it is elite power which prevents the exercise of such control.[29] Globalisation has tended to decrease inequality between countries, but increase it within them, supporting elite global players. Indeed, globalisation itself has been driven by governments de-regulating 'in the national interest' which frequently means policies "were chosen to serve the interests of social, political or economic elites."[30] Nevertheless, markets do not have the other sources of power traditionally associated with the state, that of policing, law and military power. And one prominent characteristic of world affairs in recent years has been the growth of international terrorism directed, not so much at the state, but at the foundations of global capitalism. Richard Woodward pursues these arguments in chapter five.

Curiously, it is here that protectionism, engaging the power of financial markets, has been increasingly, if unsuccessfully, deployed. Benn Steil of the Council on Foreign Relations, has argued that "America, the global power of international commerce and finance, bestows free trade agreements on nations that aid her in the war on terrorism...America also punishes with economic sanctions those who oppose her. For those large enough to be particularly irksome in their opposition, such as China, the ultimate surrogate for traditional warfare has become capital market sanctions."[31] The limited success of these moves, precipitated by the reports of two con-gressionally mandated bodies, the Cox and the Deutch Commissions respectively, perhaps illustrates both the global nature of the markets and the idea that governments, rather than remaining powerless in their wake, simply misunderstand the nature of globalisation. Capital market sanctions have merely forced overseas, listings which might have been attracted to New York, ironically accelerating the process of globalisation of financial markets. And it is not only listing which have been driven overseas. "The clear message...is that US investors go abroad to invest in foreign companies. They do not sit in 'New York City' waiting for the world to come to them."[32]

In Britain, Gordon Brown's powerful Treasury has sought to support the war on terror by tightening anti-money laundering measures in the City, including better identification of those moving capital, greater cross-border co-operation, and has been ready to freeze assets of those suspected of involvement in terrorism. Speaking at Chatham House in 2006, the Chancellor warned that "there should be no safe haven anywhere in the world for terrorists. Equally there should be no hiding place anywhere for those who finance terrorism."[33] But despite a certain jurisdiction over one of the most powerful financial centres in the world, the British government has been studiously careful to avoid intervening in the industry to either support its wider foreign policy aims or indeed to 'protect' a sector whose success has contributed greatly to the administration's ability to increase public spending over a decade since 1997. Indeed, Brown appears to value the pre-eminent role of financial services in Britain's modern economy to the detriment of other sectors and his prescription, in contrast to that of the United States, is to ensure that it remains competitive and attractive internationally. His final Budget in March 2007 saw a drop in corporation tax from 30p to 28p at an annual cost to the Exchequer of around £2 billion, covered partly by a reduction in allowances for businesses investing in machinery. Overwhelmingly it is the more upwardly mobile big banks who would benefit from this tax change and traditional manufacturers who would have to carry the can. A decade of Labour government has only extended the dominant role the City has at the heart of the British economy and not even foreign policy goals, of a proportion not seen in decades, can persuade the administration to attempt to harness its power.

The interdependence of economies and the integration of financial markets is a natural consequence of globalisation and the City of London sits at the very heart of the process. Lauren Phillips discusses one element, in the context of European supra-national bonds, in chapter six. This has implications for governance in the global as well as the national sphere. The governance of global markets is not entirely beyond societal control and the market remains reliant on the legal and military power of traditional government. But even a super-power like the United States is incapable of harnessing the global market's power as a means of coercing others on the global stage. For decades the wealthy West has driven and profited from the globalisation agenda, forcing fragile, developing markets to open while continuing to protect its own. The sheer size of China frightens some who want to retain control of the agenda and instinctively reach for the shield of protectionism. But such a move would only harm the vast financial services industry centred in the City of London as can be seen (for different reasons) by the partial exodus of business from New York. London can continue to prosper in the new global world so long as it remains open and innovative. It can take advantage of the growth potential of China, India and other emerging economies. But it can only do this by engaging with them.

Notes

1   Steingart, G. "Protectionism! The West Must Defend Itself", *Spiegel Online*, 17/10/06. The article formed part of a series of translated excerpts from Gabor Steingart's German best-selling book, *World War for Prosperity*. The excerpts appear as inconsistent, economic conjecture which, while undoubtedly populist, do not stand up to scrutiny. Among the pieces he states that 'in the global conflict for wealth, Asia is on the attack using brutal methods'. Elsewhere he condescendingly claims, 'Western economists…think the best of people and are therefore dangerous'; Steingart worries for his own standard of living and welfare provision in Europe, hiding behind concerns for worker remuneration in China and elsewhere. His fear is rather given away in one sentence 'around 7 million Chinese children are sent out to work…they weave carpets, carry heavy loads, build plastic toys – *but most of all, they drive down prices*' (emphasis added).

2   Although it is a side issue for financial services, it is noteworthy that indus-trialisation across the Western world led to a rapid decrease in child labour since it is in pre-industrialised agricultural work that child labour is harder to tackle as there is no creation of affluence. See for instance Nardinelli, C. "Child Labor and the Factory Acts." *Journal of Economic History*, December 1980. A similar situation can be found more recently in Vietnam which saw child labour decline from 57% to 38% during the five years from 1993 to 1998 as the market was opened to competition. Edmonds, E. and Pavcnik N. 2002, *Does Globalization Increase Child Labor? Evidence from Vietnam.* NBER Working Paper W8760. Cambridge, MA. Recent evidence from China appears to support the view given that, according to JP Morgan, the country has seen accelerating personal income levels since the 1980s. Between 2001 and 2005 alone urban income increased by 53% and was almost three times that of rural income which has also grown significantly. It is noteworthy, nevertheless, that the gap between urban and rural pay (which was once narrow) has widened considerably over the twenty years since the mid-1980s. Raising trade barriers with China would not tackle the issue of child labour. According to the International Labour Organisation, Indonesia heads the international list with 700,000 child workers, followed by Brazil with 559,000, Bangladesh with 300,000 and Pakistan with 264,000. Elsewhere, child slavery on the west coast

15

of Africa in the production of cocoa beans has led to a law suit filed by the International Labour Rights Fund against the companies Nestlé, Archer Daniels Midland, and Cargill in Los Angeles on behalf of a class of Malian children who were trafficked from Mali into the Ivory Coast. Steingart appears unconcerned about such slavery in economies which pose little serious threat to his way of life. The form of Steingart's argument is also misleading since he suggests that it is Asian companies which are doing the running. In fact, poverty labour is also undertaken at the behest of Western companies operating in these countries. It is here that the EU and the USA could do more to hold companies, either registered in or exporting to their countries, to account. Making western consumers pay a little more (by way of home taxes) for trainers stitched together by children will do much less to change behaviour in these countries than a 'made using child slave labour' consumer warning and prosecutions.

3   Miller, L. "China an Emerging Superpower?", *Stanford Journal of International Relations*, Vol 6, issue 1, winter 2005.

4   Hutton, W. "Does the Future Really Belong to China?", *Prospect Magazine*, Issue 130, January 2007.

5   Hutton, W. "Low Wage Competition isn't to Blame for Western Job Losses and Inequality", *The Guardian*, 9/1/07

6   Peter Mandelson speaking at the launch of the Global Policy Institute, London Metropolitan University 2 February 2007.

7   Gillespie, N. "Protectionism in Politics and Prose", *Reason*, July 2004.

8   *Scenarios for India and China 2015: implications for the City of London*, City of London, October 2006.

9   Statistics drawn from Cityof London.gov.uk.

10   Oxford Economic Forecasting, November 2006, *London's Place in the UK Economy 2006-07*, City of London. P 9

11   The New York Stock Exchange and NASDAQ are the first and second largest bourses in the world when measured by volumes and market capitalisation. See Claessens, S, Glaessner, T, and Klingebiel, D. 2007, *Electronic Finance: Reshaping the Financial Landscape Around the World*, The World Bank. P 13.

12   In an attempt to rein in the seepage of Dollars seen as a major factor in the US balance of Payments deficit.See Roberts, R. and Kynaston, D. 2002, *City State*, Profile. p 89.

13   Though in an attempt to weaken the Pound which had appreciated substantially as a petro-currency in the 1970s.The move was made without consultation or indeed consideration for City interests. *City State*, op cit. p92

14   Ibid.

15   See Treanor, J. "Revolution hailed but City warned of a looming fight for supremacy", *The Guardian* 26/10/06.

16   Ibid.

17 As at 29 December 2006, Shell had a market capitalisation of £117,078m, BP £ 110,754m and HSBC £ 106,792m. The threshold for inclusion at this time was about £2.9 billion.

18 Nixon, S. "What did Big Bang do for UK Industry?", *Money Week*, 27/10/06.

19 *The Global Financial Services Index*, Corporation of London, March 2007.

20 *Sustaining New York's and the US' Global Financial Services Leadership*, McKinsey, 22/1/07.

21 "A worrying report for New York, New York", *Financial Times*, 23/1/07

22 Oxford Economic Forecasting, 2006, op cit. P 3.

23 Hutton, W. *Prospect Magazine*, 2007, op cit.

24 Ibid.

25 Colas, A, "The Limits of Imperial Power: US Hegemony in Historical Perspective", Birkbeck College Working Paper, undated. P 3.

26 Various sources. See for instance *The World Factbook 2007*, CIA; Stockholm International Peace Institute, 2005.

27 O'Brien, R. 1992, *Global financial Integration: The End of Geography*, Pinter Publishers.

28 Barber, S. "Global markets and the limits of Political Decision Making", *Contemporary European Studies Journal*, June 2007.

29 Hirst, P. and Thompson, G, 1999, *Globalisation in Question*, Polity.

30 Strange, S. "What Theory? The Theory in Mad Money", *CSGR Working paper*, December 1998. p 18.

31 Steil, B. "The Capital Market Sanctions Folly: a lesson in diplomatic dopiness", *International Economy*, Winter 2005.

32 Ibid.

33 Gordon Brown, "Meeting the terrorist challenge", speech given to Chatham House, 10 October 2006. In the speech Brown claimed "In total here in Britain since September 11th almost 200 accounts have been frozen linked to over 100 organisations with suspected connections to Al Qaeda. In 2005 alone our requirements to report suspicious activity saw banks and other businesses report over 2,000 suspicious potential terrorist transactions with 650 leading to detailed investigations resulting in not just the seizure of cash thought to be destined for terrorism in Iraq but the tracking down of individuals wanted for terrorist charges and not just here but overseas".

Chapter 2

City of London – Global Village: Understanding the Square Mile in a Post-Industrial World Economy

Kathy Pain

The Global Economy: London

Europe's competitiveness in the global economy and the contribution of its major capitals to this, have been a key policy pre-occupation since the launch of the Lisbon Strategy in the year 2000.[1] As globalisation gathers pace, the rise of the Chinese and Indian economies and their 'mega-cities' is widely seen as a major threat to the future growth and prosperity of the European region, as is discussed by Swati Raju elsewhere in this volume. Economic globalisation and world political instability appear to threaten the established geo-political alliances and trading relationships that have so far underpinned the geometry of capital accumulation in the post-industrial service economy. This has largely benefited Western countries but China and India are catching up fast. Their major investments in research and development for high technology manufacturing production are paving the way for a shift from low-revenue commoditised services to high value-added knowledge-based 'new economy' functions based in mushrooming high-rise urban infrastructures as seen in Shanghai and Mumbai.

As the limits of crude oil production approach, enormous revenues in the Middle East and volatile political relations with the West are also expected to reinstate historic 'Silk Route' trading relations[2] for Chinese manufactured products. In the context of these macro-economic changes, the challenges of demographic change and European enlargement, the sustainability of London's global role as a leading finance and business centre, is a key concern for the UK and the re-launched 2005 EU Lisbon growth agenda.[3]

The Place of 'the City' in a Network Economy
Academic commentators have theorised the changing spatial relations associated with globalisation from a variety of economic, sociology, geography and political economy standpoints. Shifting patterns of uneven world economic development – over time conceptualised variously as 'North-South', 'First-Third', 'core-periphery' 'urban-rural' and so on – are now seen to reflect digital infrastructures. Increasing poverty and mortality in Sub-Saharan Africa and contrasting living conditions in the world's richest cities including London, illustrate the complex layering of evolving contemporary global-local spatial divisions. The significance of *trans-urban networks* – constituted by supra-national business and political organisations, alliances and non-formal social networks – is recognised as transforming spatial relationships and challenging established geo-political explanatory dualisms.[4]

In the high value-added 'advanced' service economy (the key priority and focus of the Lisbon growth agenda), virtualisation of information and knowledge exchange has both facilitated and promoted the development of cross-border financial, business and professional networks that are increasingly interlinking cities across political and jurisdictional boundaries. The simultaneous geographical dispersal and concentration of activity in network organisations – first identified by Sassen[5] as a feature of the advanced service economy – leads to the agglomeration of key knowledge-intensive production functions in dense and highly clustered areas of 'global cities', such as the so-called 'Square Mile' in the City of London.[6] But networks of city-based offices in financial services and the business and professional service suppliers that interact with them – known as advanced producer services (APS) – are also sites for mobile, high-skilled employment and the infrastructure for inter-city knowledge, labour and capital flows. Given the inherent volatility of business networks in response to market change, concerns about how the City will be affected by progressive globalisation, economic liberalisation and macro-economic shifts, are sharpened. But to what extent is the City under threat from the gathering new wave of integration and the transition of Asian 'mega-cities' from manufacturing to 'global city' functions? Four major studies conducted between 2000 and 2006,[7] provide key insights into its role in the expanding global knowledge-based service economy.

Studying London as a Networked City
The starting point for the studies was much publicised speculation about London's position in Europe with the 1999 launch of the Single Currency. London's dramatic rise as a global service centre, from the 20th Century economic and population decline, following 'Big Bang',[8] has been widely attributed to a UK regulatory and legislative framework that tilted the 'playing field' to London's advantage relative to New York, Tokyo and continental Europe. With the UK outside the Eurozone and the European Central Bank (ECB) decision to locate in Germany's leading financial centre, Frankfurt, would

London lose out? Some commentators see London's position relative to Frankfurt as counterintuitive. Whereas global cities New York and Tokyo are located in the strongest national economies of the North America and Pacific Asia world regions, Europe's leading global city failed to develop in its largest Member State economy, Germany.[9]

Underpinning the debates, London-Frankfurt relationships were represented in the international financial press as a bitter contest between rivals; even within the UK, the drive for increased economic competitiveness has underscored a competition between city administrations for inward investment and power. While the European spatial strategy[10] strongly encourages territorial cooperation, its promotion of regionally balanced or 'polycentric' urban development, supported by Structural Funds, amounts to a redistributive policy in which the London agglomeration is cast as a less sustainable, 'monocentric' form of urban spatial development.

The four studies have directly addressed these policy issues, examining London's business relations at different spatial scales: First, London's connectivity to city-based APS networks world-wide, conferred by their geographical distribution of offices and business functions; second, changing APS business relations between London and Frankfurt following the introduction of the euro; third, APS business services clustering in the City of London; and fourth, APS business linkages between London, its surrounding region and seven European major city-regions.

In contrast to conventional urban analyses using data drawn from standard statistical areas, the studies have investigated London's *inter-city*, cross-border business relations through the interactions, flows and practices in knowledge-intensive APS industries: banking and financial services, insurance, accountancy, law, advertising, management and IT consulting (advanced logistics and design services were included in the large-scale North West Europe study). As discussed, APS networks have emerged as critical conduits in globalisation,

however the functional linkages and flows between cities that
they give rise to, can only be studied by gathering primary data.
A variety of sources and analytical methods were used –
business websites, postal, telephone and web-based
questionnaires, face-to-face interviews, focus group meetings
and documentary analysis – the co-operation of very senior
decision-makers in the major global service networks was thus
essential. More than 600 face-to-face interviews with major
firms, industry and government organisations have been
conducted since the year 2000. The results are reported in detail
in a series of research publications.[11] Here the key findings from
across the studies are considered at macro- and micro-spatial
scales with specific reference to the question, what makes
London successful?

Macro-Spatial Processes Affecting London
Processes of globalisation are leading to a series of local-global
operational tensions for APS firms doing business in
increasingly competitive domestic and world markets. Within
Europe, the size of the European trading block, and the volume
of business within this, means it is necessary for firms to support
a large 'primary' or origination side but production functions can
be kept in one centre and supply a large geographic area. On a
global scale, market expansion has led to a massive growth of
non-domestic and affiliated offices for APS firms world-wide,
requiring a huge geographical spread of resources also for high-
skill, high-revenue functions. This is illustrated by the
increasing number of Pacific Asia offices now listed by American
investment banks; for example, JP Morgan has 24 offices in 14
Asia Pacific countries, employing in the region of 7,000 people.
Their Asia Pacific 'footprint' extends from northern China and
Japan as far south as Melbourne. At least six related cross-
dependent global mega-trends affecting APS agglomeration in
London can be identified.

The first major strategic trend is the increasing *concentration*
of resources in as few centres as possible on the production side,

in order to reduce costs and deploy scarce specialist skills effectively. Firms need to reduce duplication and cost to remain competitive in globalising markets and this is leading to a concentration of specialist skills in as few centres as possible. This is a key issue for continental European firms who must maintain two major locations in just one region as a German banker explains,

> You have a concentration on New York, somewhere in the far East ... and you're certainly here in London traditionally and one or two satellites on the continent and you don't want to have more places than that because you can certainly supply this time zone quite easily out of one centre and already two places in Northern Europe is quite a lot. (German Bank A)

A second huge trend, the increasing exploitation of *technology*, is to an extent, a counter-trend in some business areas, for example in foreign exchange where electronic broking is taking over. But the biggest impacts of technology relate to high-volume, low-revenue retail functions. Even here,

> Some of the paradoxes work against each other. On the one hand you could say for the activity which is most dematerialised and standard, you could have the greatest propensity for relocation. Then you say, where to?...For an investment bank it looks more appealing than it would actually be in practice. (Swiss Bank B)

Production functions generally remain strongly people-driven and people-intensive. Personal contact and relationships are still essential, reinforcing agglomeration.

Increasing global dispersal is associated with a third major trend towards industry *consolidation* to reduce costs and support expensive investment in infrastructure and developing technology. Deeper global, often in combination with local, market penetration requires centralised risk management as people and resources are spread across more offices and cities. Even close to London,

The technology hasn't got to the point where we feel comfortable
from an operational risks point of view about locating people who
are assembling trades away from the people who've actually done
the trades. (German Bank C)

The benefits of proximity shouldn't be underestimated. One example
is, we started a project in Ireland, it was a technology project and it
failed and shut down and I would definitely say one of the reasons
was it didn't have enough proximity to the front office business.
(German Bank D)

At the same time, a fourth mega-trend of increasing
specialisation, required to remain competitive in local and
global markets, is leading to increasing business alliances and
the break-up of larger firms into smaller entities. In advertising
for example, creative and strategic agencies have split and sold
media departments which have then come together in new
companies, "that's the sort of typical amoeba-like way in which
agencies are dividing and then coming together again in a
different format." (Inst. Advertising)

A fifth related trend is the increased *complexity* associated
with the cross-cutting business relationships between firms and
the interdisciplinary services they provide. As an Swiss
investment bank in London's Square Mile explains, "a lot of the
complexity at the moment is reinforcing some of the very basic
things that people have taken for granted." (Swiss Bank E).

A key feature of the APS industries is that firms provide
services to each other. Their multiple cross-cutting relationships
as service providers and suppliers creates a proliferation of
dynamic business interdependencies that requires proximity
and is a further agglomeration driver.

Intra- and inter-firm relationships and working between
cities, involving transfers of knowledge, business, skills,
revenue and labour and corporate ownership of financial
markets, thus have crucial geo-political importance.
Contradicting predictions of the 'death of distance' and

'geography' with increasingly 'wired' communications,[12] the centralisation of key APS global functions in London is shown to be a crucial component of globalisation. While the use of virtual communications is shown to be intensive in all sectors, these are mainly used for digitised, commoditised and low-value exchanges, as already discussed, and for intra-firm (as opposed to external) communications within and between offices in the same network. Increasing complexity for management and high value-added production functions – for example, mergers and acquisitions and investment banking – is actually increasing the need for proximity and agglomeration.

Agglomeration and London Global Connectivity
These trends, driven by global strategy, explain the mutually reinforcing tendencies between global dispersal and centralisation and continuing agglomeration in London. But a sixth mega-trend is seen by firms as even more important in explaining London's role as a premier location for global business. Before turning to consider this, London's global position as an APS cluster two years after the introduction of the Single Currency, is briefly considered.

2001 data on the organisation of 100 major APS firms across 315 cities world-wide,[13] showed London to be the most highly connected financial and business services cluster in the world, followed by New York, on the basis of the global service functions located there. Comparing London's global network connectivity with other European cities, London (ranked 1) was followed by Paris (6) and Frankfurt (7) for financial services connectivity, while Paris (4) proved much more strongly connected than Frankfurt (14) as an all-round business services cluster.[14]

Questionnaire and interview evidence from subsequent studies indicates that London's position as a global service centre has not diminished in spite of the UK remaining outside the Eurozone with 25 countries turning to the ECB in Frankfurt since 2004. This view is reinforced elsewhere in the book. London is unanimously still considered the unique European

production centre and platform, or interface, for international
flows and interactions in global service networks. But
agglomeration is a fluid, not a fixed state.

New economy clustering is constituted by flows and transfers
of information, ideas and people rather than material
concentrations in any fixed physical or territorial sense. The
high-value international communications and transactions
articulated *in* London circulate *through* inter-city corporate
networks. All parties meetings conducted in London may, for
example, be interactions between New York and Hong Kong or
Amsterdam and Dublin. The collective specialist skills and
intelligence of global experts in any one field are present in the
City. Similarly, technology allows banks headquartered in
Europe, including German banks, to access European and global
markets from their offices in London, by-passing Frankfurt,
because London is seen as the more efficient place to conduct
international transactions.

Growth and contraction are signs of a healthy cluster but, in
the context of macro-economic instability, it is vitally important
to understand London's specific strengths. These evidently do
not relate to the relative size of the German and UK economies;
equally the euro is regarded as making no difference. It is seen
as 'just another currency' with London benefiting from the new
euromarkets. Global connectivity is clearly more than a matter
of national economic strength or a currency.

But attempts to model new economy service agglomeration
are found to be unable to take satisfactory account of the
dynamic cross-border and supra-city relationships, and the
human social and cultural processes that influence network
flows and localised clustering.[15] Office locations tend to be
relatively fixed over time and relocation is generally within
centralised and local cluster extensions, but flows of key APS
production assets – labour and business intelligence – are
much more difficult to elicit. As the senior manager of one
German headquartered bank who operates a virtual office in
London and Frankfurt explained,

> All those 100% are operating together as one team – they're a European team with one head, there are no two heads any more…How big is our office in Frankfurt and London? I don't know. It's as big as that today and its smaller or larger…we increasingly get to the point where we say it doesn't matter. (German Bank F)

This increasing fluidity – a product of the need for firms to be agile – is reflected in present requirements for flexible office space as well as flexible and mobile labour.

This leads to the sixth mega-trend, regarded as most important by interviewees in explaining London's success as a global APS cluster – *infrastructure*. In part this relates to the increasing dependence on high-density technology but the key concern is people – where talent can be found? "Where do I get the people from? Where do they sit and where are they available?" (German Bank G). Most importantly, London's trans-national talent pool is regarded as unique. For an American investment bank in EC2, "what we're interested in is the infrastructure of where we are but the primary driver is workforce" (US Bank H). Traditionally flexible UK employment legislation has allowed contracts to be structured appropriately according to business so that firms are willing to take risks in expanding in London. This is an incentive to locate business in London but it is not a complete explanation. More importantly, talent and business intelligence – the inputs and products of APS – are mobile, and they are currently found in London. UK personal taxation regimes are an important incentive for some to work in London but the interview results indicate that other 'soft' micro-processes are also crucial.

Micro-Processes: Interaction in the New Space-Economy
At a micro-scale of the new service economy, it is clear that transaction costs – office space and transport – are 'fuzzy' locational determinants in APS production.

> Very, very few foreign players actually make money in London. The vast majority of them are losing money, so why are they here?…I'm

not talking about people like Deutsche and Chase and ABN Amro
but the vast swathes of small banks. (Inst. Banking)

And, for firms engaged in wholesale production activity, the
need for a central London location is not simply a matter of
needing a prestigious City address for market credibility in
building a global brand, important though this is. Integration
into *localised* trans-national labour markets and social and
cultural networks is regarded essential for knowledge
production, transfer and innovation in international business,
and this requires a substantive human presence. For global
functions, the simple 'need to be there' for relationships, trust
and a 'sense of team', is impossible to quantify or model
mathematically satisfactorily. Here, the restricted area of the
City of London and its Square Mile play a crucial role in
generating global agglomeration economies for the new space
economy. *Supranational* tacit knowledge exchange is made
possible through the Square Mile's 'global village' social
networks.

The advantages of close proximity for face-to-face contact are
well-established but the studies show that these apply
especially to APS wholesale functions, which have a different
locational logic from that of other 'hi-tech' and retail business
services that have a more dispersed cluster geography. Banking
and a wide range of specialist auxiliary financial services are
identified as a key anchor in London cross-sector business
clustering. The need to be close also applies to segments within
one entity. For one American bank,

Connecting the dots...all those people who can provide the very best
advice and the very best service, that requires them to talk to each
other, to see each other and that means equity fixing, investment
banking, private wealth management, commodities, foreign
exchange, private equity, all need to know what they're doing
somewhere or at least co-ordinate the services they're providing to
the same client or to related clients. That means we've strongly

resisted the decentralisation of our businesses...we need to have
everybody together. (US Bank I)

The insurance cluster appears relatively self-contained
physically, "you've only got to go two or three blocks away and
you won't find any insurance businesses at all" (UK Insurance
J). However, the increasing need to spread risk across
institutions, also requires proximity between the financial and
insurance sectors. Both sectors have multiple cross-
dependencies with specialised 'City' law and accountancy
firms, clustered close by and to the west of the Square Mile.

All businesses need banks [and] so many ancillary businesses feed
off insurance – law, accountancy particularly in this place because of
our accounting systems, loss adjusters, surveyors, all sorts of support
services like software houses specialising in insurance. There's a lot
of people round here who aren't actually in the business of
underwriting or broking but who nonetheless feed off it and equally
suppliers are close. (UK Insurance K)

Increasing transaction size, for example in mergers and
acquisitions, requires proximity for frequent, and often
protracted, face-to-face interaction between multiple sectors
and multiple actors within these, including corporate,
government and institutional clients, "round table meetings that
go on non-stop, day and night for days on end" (UK Law L).
Because client teams need representation by the top global
specialists in any given market, not just one, several top law
firms may be involved in the same transaction.

Very close proximity between global service suppliers enables
relationships of reciprocity to be established between senior
managers and specialists which is crucial for high-value
knowledge transfer and innovation. While the costs of supporting
a City location are high, these can be offset by network capacities
for virtual working. For foreign firms, the City is also a back office.
For example, in a Swiss investment bank in EC2, "we run systems

here for use in other locations" (Swiss Bank M). A Dutch
investment bank's London office is creating economies of scale by
providing,

> hub back office activities, particularly things like settlement. And
> London is one of those hubs for our global network so, from an IT
> and a settlement perspective, and for some of the front office
> equities for example, we're hubbing a lot of the processing power
> and sort of back office activity in London and servicing,
> particularly Europe, but, in some cases, Asia and the United States.
> (Swiss Bank N)

Similarly, a French bank undertakes back office activities
overnight for an Asian subsidiary. These activities are fluid and
move invisibly between cities and countries in networks.

> We could clearly be doing those either in Paris, where it's cheaper
> anyway, or in various other locations. But, increasingly upstairs,
> we're doing certain back office activities for our Far Eastern offices,
> which is the opposite way round to what you'd expect. But that's
> because we've got the systems and the space is free at night…I'm
> sure people are more expensive here but here we are doing Tokyo
> and Singapore in London. (French Bank O)

Paradoxically, for the insurance sector, a single tightly
clustered City location is necessary for the global functioning
of virtual insurance markets. Accounting and consulting are
the least centralised, and also the most regionalised non-retail,
APS sectors. Both law and accountancy straddle between the
Square Mile and central London, to the law courts and the
West End, where high-value private, corporate and
institutional clients are located. Canary Wharf to the east, has
become established as a non-contiguous City cluster extension
for banks and financial services, "in effect, a single business
cluster" (US Bank P), providing office space that has been
deficient in the Square Mile,

> The problem with the City is, it has some great buildings, but floor-plates are a problem and always will be...you have a multiplicity of landlords who don't have the focus these guys have. (French Bank Q)

But the benefits of a Square Mile location remain an overriding locational determinant for many banks and financial services firms. Firms that have moved to Canary Wharf have pressed for better accessibility to the west for interface with the City, the West End and Heathrow airport; some have retained the use of offices in the City for meetings there. A senior manager of a German bank located in EC2 regards the distance between the City and Canary Wharf as a barrier, "I haven't been for a meeting in Canary Wharf for ages. It may be that meetings are just not taking place in consequence." (German Bank R).

A sense of 'place' remains important for production in globalising services because of their essential nature as 'people' and 'relationships' businesses. And the need for close proximity goes beyond practical reasons, such as the need for firms to build relationships of trust or conduct complex negotiations. The 'atmosphere' of the City, the proximity of its financial and creative milieu and of central London's lifestyle offerings, are much discussed as material assets. For example in advertising,

> That is why London is the centre of UK advertising, because it has got the most intense aggregation of people, businesses and stimuli around it and it feeds off itself and it gets better and better. (Inst. Financial Services)

Being in the right environment matters. A move to Canary Wharf was seen as "disastrous" for one major advertising firm because this is considered, "a banking environment ...not the ideal environment for an advertising agency" (US Advertising S); "the reason it's struggling is that they can't get people to work there...clients don't want to go down there" (Inst. Advertising).

The contrast with Frankfurt is notable. In terms of its size and development, it fails to offer the scope of employment opportunities and cosmopolitan environment needed to attract the young, talented and ambitious people from around the world who are essential inputs to London's synergistic, multi-sector APS clustering.

> If you have a young Italian sitting in Milan and his boss calls three of them in and says to two of them, you're going to London, and one of them is going to Frankfurt, the one whose going to Frankfurt…he may get paid the same but he'll say what have I done wrong? (Inst. Financial Services)

A recurrent complaint in interviews undertaken in Frankfurt is the difficulty of getting good people to work there; even within Germany, other cities are preferred. Work-lifestyle choices are shown to have contradictory spatio-economic outcomes in these two cities that reflects their historical development paths. Frankfurt's position as an international financial centre seems held back, in comparison to London, by its lack of 'single city focus' and 'institutional thickness' within Germany, influencing its attractiveness as a space for consumption and production in APS networks. And the effects extend to the cities' respective regional hinterlands where APS clusters in South East England are found to be functionally inter-linked to central London and to each other, making this a more *functionally* polycentric region than the Rhine-Main and other major city-regions studied in North West Europe.[16]

Conclusion: New Directions – Risks and Opportunities
A crucial finding from the recent North West Europe fourth study is that, even in regions that appear polycentric in terms of the size and morphological distribution of their towns and cities, global APS functions are concentrated in just one city in all cases. The phenomenon of centrality, at a city-region scale of the European service economy, overturns previous theorisation in spatial policy

that aligns objectives for growth with those of morphologically polycentric development. Furthermore, urban polycentricity is not found to promote more balanced or environmentally sustainable development in any of the regions studied.[17]

Contrary to its representation in the ESDP, far from being a monocentric city, London is shown to be highly functionally connected through APS business flows within the UK, within the European region and globally – a product of, and contributor to, functionally polycentric *inter-city* relationships.[18] The sustainability of London's global connectivity thus has far-reaching economic and employment implications outside the City and beyond the South East. In addition to direct links between clustered central London APS functions and business conducted across the country, benefits within the UK include tax revenues and a raft of invisible earnings from supply chain linkages that are impossible to trace and map accurately.

Whereas the globalisation discourse has typically focused on dualistic territorial power relations, the results from the four studies indicate that a complex geo-political frame is emerging. As globalisation progresses, intensifying market competition at all scales appears to be thickening and extending trans-urban network linkages. Firms increasingly need to work *across* cities to remain competitive, leading to *synergistic* inter-city relations. Potentially this presages a shift from low-value, off-shored, commoditised activity to the development of high-skill, high-revenue functions in integration zones such as Eastern Europe and Asia, reflecting their market development as opposed to their low-cost labour. Morgan Stanley, for example, has the first Chinese language site by an international investment bank communicating its best practices in finance, management, operations, infrastructure, communications and capital market development.

But current European and UK spatial policy aimed at promoting central London activities in areas lacking development, fails to appreciate the specific geographical logic of APS industries, for which dispersal and centralisation are 'two sides of one ball'. A law firm explains the dilemma.

Is there any way of moving some of that outside London, no, there isn't. If we were to move anywhere outside the City, or even to Birmingham, those would be lost. We wouldn't be able to create wealth...It isn't just a question of, can we have a little bit more of it please elsewhere?...We wouldn't be able to bring in the business in order to do it. We can only do it because we're in the City. (UK Law T)

Improved understanding of cluster dynamics and the functional specialisation between wholesale and retail, complex and commoditised functions across space, would allow a sharper focus on investments to support inter-city complementarities. According to the City, the Government will ignore London's needs at the entire country's peril.

We won't be able to afford to put up new infrastructure in Huddersfield or Glasgow if the UK plc doesn't make the money that it needs to London...some advisers still have the wrong misguided 1970s version...businesses at the end of the day are rational entities and they will go where it makes sense for them to go. You can do anything you want and they're like squeezing a bar of soap, they'll pop up where they think the most essential.. (US Bank U)

Key issues – transport and regulation – require multi-layered approaches and investment in London and its city-region, cutting across government departmental and jurisdictional boundaries. The strongest warnings come from the major foreign investment banks that are critical to London clustering.

London's becoming a third world country in terms of transportation...public transportation can't cope. It's increasingly problematic...it's almost easier to have cross-industry meetings in another city. (US Bank V)

We talk about a gradual erosion of London's attractiveness as a place in which to do business...whether it's about tax, or transport, the cost of people, the cost of living, European legislation, employment and social, is a nightmare – it worries us and it's part of the chipping away…you start asking the question – well is this really the best place to be? (US Bank W)

Do we get to the point where we're so regulated, or its so difficult for us to actually make money that we're doing all this regulatory stuff [and] we're not making any money, that it could tip over the brink and somewhere else picks up the call? (Swiss Bank X)

The Chief Operating Officer is American. The Chairman and senior executives, they love London, they all like living here but they don't have a natural loyalty…and the way we're seeing it is we're not bringing a single new job to London and, where we can move jobs out, we are, and that's the reality…in ten years time London is going to grind to a halt…key functions are always going to be here but if all the non-essential people go, even if we're left with 2,000 here, that's still a big impact on London. (US Bank Y)

The overriding message arising for policy is the need to maintain London's historic openness to flows that has made the City the 'Wimbledon' for top international players.[19] And this will be all the more important as demographic change increasingly constrains the supply of young talented labour for service providers and places greater burdens on public sector expenditure. For a London based consultancy the skills shortage already constitutes a serious problem,

Our constraint is getting people of the right calibre to do it…there's a limit to how much longer you can go on, so you've got to diversify, you know overseas where there are more people…the Indias and the Chinas and you've got to go into non-people in terms of businesses, intellectual property and asset driven businesses. (US Consulting Z)

Returning to overarching questions – To what extent is the City under threat from the Asianisation of the global economy? Will emergent economic circuits bypass Europe and London? The

answers would seem to depend, to a large extent, on appropriate
UK and European governance. There are big opportunities for
both East and West. While Asia has large capital savings, it lacks
relevant expertise and experience that the City can offer; at the
same time, Europe constitutes an expanding market for China.
But policy needs to provide a stable local environment and
infrastructure for globally traded service sectors.

Notes

1   European Council, 2000, *Presidency Conclusions – Lisbon European Council*,
    23 and 24 March. http://ue.eu.int/ueDocs/cms_Data/docs/pressData/
    en/ec/00100-r1.en0.htm.

2   The so-called 'Silk Route' was an interconnected series of trading routes
    between the Far and Middle East, across Southern Asia

3   Commission of the European Communities (CEC), 2005b, *Common Actions for
    Growth and Employment: The Community Lisbon Programme*. Communication
    from the Commission to the Council and the European Parliament, SEC 2005
    981, July 2005, COM 2005 330 http://europa.eu.int/growthandjobs/
    pdf/COM2005_330_en.pdf.

4   Pain, K. 2007, "Core-Periphery Relationships in a Global City-Region: The
    Case of London and South East England", in Hoyler, M., Kloosterman, R. and
    Sokol, M. (eds.), *Globalisation, City-regions and Polycentricity in North West
    Europe*, Regional Studies (forthcoming).

5   Sassen, S. 1991, 2001, *The Global City*, Princeton University Press, Princeton;
    Sassen, S. 1994, 2000 *Cities in a World Economy*, Pine Forge Press, London.
    See also, Castells, M. 1996, 2000, *The Information Age: Economy, Society and
    Culture*. Vol. I: *The Rise of the Network Society*. Blackwell, Oxford.

6   The 'City of London' is London's 'central business and financial district,' is
    also referred to as 'the City' or 'the Square Mile', as it is approximately one
    square mile (2.6 km) in area.

7   Taylor et al. 2001, *World City Network Formation in a Space of Flows*,
    Economic and Social Research Council; Beaverstock et al., 2001, *Comparing
    London and Frankfurt as World Cities: a relational study of contemporary
    urban change*, Anglo-German Foundation; Taylor et al., 2003, *The City of
    London and Research into Business Clusters*, Corporation of London; Hall and
    Pain, 2006, INTERREG IIIB North-West Europe *POLYNET Sustainable
    Management of European Polycentric Mega-City Regions*.

8   'The Big Bang' refers to the sudden UK government deregulation of the City's
    financial markets in 1986.

9   See Beaverstock, J.V., Hoyler, M., Pain, K., Taylor, P.J. 2003, "London and
    Frankfurt: Competition or Synergy?", in: Shearlock, P., (ed) *International*

Investor, March 2003, 225-229. Sovereign Publications, London.

10 European Commission (EC), 1999, *ESDP: European Spatial Development Perspective: Towards Balanced and Sustainable Development of the Territory of the European Union*. European Commission, Brussels. (Supported by the European Union 'INTERREG' and 'ESPON' programmes.)

11 Taylor, P. J., Catalano, G. and Walker, D. R. F. 2002, "Measurement of the world city network". *Urban Studies*, Vol 39, pp2367-2376; Beaverstock, J. V., Hoyler, M., Pain, K. and Taylor, P. J. 2001, *Comparing London and Frankfurt as World Cities: A Relational Study of Contemporary Urban Change*, Anglo-German Foundation, London:; Taylor, P., Beaverstock, J., Cook, G., Pandit, N., Pain, K. and Greenwood, H. 2003, *Financial Services Clustering and its Significance for London*. Corporation of London, London; Hall, P. and Pain, K. 2006, (eds) *The Polycentric Metropolis: Learning from Mega-City Regions in Europe*, Earthscan, London.

12 For example Cairncross, F. 1997, *The death of distance: How the communications revolution will change our lives*, Orion Business Books, London.

13 Taylor, P. J., Catalano, G. and Walker, D. R. F. 2002, "Measurement of the world city network" in *Urban Studies*, Vol 39, pp2367-2376.

14 Taylor, P. J. 2003, "European Cities in the World Network" in Dijk, H. van (ed.) *The European Metropolis 1920-2000*, Erasmus Universiteit, Rotterdam. http://hdl.handle.net/1765/1021.

15 Discussed in Pain, K. 2007, "Core-Periphery Relationships in a Global City-Region: The Case of London and South East England", in Hoyler, M., Kloosterman, R. and Sokol, M. (eds.) *Globalisation, City-regions and Polycentricity in North West Europe*, Regional Studies (forthcoming).

16 Pain, K. 2006, "Policy Challenges of Functional Polycentricity in a Global Mega-City Region: South East England" *Built Environment* 32, 2, 194-205.

17 Pain, K., Hall, P., Potts, G. and Walker, D. 2006, "South East England: Global Constellation" in Hall, P. and Pain, K. 2006, (eds), *The Polycentric Metropolis: Learning from mega-city regions in Europe*, James & James Ltd / Earthscan, London, pp.125-136.

18 Taylor, P., Evans, D. and Pain, K. 2007, "Application of the Inter-Locking Network Model to Mega City-Regions: Measuring Polycentricity within and beyond City-regions" Regional Studies (forthcoming).

19 The 'Wimbledonisation' of the City refers to its role as a playing field for the world's top foreign players.

Chapter 3

The City and the End of Geographical Proximity

David Lascelles

Back in 1998, when Britain was agonising over whether to join the euro, Lord Levene, then Lord Mayor of the City of London, issued the following warning:

> A significant number of responsible and acute observers in Europe believe that London's business will, in time, be eroded if the UK's entry into [the euro] is long delayed. The time horizon most often mentioned to me was three to four years.

Interestingly, when it subsequently became clear that the UK intended to stay out, Mr Rolf Breuer, the chairman of Deutsche Bank, made a speech which contained the words:

> London will no doubt remain the leading centre in Europe thanks to
> its advantages of size, excellently qualified personnel, and the
> attractive tax, legal and cultural environment.

Eight years later, twice the time frame mentioned by the City's
erstwhile leader, we know that his acute observations were
wrong and the German banker was right. All the evidence shows
that London has romped ahead of Frankfurt and Paris as a
financial centre, so much so that it now claims to be not only the
leading financial centre in Europe, but in the world.

We will examine the strength of this claim in a moment. But
regardless of its truth, the last few years really have been
astonishing ones for the City – in all senses, in growth, innovation,
wealth generation and the sheer visual impact of soaring towers of
stone, steel and glass. For many of those fortunate enough to work
there, they have delivered exhilarating careers and glittering
fortunes, and transformed the once humdrum financial services
industry into one of the fastest-growing and most exciting around.
All those banks in Paris and Frankfurt to which London's business
was expected to flood away have done the opposite and flooded
over to the City to share in the bonanza.

The years since 1998 have also provided much food for thought
for those interested in the question of what makes a successful
financial centre – from policymakers and academics to consultants
and businesses that have to decide where to locate themselves.
Broadly speaking, the evidence suggests that this period has
witnessed a strong shift away from the traditional Levene-style
view which says that it is all about geography, to the Breuer view
which holds that it is all about the operating environment. If so,
this has clear implications for government policy and business
strategy – and for the ambitions of new financial centres.

London's claim to world pre-eminence in financial services is
based on two sets of evidence. The first is quantitative. The
numbers show that London has more foreign banks, lists more
foreign companies, issues more international bonds, trades
more foreign exchange, turns over more foreign shares et cetera

than anywhere else. This has actually long been the case. But there are indications that the City has strengthened its position in some markets, for example foreign exchange.

Table 1: London's share of key markets (%)

	UK	US
Cross-border bank lending	20	9
Foreign equities turnover	43	31
Foreign exchange turnover	31	19
Derivatives turnover		
• exchange traded	6	34
• over-the-counter	43	24
International bonds	70	–
Hedge fund assets	20	62

Source: International Financial Services London, April 2006

The second is perceptual. The Corporation of London has commissioned two successive independent surveys of international financiers' perceptions of financial centres in recent years. Both used the same methodology: asking people what they considered the key attributes of a financial centre to be, and getting them to score each centre against them. The first,[1] in 2003, put New York at the top with London hot on its heels. Paris and Frankfurt were distant third and fourth. The second[2] two years later put London just ahead of New York with the two continental centres, again, trailing the field (though with Frankfurt overtaking Paris).

Table 2: Comparative ranking of the major financial centres

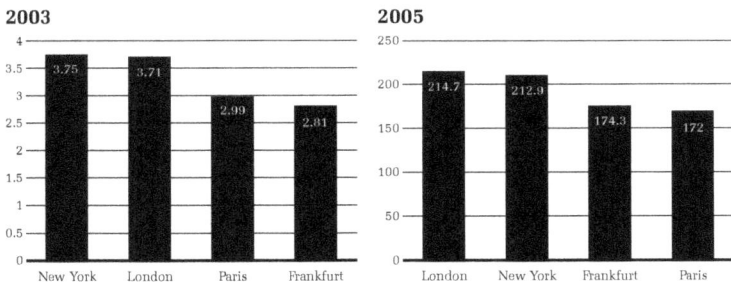

It might be possible to dismiss these studies as too subjective to be of significance. But perceptions are important because so much of the finance business is built on fashion: being in the right place, knowing the right people, and serving up products which earn the respect of customers and competitors. Indeed, this is one of the symptoms of the shift mentioned earlier.

Thus there is good evidence to support London's claim, though to anyone in the business there would be little surprise in these findings. London's pre-eminence is supported by numerous other indicators: the breadth of foreign ownership of City "business", the large number of non-British people working there, and its magnetic attraction to the ambitious young seeking international financial careers. It is probably no exaggeration to say that any aspiring banker must now spend time in London to advance his/her prospects, else risk being cast as "provincial".

The Levene View
The study of financial centres has a long history because financial centres have been around for a long time. And usually, what might be called the Levene school of thought has prevailed. Financial centres were in a particular place because they were geographically convenient and close to sources of business. Academic studies tended to stress geography, and with good reason because it was clear that centres such as New York, Zurich, Hong Kong and Tokyo served a well-defined geographic region. Moreover, their business was dominated by local firms, their regulatory and tax framework was entirely local and uninfluenced by considerations of international competitiveness. A healthy economic hinterland provided the necessary markets.

London was always a bit of an exception to the theory of geographical proximity. In the 19th century it had a big business financing development projects in far-flung corners of the world – which it managed to do not because it was close to the project, but because it knew where to find the money. It was also an exception to the economic hinterland argument, at least in the 1960s and 1970s, though the UK's economic weakness in those decades probably worked to the City's advantage by forcing it to find markets elsewhere and become more international. London's history has therefore been more one of expertise than economic strength: it knew how to do it, and in that regard it has a different tradition from New York and Tokyo which were built on weight of money and local business, (Zurich is a bit of an exception, too, for similar reasons: it made a speciality of taking in private savings).

The Levene view also took account of politics. It understood that the character of a financial centre could be strongly influenced by the local political environment: that government had the power to direct the course of business, to erect or dismantle barriers, to dictate ownership, in short to say yeah or nay. Again, London was the exception: British governments of either hue tended not to get too involved with the City, and respected its independence.

So it is easy to understand why some people became anxious about the City's position in 1998: the financial map of Europe was about to change, an exciting new geographical entity – the eurozone – loomed, and London was outside it. It was logical to suppose that the City would be the loser.

The Breuer View

But the financial services industry was also changing. In particular the vast improvement in communications – both electronic and travel – rendered geographical proximity of the traditional kind much less important, even irrelevant. It became possible for banks to choose their locations on other types of criteria, and mostly they chose ease of doing business. This included the quality of the regulatory and tax environments, the ease with which foreign banks could set up shop, whether incoming banks were treated the same as local banks, whether it was easy to get staff, and so on.

These criteria were highlighted by the two perception

surveys commissioned by the Corporation. The criteria were based on input from several hundred institutions, the majority of which were under non-British ownership, so they reflected an international point of view.

Table 3: Top attributes of a successful financial centre

	2003 survey	2005 survey
1	A pool of skilled labour	Availability of skilled personnel
2	A competent regulator	The regulatory environment
3	A favourable tax regime	Access to international financial markets
4	A responsive government	Availability of business infrastructure
5	A light regulatory touch	Access to customers
6	An attractive living environment	A fair and just business environment

Source: CSFI, Z/Yen op.cit.

What is striking is that both surveys identified human capital as the top consideration – a factor which barely featured in earlier surveys. This reflects an important change in the nature of a financial centre – from the olden days when a foreign bank dispatched a promising young chap to London to run the branch and hire a few local bods, to today's world when success in international finance relies crucially on having the very best traders, IT professionals and managers, regardless of where they come from. Closer research on this theme also revealed that it was not only the ability to hire people, but also to fire them that counted. In this regard, London and New York with their relatively light labour regulation, scored much better than Paris and Frankfurt with their tough labour laws.

Both surveys also highlighted the importance of the regulatory environment. Here London scored strongly because of its perceived "lightness of touch", and the streamlined structure of the Financial Services Authority. One reason why

London snatched first place from New York in the 2005 survey was that the US centre was seen to be losing its appeal because of the regulatory intrusiveness of Sarbanes-Oxley.[3]

Also common to both surveys is what does not appear high on the list: notably quality of life-type considerations. Although Paris and Frankfurt both scored well on these criteria while London did not, it was not enough to tilt the balance. Although Londoners bellyache about awful transport, it doesn't actually weigh heavily in the equation. If you ask a foreign banker: "Is transport more important than the regulatory environment/ tax/ human talent/ market access?", the answer is always no – and already transport is down at number five on the list. Much though it pains one to say it, Gordon Brown may be right to drag his feet over funding for Crossrail, the proposed quick link between the City and Heathrow. It's just not that important.

Further points emerge from the surveys, but they are rather abstract and are not directly quantified.

One is what might be called "the quality of the welcome". The elements of a good welcome include blindness to nationality (it doesn't matter where you come from), equal political and regulatory treatment for all (no favours for the locals), and respect for the independence of the centre (the politicians don't interfere). London came out well on these points, the Continental centres less so because business conditions there are perceived to be tilted in favour of the locals and subject to political influence (particularly Paris).

Another abstract point is what might be termed "being where it's at". Despite modern communications, the financial services industry remains very gregarious and contact-driven. Personal relations, confidence and trust play an important role. Being in the right location not only leads to business, it confers credibility on an institution, it says that a bank is well-connected and knows its stuff. Any bank with international ambitions has to be in London. If it is not, the onus is on that bank to explain why not. This is a very valuable attribute and

45

one which it is extremely difficult for aspiring financial centres to acquire.

A third is the culture of international finance, usually labelled these days as "Anglo-Saxon", by which is meant an emphasis on open markets, equity-style investments, an acceptance of the need for takeovers and mergers, and minimal government involvement. Because the Anglo-Saxon style is dominated by the Americans and the British, it also means use of the English language. Both Paris and Frankfurt suffer distinct disadvantages in this respect: they are perceived to be cautious about giving markets too free a rein, and vulnerable to negative public and political opinion. Although the City is controversial in terms of UK public opinion, this has not led to serious curbs on its activities or to political interference. Indeed the political "independence" of the City is one of its strongest attractions.

Having considered this shift in attributes, we can now take a fresh look at the Levene warning and see where it erred. The line of thought that lay behind it must have run something as follows:

'Financial centres prefer to be close to the source of business. The eurozone, itself a financial project, holds out the prospect of dynamic growth and innovation, so it will attract international banks. It will need a financial centre which is rooted in its economy. Frankfurt is the obvious location because the European Central Bank is there. The politics of the euro will influence banks to do business inside the eurozone. The obvious loser from all of this is London because it is geographically outside the eurozone, and because the UK has weakened its political influence by staying outside the single currency.'

One can see several flaws in the reasoning.

1. "Financial centres prefer to be close to the source of business..." This view is now outdated. Geographical proximity has ceased to be a draw.

2. "The eurozone, itself a financial project, holds out the prospect of dynamic growth and innovation, so it will attract international banks…" This is a variation of the geographical proximity argument. Financial centres have no need to be near dynamic economies or even central banks so long as they can access them by other means. Most banks would rather be in a "good" centre than in a dynamic economy.

3. "The politics of the euro will influence banks to do business inside the eurozone…" This view betrays an imperfect understanding of how financial markets think. There is little they hate more than politically-driven projects, particularly ones which are likely to put pressure on them to behave in chosen ways. If anything, the fact that London was outside the eurozone was seen in the City as a political plus, as offering the hope that the City's independence would remain unscathed.

Where Geography Still Counts

The argument that geography has diminished in importance and been replaced by operating considerations needs to be qualified in some respects, both positive and negative for London.

Two positive points.

The improvement in communications has allowed international banks to centralise many operations which were previously dispersed among several locations, such as research, risk management and back office. In Europe, it has made sense for banks to centralise these operations in London, which means that many of them now have *smaller* operations on the Continent, relatively speaking, than they had before. (See table 4) Ironically, the introduction of the euro has hastened this process. Many banks actually manage their euro trading businesses from a centralised position in London. If ever there was an indication of the demotion of geography, this must surely be it.

Table 4: Relationship between European financial centres

Before 2000   **Since 2000**

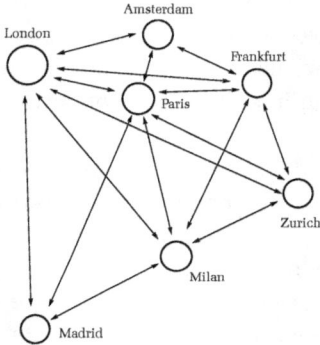 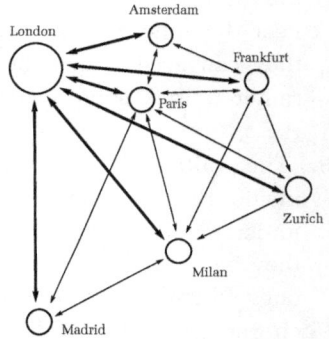

Before 2000, the relationships between European financial centres were dispersed and balanced, though London already occupied a leading position. Since 2000, the structure has become much more centred on London, which has grown while other centres have shrunk by comparison. London has emerged clearly as the hub of European finance.

The second point is an amplification of an observation already made: that finance remains a highly gregarious business. Although it is theoretically possible these days for people to deal in the markets from a log cabin in Montana or a beach hut in the Caribbean, the reality is that very few of them do. The vast majority prefer to be "where it's at" even if it means living in an overpriced London house and fighting one's way to work on an unreliable Underground system in the pouring rain. The reasons are variously given as "the buzz", access to business, gossip, credibility, office politics and so on. In this sense, geography remains critical, though the impulse is a negative one: the fear of being left out. The City remains a herd.

In one respect, the Levene reasoning touched on a real concern, and that was in suggesting that conditions could emerge which might create a shift in preference between the City and the Continent – a powerful geographic negative. Were this to happen, this herding instinct would certainly drive much of the flock out of London, though whether the financial services industry is as mobile as is often said is moot. The City's largest international banks have invested hugely in their London presence, and it would be costly if not technically very difficult for them suddenly to up sticks and move.

London also benefits from geography in that it straddles all three of the world's major time zones. It is the only major centre where you can deal with the Far East, Europe and the Americas without stretching your day into uncivilised hours. However one should not make too much of this advantage. It is God-given and can never be snatched away. The threat is the appearance of a more attractive competitor in the same time zone. But Frankfurt and Paris have had their chance, and failed to take London's crown.

Indeed, the shift away from geographical considerations to ones of operating environment arguably works to London's advantage. The geographical factor is beyond the financial centre's control: you are where you are. History is littered with examples of once prosperous trading centres which vanished under the sands because the camel trains went elsewhere.

But the operating environment *is* under a financial centre's control. The City today has much firmer grip on its destiny than before because it has the means to ensure that regulation is good, that talent is present, that access to markets can be provided. If it loses business, it will most likely be because of some self-inflicted damage. The US has twice done this to itself, once in the 1960s when it introduced the interest equalisation tax and drove the eurobond business to London, and more recently with Sarbanes-Oxley.

This does also mean, however, that aspiring centres have the means to mount a challenge to London. They do not have to be at the cross-roads of financial trade routes to succeed; all they need is to identify what the markets want, and provide it. However it is not quite as easy as that. They can certainly put out a good welcome mat and make the visitors feel at home. And many budding financial centres are essaying this route: Dublin, Dubai, Mumbai, Shanghai. But they will also need to create the sense of being "where it's at", which is much more difficult.

The phrase "critical mass" has been used to describe London's advantages. People come to the City because of what is already there. The more they come, the larger the critical mass becomes, and the more fresh people are attracted. It works as a virtuous circle. How does a new financial centre set this circle spinning, become "where it's at"?

No one has a clear answer to this question, one reason being that London's success has not been the product of a master plan, in which its objectives were identified, thought through and reached for – and the lessons learnt and copied by others Like most things British, the City has succeeded in a haphazard way, getting some things wrong but most things right, and creating in the process a flexible, very workable system which adapts readily to changing demands. But it is not only the flexiblility that is London's appeal. It is precisely the absence of a master plan that draws people to it. One might argue that Frankfurt and Paris failed in their challenge to the City because there was a master plan which reduced flexibility – and conveyed to the markets the unwelcome message that "Government Is Involved". Both Frankfurt and Paris laid on expensively funded promotion campaigns which had little effect. Yet when the Corporation of London thought it would be a good idea to open an office in Brussels to fight the City's cause, the City baulked at this forwardness. The office went ahead, but without the City's enthusiastic backing. For the same reason, there is unease in the City about Gordon Brown's loudly proclaimed "City Competitiveness Initiative". Though doubtless well-intentioned, it comes a bit late in the day and could convey the wrong message about the government's role.

Could it Go Wrong?
The logical conclusion from these observations is that the City is strongly placed, with much going for it and its closest

competitors flagging. In the near term (next five years?), that must be the correct view: it is hard to see what could take away London's crown. But no financial centre has lived for ever, and any analysis of the City must try to identify the threats it faces.

Table 5: UK insurance sector net exports £m

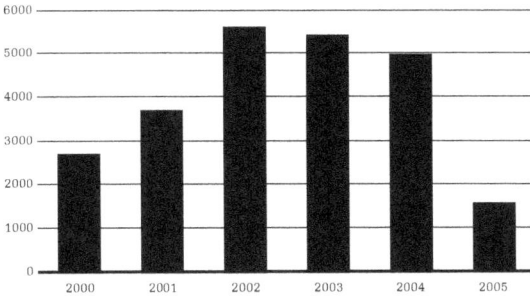

Source: UK Financial sector net exports. IFSL July 2006

The City is not immune to disasters. One example is the sudden decline of the international insurance business. In the year 2002, net exports of the UK insurance industry were £5.6bn. By 2005 they had collapsed to £1.6bn, a fall of two thirds. Part of this was due to hurricane claims. But a deeper reason lies in the London's insurance market's loss of business to Bermuda, which has set itself up as a specialist centre for wholesale insurance. This supports the broad thesis of this piece: it is all about operating environment and little to do with geography. A determined financial centre with a clear focus and the ability to deliver what the market wants can make inroads, even against as formidable an opponent as London. It has to be said that very little actual business goes on in Bermuda: there are not thousands of insurance people running around doing deals. It is more a booking centre for deals generated in London, so it has not affected employment or salaries in the City. But it has bitten a big chunk out of the UK's invisible earnings overseas and, in 2005, contributed to the first decline in these earnings in more than 10 years.

51

Bermuda is not the only example. Using special tax advantages, Dublin has successfully lured away a lot of London's fund management business, though what has gone is not so much the City's high value-added front end as the back office and the processing side. Still, every job that goes to Dublin is one fewer in the City. Dubai has also mounted a determined effort to win listing business from the London Stock Exchange, but it is too early to measure its success. Meanwhile, Paris and Frankfurt have dropped any ambition to become the financial centre of Europe, even of the eurozone, and focused on regional business and specialist areas such as, in Paris' case, derivatives.

A further threat comes from technology, particularly communications. Might there be, at some point in the future, a further step in centralisation of the kind that benefited London within Europe – but this time at a global level, and to New York? It is possible. But this possibility also poses a threat to New York. Supposing the centralisation occurred in London, which is already at the hub of a much greater international network than New York. At the moment, the trends favour this outcome.

Centrifugal forces might also arise to counter the gravitational effect of London's critical mass. Again, communications technology could trigger these by making it possible to achieve the "where it's at" effect in a virtualised form. You really could be part of the London buzz as you sat in your Montana log cabin. But this is getting us into the realms of fantasy, and would in any case require a profound change in the City's herding mentality. A different type of centrifugal force might be driven by concentration concerns. In a terrorist-threatened age, the presence of so much know-how and processing power in one place might seem imprudent, and could trigger an urge to disperse. This is already happening at some levels: data and processing have been split up. But the people are still there, being "where it's at".

Much the greatest threat, [in the view of this writer,] lies in self-inflicted damage. The shift in considerations from geography to environment has not only put control over a financial centre's fortunes firmly in its own hands. It has also made these considerations a competitive issue. The financial centre winners are those which are perceived to have the best regulation and tax regimes, which attract the best talent and provide the best professional support, and these can all be achieved with the right policies and attitudes. Regulation and tax are both becoming more onerous in London, blunting its competitive edge. But fortunately for London, these features are becoming even worse elsewhere, so relatively speaking London still comes out on top. One could never rule out the possibility that a British government would severely damage the City's advantages. But it hasn't happened yet.

Perhaps one sign of the City's healthy attitudes is the amount of *Angst* there is currently there about its future. Numerous working groups, promoted by the Corporation, the regulators, academia and private organisations are staring hard into the future, trying to spot the disruptive technologies or seismic shifts that might bring about dramatic change. But in some ways, the more they stare, the more reassured they become, for it is that it is very hard to identify a silver bullet or a seeping trend that could undermine the City's position in the near to medium term. Perhaps one of the secrets of financial centre success is eternal vigilance.

Notes

1   *Sizing up the City*. Centre for the Study of Financial Innovation. June 2003. The report was written by the author of this chapter.

2   The competitive position of London as a global financial centre. Z/Yen. November 2005.

3   Public Company Accounting Reform and Investor Protection Act, 2002 (US).

Chapter 4

London as a Global City[1]

Sam Whimster

When, in the late 1980s, I was putting together a collection of essays on the new London of de-regulation, integrated finance houses, financial instruments, popular capitalism, yuppies, and the revival of the inner city, my co-editor Leslie Budd and I were confident enough to call the book *Global Finance and Urban Living*. It was pretty clear then that a new form of the money economy had arrived which brought with it a new sociology of how people behaved in relation to consumption, saving, career, culture, one another, their housing, and their urban environment. We did not use the term 'London as a global city', thinking this rather premature in the face of London's obvious continuities with its role as an ex-imperial capital city and its inheritance of decline. Returning to the subject today, this hesitation is borne out. Our book was published in 1992 and it was only *after* this time that London started to demonstrate the growth trends in wealth, jobs and their value added component, and population – and that it was turning around its previous history of decline. We can be more assured today that the financial services really are an industry with a large permanent workforce, a technology, major profitability, and a large physical office presence in the centre of London.

Our other hesitation, indeed silence, was about London's governance. The Thatcher administration had abolished the GLC, most local councils in the inner city did not inspire confidence, and Canary Wharf had just done the development equivalent of a vertical take-off plane. Watch, observe and analyse seemed the best tactic. In this chapter, I assume that London has attained global city status through design, innovation and political intent – but also that the older cities still exist: the administrative and metropolitan city, the manufacturing city, the service-sector city, the immigrant city. My feeling today is that London's governance still has some way to go, despite the inception of the GLA, before it is politically responsive and accountable to all its constituencies and economic sectors. In particular, I do not think the full socio-economic implications of what being global demands, in terms of policy, planning and political virtue, have been fully grasped. And I have dug slightly deeper into classical sociological analysis, which has been neglected by the consensualist assumptions of third-way thinking. I turn first to social cohesion and the recent and disturbing appearance of streets closed off with yellow police tape – another gun incident, another homicide.

Crime and Cohesion in the City
In the second week of February 2007, three teenagers were fatally shot – Billy Cox, aged 15, in his home in Clapham North, Michael Dosunmu, 15, in his home in Peckham, and James Smartt-Ford in Streatham Ice Arena. These deaths represented a new lowering of the age of victims of a lethal gun culture and were part of a rising trend of drug related crime in London and other metropolitan cities. David Cameron, Leader of the

Opposition, used these events, coupled with a Unicef report on the well-being of children in industrialised nations that placed the UK bottom of the league, to launch into a sociological account of the malaise affecting our cities. Further savage murders of teenagers and young men have followed. It is worth taking a hard look at London's urban sociology.

Cameron lifted the blame off the teenagers themselves and placed it with parents, families, communities and society. He did not accept "for a moment that these terrible statistics are the 'fault' of children themselves." Along with the Unicef report he took the events as a wake-up call "to do what is necessary to save our society." The situation would not be rectified by resources, alone, but by 'relationships'. Businesses had to show corporate responsibility on the work-life balance. Quality of life, family life and the taking of personal responsibility were, he said, essential. Personal responsibility was part of the 'good society'. "A good society is one in which everyone takes his or her own responsibility – as parents, as professionals, as business people, as neighbours. The good society is the responsible society." At the level of relationships in the family and community, Cameron called for authority with settled rules and understandings that was a 'system of natural boundaries' – what Burke termed 'moral chains upon our appetites'. This could not be authoritarian because children and teenagers should be treated with respect and the assumption made that they are 'reasonable people'. Noting his party once stood for economic revival, Cameron concluded that: "We now stand for social revival. We used to stand for the individual. Now we stand for the family, for the neighbourhood – in a word, for society."[2]

You have to pinch yourself that this is a speech by the Leader of the Conservative Party – at least of the contemporary Conservative Party, for it can, without much difficulty, be aligned with an older and longer tradition of conservatism. But it jars mightily with the neo-liberalism of the 1980s and 1990s where the market was the prime determinant of all policy. And it contrasts strongly with New Labour's approach to crime and disorder. In 1993 when Blair was at roughly the same point of political ascent as Cameron, he was faced with the Jeremy Bulger murder case. Blair took a stern line – "you've got to be prepared to punish", as he said in a radio interview.[3] He abjured the line of sociological understanding of *tout pardonné*, developing instead the ideology of citizens having both rights and obligations. The temptation to blame the Thatcher administration for the destruction of community – and the resulting ills – must have been strong. It is reported that a decision was made by the Blair coterie to write off the deprived generation of Thatcher's children as a lost cause and stay with the widespread revulsion to the Bulger murder and, beyond that, to support a populist punitiveness as the new political realism.[4] Cameron has done the opposite. He is placing his political fortunes on saving an endangered generation; of attacking New Labour's failure to be tough on the causes of crime and their over-reliance on the failed efficacy of new public management and its 'tick-box' approach to administration and governance.

The Cameron speech may turn out to be a sociological trojan horse with all the usual suspects leaping out on taking control of the citadel. But for the purposes of this analysis I will treat it as a sociological gift-horse. One bona fide immediate effect of the speech is not to have contributed to a moral panic or to ratchet up the new punitiveness. On the other hand creating the 'good society' – and here the reference point is the inner city – is quite a big 'ask'. The good society is an aspiration that by most political philosophies extends the conceptions of citizens' action beyond that of personal responsibility. The good society is usually conceived of as an end in itself over and above the behavioural virtues of parents and communities. Some sort of descriptor of the good has to be inserted. For Plato it was justice, for Christians charity, for Muslims "the umma", for the political philosopher Wilhelm Hennis the conduct of life. It is difficult to believe that any contemporary UK political party would stray beyond the 'methodological individualism' of the citizen and to ascend to the higher ground: that the citizens living together should actively work towards a higher good beyond their role as parents or neighbours.

An additional difficulty with the pursuit of the good society is the sociological medium through which it is to be achieved. The inner city is an ambitious place to start. Referring to mainstream institutions like community and family is an obvious starting point, but raises the question as to what sociological entity these are embedded within. The two main possibilities are the nation and the city, both problematic and, as I shall show, confusingly intertwined. The modern city is, in much sociology, the site of dislocation, alienation, and the melancholic loss of community. The modern nation has always been something of a neologism, constructing a retrospective cultural community while processing the business of modernisation; that is, breaking up traditional communities, severing the link to village and hometowns, and downgrading regionalism and its culture in favour of the artificially created nation-state whose common purpose is articulated as patriotism in times of war or sporting contest. Neither the modern city nor nation-state have existed primarily to nurture the good society.

Nevertheless, it is an intriguing idea to pursue: what is the good society and how should it be pursued through the jungle of modern sociological entities – of nation, state, class, status, culture, identity, market, organisation, firm etc.? Emboldened that a leading politician should raise the issue of the good society, my answer is to take equally seriously the global city as the city-state within which political virtue should be exercised. This was citizen Machiavelli's great theme, but first, more has to be said about sociological forces in the city.

In invoking institutions that have 'settled rules and understandings' with 'natural boundaries' Cameron (or his speechwriter) would seem to be drawing on the great Emile Durkheim (1858-1917). In the transition to modernity Durkheim observed that the old collective solidarities provided by religion and tribal loyalties are attenuated. As a French republican who sought to reinforce the sense of order in modern society, Durkheim searched out those institutions which could foster new social solidarities. Foremost was the process of education, which had the capacity to induce a sense of national identity – or what Durkheim termed the *conscience collective* – in the face of the individualising tendencies of modern society. Durkheim was also a forerunner of the necessity of intermediate groups as providing the institutional infrastructure much required in mass societies. The Blairite notion of the citizen's obligation, or Cameron's call for authority and responsibility in the family, however, fall considerably short of Durkheim's conceptualisation of how solidarity is generated. Obligation, whether as citizen or parent, comes from a force external to the individual. It is for Durkheim an external constraint. It cannot so to speak be bootstrapped by the individual. The duty of responsibility as a father or mother pre-exists the individual, i.e. it is handed down through the institution of the family from generation to generation. The Conservative Party of the 1980s and 90s in its neo-liberal guise effectively eroded this heritage in which 'family' values resided. De-industrialisation, unemployment, the antipathy to public service and public expenditure, and the attack on local government undermined civil society and the robustness of the family as a social unit.

New Labour has played with ideas of intermediate groups – the so-called civil society agenda of Etzioni and Putnam stamp. Ideas like these seek to offer new bases of social cohesion with the fading of traditional middle class and working class structures and their strong orientation to class-based work and family values. Creating new institutions that can exert constraint on individual's behaviour is no easy matter. The good society is not created by people willing themselves to be good. In Durkheimian terms it would be an innate force coming from outside the individual, ordering and specifying what constituted the good. It is glibly said that we are all middle class now. This is only partially true by dint of occupational definition. The old working class jobs have been lost; the new jobs – in services –

are classified as middle class. Similarly, many middle class occupations have lost prestige, relative earning power, and respect.[5]

Durkheim's other key theme was the division of labour in society. In its abnormal form its influence in modern society undermined social solidarities, creating atomised social relationships that veered towards the pathologies of egoism and anomie. In its normal form, realised in complex urban society, it offered both freedom and integration through interdependence. Unlike the traditional countryside, a person in the town could find a specialism in line with his skills and aspirations and he did not have to resort to exclusionary strategies to secure himself employment. This is a line of social theory that Durkheim learnt from Herbert Spencer and that goes back to Adam Smith. The opening up of markets in place of the restrictive practices and tariffs of late feudal society creates new dimensions of freedom and opportunity. What then distinguishes an abnormal division of labour from a normal division of labour? Much hangs of the answer – the difference, for instance, between current crime levels in Los Angeles and New York.

An abnormal division of labour occurs with unchecked markets, the degradation of work, and a system of unjust rewards. By unchecked markets Durkheim was thinking of economic cycles of boom and bust, which afflicted all late nineteenth century industrial societies – what we in a post-Keynesian age refer to as volatility. The degradation of work could be seen in the factory system and sweatshops. For Durkheim, a normal division of labour would allow a spontaneous allocation of people to occupations (rather than a forced allocation, as in traditional and feudal societies).

The *conscience collective* (which combines both conscience and consciousness) also had an important part to play in normal advanced societies. Religion and tradition could no longer perform the binding function they did at the level of ideas with which the world was perceived. There were, however, secular

61

equivalents. Modern society is characterised by individualism. Each person knows this in his or her head and respects the right of all people to their individuality. The same idea has been culturally extended in the idea of respect of the other. If there is a modern "I" there is also an "other", and in a global age this other is not just your urban neighbour but anyone. A similar extension of Durkheim's thinking is the development of human rights, as the contemporary legal form consonant with individualism. Again, much depends on how a *conscience collective* is fostered (and its absence leads to the pathology of Hobbesian egoism).

The abnormal division of labour links directly to inequality and stratification. Max Weber (1864-1920) worked these linkages out more precisely than Durkheim. The division of roles within production, for example in a factory, he referred to as the technical division of labour – and this is the analytic starting point for investigating alienation or satisfaction at/with work. In addition, he had a category of the social division of labour. All units of production require inputs from society. In modern production these are labour, management and owners. Labour could be free, free and unionised, indentured, forced or slave labour – all forms of the modern labour condition. Ownership can vary from unencumbered share ownership, cooperative ventures, state ownership and people's ownership. Managers stand in varying ways to control and profit-take from the firm. In Weber's social-economics, these issues are always complex and changing, reflecting the nature of the empirical world. Weber also added in the accountancy procedures – how profit is calculated and for what end wealth is being generated.[6] Today, where securitisation and private equity consortia have been developed, alongside the partnership and public limited company, this feature cannot be ignored.

Weber's division of labour generates the pattern of occupational differentiation and this in turn determines the social stratification in a society – the divisions in wealth, income, opportunities, and social status. It is not hard to see how the social division of labour is directly linked to stratification. This places us in a better analytic position to return to Durkheim's distinction between normal and abnormal division of labour in society. Inequality and complexity in the division of labour are not in themselves factors leading to an abnormal division of labour – and the pathologies of crime and suicide. The bias in Durkheim's analysis (at least in his first work *The Division of Labour in Society*, 1892) tends to a benign outcome. He imported his understanding of the division of labour from Herbert Spencer, who saw it as a self-moving and self-organising process directly equivalent to evolution in the natural world. There was an ineluctable movement from simple to complex structures accompanied by functional differentiation in the organisation of societies. Spencer was a blithe and great believer in the efficacy of the interdependence and functionality created by the complex modern division of labour. These points are worth emphasising since globalisation brings with it an increasingly complex division of labour in all its Weberian aspects, greater stratification, and a relentless urbanisation. Sociologically, pessimism is not always the default position.

In third-way politics the assumption is made that globalisation, sustainable communities and social cohesion are all jointly feasible. The same idea occurs in Cameron's speech where he demands both flexible labour and a better work/life balance. There is an element of Spencerian blitheness in third-way discourse in its assumption of the compatibility of what are separate and probably discrepant goals. The causal processes need to be modelled analytically and tested against the evidence. Obtaining cohesion and community by pursuing globalisation may involve some interventionist social-engineering – something Durkheim demanded later observing the trajectory of modernising society. In our day it almost certainly will require the shaping of globalisation itself, as recently emphasized by the European Union Trade Commissioner.[7]

63

Global City Analysis

The aim of this chapter is to raise questions about London as a global city – not just questions of crime but of London's identity and cohesion while it pursues a dominant place in the global division of labour. Cities are themselves part of the social division of labour. Durkheim more or less assumed that modern society was coterminous with the modern city, and the place where the occupational specialism and the division of labour had developed furthest. Society itself comes to "resemble a great city which contains the entire population within its walls", wrote Durkheim.[8] For the geographer, the division of labour is between town and countryside, city and its hinterland. Weber was in part reliant on Karl Bücher for his understanding of how cities fitted within the division of labour.[9] Bücher, as an economic historian, argued for an upward economic progress from the manor and village economy, to the medieval town and its trading patterns with other towns and the countryside, to the rise of the national economy with its industrial cities, and finally an international economy with entrepôt cities, like London, Amsterdam, and New York handling wholesale trade. In this schema an entrepôt city, like London, will stand out as having a more complex division of labour, than say a regional city which will contain a range of occupations oriented to its own region and economic needs.

Global cities, as developed by economic geographers over the last 20 years, break with this paradigm. Global cities have no 'natural' hinterland in the way a town has its surrounding countryside, or regional centre has its region, or a capital city its national economy. In the old paradigm, the rise of trade – from local right through to international – goes hand in hand with the increasing specialisation of labour in the town and city (and also in their hinterlands). Adam Smith would have been able to comprehend this production and trade-based (market) model. Global cities, however, restructure and re-organise patterns of trade and production to their own advantage. They do not so much offer a specialist service as just one more bit in a complex division of labour, they actually control and shape the international division of labour according to their interests. In doing this, they re-order production sites and consumption across the world in entirely new ways.[10]

The geographer John Friedman, in 1986, was one of the first to see a new economic function in certain cities: "leading cities were conceptualised as the *global command centres* because they were "bussing points" between world production and world markets."[11] Certain cities had levered themselves into a position of controlling the major arteries of world commerce, and with this capability came a new breed of professionals (known in their halcyon days in the 1980s as young urban professionals). As 'command posts' they stand at the apex of the economic system – they control production and markets and are not too bothered where production takes place or markets occur. All that matters is that this happens through finance, branding, advertising, and sale.

Saskia Sassen points out that not only do global cities have no traditional hinterlands of production and trade, but they have become the core structures in the world economy replacing the national economy.[12] She outlines a two-stage diminution of the national economy. First, by the large transnational companies whose ascendancy came to an end in the 1980s; secondly, the displacement of those companies by financial and management coordination centres, in global cities, whose function was to integrate increasingly dispersed production activities. For Sassen, the financial and management services are an industry, concentrated in three main centres – New York, London, and Tokyo. It has a concentration or agglomeration of professionals in one area, unlike production activities which are dispersed and scattered through outsourcing and delayering. Both control at the centre and integration of dispersed production are made possible by increasingly sophisticated ICTs. Global cities accrete high-value professional services: in finance, banking, management, law, accountancy, advertising and computing. This is the advantage of 'agglomeration'. Global cities trade with each other and lesser financial centres. The prime example in London is trading in foreign exchange and their options and derivatives. Global cities maintain their superiority through innovation of financial instruments and aggressive trading.

The last proposition relates more to London as a world city than a global city. World cities are attractors in terms of their size, cultural artefacts and institutions, ambience, range of services on offer. Their most obvious feature is tourism and travel, greatly facilitated by cheap air travel. London has the additional advantage that it has an important inter-lining airport (Heathrow), making it a major hub of air transport. To what extent corporate HQs locate in London because of its world city status or the sorts of financial, professional and business services offered in the City of London remains an open question. When seen from the theory of agglomeration, it is not necessary to answer. Being a world city and a global financial centre is mutually reinforcing – either way there is a dynamic concentration of skills. However, in a world of foot-loose capital, and the ability of companies and personnel to relocate quite easily, London as a global and/or world city has constantly to look over its shoulder to see whether any other competitor city might prove cheaper and more alluring.

The available statistics show that London is doing very well as a global city. Employment is rising, productivity is increasing, and London's population has since the early 1990s reversed its downward trend. 450,000 new jobs will be created, it is predicted, by 2016. Population is forecast to rise by 700,000 to 8.3 million by 2016. Much of this will be driven by net international migration, which in 2005 was officially 126,000. The population increase from 1991-2001 of half a million was due mostly to migration.[13] "Between 1993 and 2002 the population of London grew by 0.6 per cent per annum (compared to a national average of 0.2 percent) driven principally by net international in-migration."[14] The gross value added to each London job in 2005 was 26% higher than the UK average, reflecting the high productivity and knowledge component of the majority of jobs.[15] Out of this comes a number of success-related problems, alongside some of the more enduring problems in relation to sectoral decline that London has suffered since the 1970s. These problems can be analysed by using the division of labour as a conceptual aid. Weber's analysis of stratification and Durkheim's concern with cohesion and order still remain valid ways of proceeding, even though the exact form of the new global division of labour was not anticipated by them.

The top layer of the economy belongs to the circuits of international business and finance. It relates to the British economy only to the extent that UK companies and domestic banking and finance are worthy of consideration. Its continuation and success is dependent on maintaining its command and control capacities against international competitors. The next level down in the London economy is the so-called cultural industries: media, films, publishing, creative industries. This is a success story that is more authentically English – or rather, London's sense of multiculturalism – than the City of London. Then there is the administrative city with its range of civil servant, local government and non-governmental organisation jobs. The manufacturing sector is now reduced to an adjunct to the first two sectors, mainly printing and publishing. Finally, there is a new service class, comprising high-end occupations like architects and designers through to the world of flexible labour markets – retail assistants, office cleaners, security guards, entertainment etc. This new social division of labour, and the way it is coordinated and layered, produces the peculiar occupational structure now evidenced in the statistics. The financial and business services sector accounted for almost 26.5% of employment in London in 2001 compared with 16% in 1971. In 1971 over 22% of all London jobs were in manufacturing whereas in 2001 it was 6.5%; a reduction in jobs from 1 million to 230,000.[16] (It has to be remembered that occupational statistics are a classification, bringing together only roughly similar jobs, when viewed from each specific economic sector. The concept of division of labour is required to understand the drivers of these trends.)

The stratification effects of this new patterning of London's economic division of labour are novel – and still open to sociological debate. At the top is a new cosmopolitan business elite, whose outlook is international rather than national. The cultural industries are indigenous, offering every sort of employment from the super-rich through to casual employment. The service sector is predominantly poorly paid and suggests the new proletariat. The unemployed and under-employed form around 10% of the workforce. It can be divided into older workers in the manufacturing sectors whose jobs have disappeared – especially in the eastern boroughs of Newham, Tower Hamlets, and Hackney; and younger workers whose lack of educational qualifications discount them for the new sorts of jobs.[17] There is an ongoing argument about whether London's stratification has diminished the middle class occupations, salaries and conditions of work in place of highly paid elites and lowly placed service class; or whether the cultural industries and service industries benefit substantially from the super-rich and that a different sort of middle class is emerging.[18] Economic migrants, both legal and illegal, enter all levels of these social strata.

London then has entered into a new division of labour, led by global (financial) trade and commerce, with the English economy assuming a subaltern service role to London rather than a predominantly independent economic force. London's social stratification, driven by the dynamics of London's global economic outreach and attraction, is being re-stratified with new sets of inequalities being established. There is a large and expanding cosmopolitan elite who can buy the best an increasingly sophisticated services market can offer – housing, schooling, entertainment, and cultural habitus. The national and metropolitan middle class are being priced out of the markets that until very recently they were able to buy into, i.e.

housing, education, cultural habitus. The first wave of gentrification in the late 1960s and 1970s was beneficial because it was regenerating areas of London that had de-populated or had an ageing demographic. London has now 'filled up' and its housing provision is unable to keep up. The new young professional middle classes are in competition in the housing markets with the large service sector. Gentrification of inner city and eastern suburbs involves displacement of key workers into the low cost areas of Kent, Essex and beyond. The recent study *The New East End: Kinship, Race and Conflict* (2006) by Geoff Dench, Kate Gavron and Michael Young documents the desperate pressures of different social groups competing for inner city housing and the tensions thereby generated. Chris Hamnett in *Unequal London* acknowledges that affordable housing has become a major problem in London, but he rejects the thesis that this is "gentrification-induced displacement". Given the period for when he was collecting empirical data, this is probably true – the gentrifiers were moving into the spaces left by de-industrialisation and de-population. Post 2002, in a very tight housing market, it is middle class incomes that are now forcing lower income earners further afield.[19]

Does this amount to Durkheim's abnormal division of labour? There has been the dotcom bust that lost 100,000 plus jobs which would count as an unchecked market. Any repeat of the 1987 crash would have a far greater effect on London's prosperity – given its increased reliance on financial services. There is much degradation of work in low paid service jobs and loss of respect for experience and skill across a range of jobs.[20] There is a situation of unjust rewards in that the talented inner city school student would find it difficult to break into the new cosmopolitan elite, and the best paid jobs can always be filled by incoming workers. Income inequality is systematically correlated with background, not merit. The question of just allocation of jobs against talent requires updating to that of social justice. W.G. Runciman has shown – for some time – that this has to be understood in terms of relative deprivation.[21] Increased stratification produces greater relative deprivation, and London as a global city finds it increasingly difficult to deliver equality of opportunity. On balance this then suggests an abnormal division of labour. Is London able as a global city to rectify the situation with its many but related dimensions of inequality in power, status, income and wealth? And does it have the ability to create a sense of identity that could transcend those inequalities?

London's Governance

London's governance is shared between central government, local boroughs, and the Greater London Authority. Central government controls and makes most of the strategic decisions, local boroughs deliver the essential services, and the Mayor and the GLA have some pan-London powers and rather more responsibilities. I will argue in this section that London's combined governance is not designed or equipped to rectify the many problems London faces, especially those that stem from its global city status. It can be further argued that London's governance is constituted to advance its global business standing at the expense of issues of coordination, social cohesion and social justice.

All eyes are on the Mayor's Office and the GLA which came into existence in July 2000, replacing in a different form the Greater London Council, which was abolished in 1986 by Mrs Thatcher's Conservative government. The missing years of any overall London governance were of course those of the new ascendancy of financial and business services and the prosperity that went with it. As already noted, London reversed the trend of decline – demographically, economically, and in world city status. New pressures and stresses accompanied these growth trends, and the Mayor and GLA were expected to relieve the pressure and offer better coordination for London-wide issues.

It is, however, a common observation that the Mayor and the

GLA have limited statutory powers in tackling London's problems. The Assembly has strategic oversight of the Metropolitan Police Authority and it was given similar control over the London Planning and Emergency Planning Authority, the London Development Agency, Transport for London, and the London Pensions Fund Authority. These competencies do not provide the GLA with the levers to re-engineer neighbourhood and family policies, to redress the entrenched patterns of inequality highlighted in the Mayor's commissioned report *London Divided. Income Inequality and Poverty in the Capital* (2004), or to sort out major planning issues of housing, transport and the environment. Most of those levers remain in the hands of central government. The necessary fiscal measures lie with the Chancellor of the Exchequer, schools policy with the Department for Education and Skills, and planning and the environment with (in the recent period) the Office of the Deputy Prime Minister (ODPM). The government's large regeneration budget is administered through Government Office for London, and this need not coincide with the London Development Agency's identification of priority areas.[22] The Mayor and the GLA have very limited tax-raising powers and no input into the taxation and benefit system, which they might wish to have in order to target the large and deep pockets of deprivation that occur within London. The GLA have to insert a precept into Londoners council tax bills in order to raise funds – probably the most unpopular way of raising tax (whose bulk comes from central government anyway). Only 10% of public spending in London goes through the GLA, and very little of this is discretionary spending on new plans and policy – rather existing commitments it inherited. This can be compared to New York, where 70% of the city's funding comes from local taxation and the mayor and the city council are "responsible for police, fire, hospitals, personal social services, social housing, refuse collection, local streets and lighting, cleansing, sport and planning." Education is also funded by the mayor.[23] London's Mayor can highlight deprivation but can do little to change the

71

circumstances that produce inequality. London's state schooling system is generally judged to deliver a lower level of educational attainment than neighbouring counties, and in certain areas of inner London markedly worse attainment levels. This matters, even more, because the job market demands not unskilled labour power, as in much of London's old manufacturing sector, but a high knowledge component. Being a global city pushes the job requirements ever higher, along with salaries. Yet in many inner city areas the London school student is left stranded with inadequate education, skills and – unsurprisingly – low expectations. The high value jobs are filled by incomers – from the rest of the UK and abroad.[24] In the matter of youth crime, it would seem the Home Office has more say in the deployment of the Metropolitan Police – its priority being guarding against terrorism rather than a police presence in areas of known youth crime.

The mayoral system tends to disguise this absence of effective power. Mayoral candidates will always be politicians of national reputation, and their political personalities will belong to the national stage as much as to London itself.[25] The London Assembly is not a legislative body, rather it is confined to oversight of the Mayor's appointments and strategy plans. It takes a two-thirds majority of its members to overturn a decision of the Mayor. This emphasises the leadership principle incorporated in the arrangements for the GLA and Mayor, adding to the high political profile of the Mayor's office.

Historically, central government has always been loath to provide adequate self-governing powers to London, fearing, so to speak, the big boots of Dick Whittington and the immensity of London as a counterweight to Westminster. The incoming Labour government of 1997 was obliged by its electoral promises to replace in some form the Greater London Council. The legislation restricted the Mayor and the GLA from encroaching on existing London boroughs' delivery of service and confined them to informing strategic decisions "and to assist in the delivery of 'agreed London-wide policies'". This agreement includes not only London boroughs but the Government Office of London, which is directly responsible to the Cabinet. The GLA bureaucracy was envisaged as no more that 250 – hence the small size of the original London Assembly buildings. And the GLA was specifically prohibited "from incurring any expenditure in providing any housing, education, social services, or health services…".[26] Martin Pilgrim quotes the Prime Minister's Strategy Unit which in 2003 wrote, "Central government has by far the greatest impact on the strategic issues facing London". Pilgrim provides in his article a "wiring diagram" of London's government which illustrates how densely and how completely the GLA is circumscribed by other statutory bodies. In his view, the chart showed "that in key areas such as infrastructure, skills, people, economy and service provision, the Mayor of London has less power than central government and in many cases less power than local government".[27] The local government expert Tony Travers is more scathing: "Only if central government devolved financial and political power to London (or other regions) would there be any real change that Britain's abject record of developing major projects could be put to an end."[28]

Perhaps in recognition of this, a government bill was passed in November 2006, granting the Mayor additional powers over planning, housing and waste management. These are not negligible additions in regard to local boroughs, for they empower the Mayor to override local planning priorities in favour of what he regards as a strategic necessity – for example, high density and high rise housing in the inner city. Central government, though, has written into every clause of these new powers that they are subject to Secretary of State and have to conform to national policy. Effectively, the Mayor becomes the agent of central government. In seeking to meet the London Plan targets without sufficient means, there is a danger that the Mayor pushes the burden onto boroughs least able to resist. The London Plan envisages 458,000 additional housing units by 2016.[29] The target for affordable housing in the 2007 Monitoring Report undershot by 5,000 units. The overall new homes target, which is meant to include a 50% affordable target, was met. But there is evidence that housing densities went over the maximum in boroughs like Hackney and Southwark, but remained under the recommended targets in the outer boroughs.[30] Dalston in the heart of Hackney, and one of the most dense areas in London, is targeted for high rise towers – after a period of urban renewal which had removed them from the area. This would seem to be a misinterpretation of the Richard Rogers high density doctrine, which was originally aimed at low density urban settlement, and as such it will be interesting to note the view of the Commission for Architecture and the Built Environment on this type of development.[31] Growth targets in economic activity and population growth are being met – but these are exogenous to the Plan; housing, transport infrastructure, waste disposal and pollution prove more difficult.[32]

In one sense this is consistent with central government's national economic policies since the 1980s. London's economic standing today results from the raft of neo-liberal policies introduced by the Conservative administration of Mrs Thatcher, which included the liberalisation of markets, deregulation, privatisation, market provision of previously state provided services, tax reductions, and internationalisation of labour and capital markets. In theory, these measures could have galvanised all sectors of London's economy, and did so for the services sector broadly defined. Manufacturing, however, followed a declining trend of investment. It was unattractive for its low value-added value and productivity, and the exigency of very high pound to dollar rate made it less attractive, so leading to the de-industrialisation of the London economy. Neo-liberal policies were effective for and beneficial to the City of London. As Jessop and Stones note of this period: "Thatcherite policies have reinforced the concentration of financial power in the City by abolishing exchange controls, deregulating financial institutions and services, generating business through privatisation, encouraging a free flow of inward and outward investment by multinationals, sponsoring small business expansion, providing favourable tax treatment for some financial instruments as well as reducing levels of personal and corporate taxation, and promoting popular capitalism."[33] London's current growth trend of massive inward investment by foreign banks, finance houses and corporations is to be dated to the state's policies of the mid-1980s. Dirigiste state policies on regionalism and the modernisation of industry were abandoned. The Greater London Enterprise Board of the early 1980s and its scheme to re-invigorate Docklands is now a forgotten industrial policy in the face of the miraculous ascent of Canary Wharf.

The connection is not quite as direct as the above paragraph might suggest. Neo-liberal policies provided a favourable environment for financial services (and a hostile one to manufacturing). Innovation, creativity, investment and risk-taking, and a high-knowledge input were all required to get London's financial revolution underway; just as those same factors were at work in the property sector, consumer services, and the creative industries. There is a large element of self-organisation in the urban economy that cannot be reduced to the determination of prime movers. That said, it was economic policies of central government that enabled the financial revolution of Big Bang, and its continuing policies of non-intervention, which is so evident in the present government's reluctance to re-equilibrate the heated growth trends of London and the south east in favour of the north of England and Scotland. London is now the motor of the British economy. London has a surplus of £13 billion in 2005 in its balance of trade with the rest of the UK economy. London imports "substantially more manufactures and other goods than it exports, underlining the extent to which London acts as the hub of financial and business services for the UK."[34] In 2005 it dragged in over £110 billion of goods and services from the rest of the UK economy – and that's a lot of white van traffic on the motorways, bringing the builders, shop-fitters, carpet layers, security experts etc. as well as London's daily need for consumable goods. London is a net contributor to UK public finances of between £6 and £20 billion in 2004-05 (depending on method of calculation).[35] If London should catch a cold, there would be no offsetting economic sector to take the load. (The 2000-2002 downturn was, fortuitously, offset by increased public service expenditure.)

London's many problems – especially those that stem from its recent successes – are therefore the outcome of national policy. But those problems are not as much a concern for Westminster as they are to the Mayor, the London boroughs, and London's population and commuters. London is a cash cow – well, more of a spurting bull – whose overheated economy and stressed environment is not the first concern of national politicians. The important point about London is not simply that it is disadvantaged fiscally from what it gets back in expenditure, but disadvantaged through the electoral arithmetic that London MPs, from who no caucus has appeared, amount to very little in the face of the body of UK MPs.

This gives rise to the paradox that London is moving towards an economy centred on its global connections, yet this trend was put in place and furthered by a central, national government. The present mayor, as we will see, goes along with these policies, but he did not originate them. London is a global city, but it will always be denied the polity of a global city state.

This matters on a number of counts: planning, policy and political virtue. It is legitimate for a London-wide government to institute measures in education, housing, transport, and the environment that in some ways offset the changes in the social division of labour that are concomitant with its global economic position. It has no such powers. London as a global city now dominates the south east region and raises immense issues on infrastructural investment and planning. London's interest in these issues always has to be formulated, through the London Development Agency, in terms of *national* policy guidelines on transport, housing, utilities, and economic policy. The London region, i.e. the 32 boroughs, the City of London, *and* its regional commuter belt, is not allowed to act as a unitary authority to solve their common problems. Given the sheer wealth of the "London region" – one of the richest regions in the world, it would not lack the resources, will and capacity to sort out its problems in a proactive way. Had such a self-governing regional London existed from the early 1990s, when the global trend became apparent, it would have uprated London's commuter transit system, built new tube lines and Crossrail, put in the infrastructure for brownfield sites like Thames Gateway so bringing on stream desperately needed new housing, and lastly, it would have taken a more interventionist line over the London region's precarious water supply (precarious because it is reliant on riverine abstraction). It could have also instituted a training and skills programme specifically oriented to the labour requirements of infrastructural investment, so re-skilling the unemployed and underemployed for construction led jobs.

All of these things are endlessly talked about in the welter of organisations that worked under the umbrella of the Office of the Deputy Prime Minister. But the ODPM appears not to have had the competence or political backing to progress these badly needed solutions. Instead these measures are pursued in a reactive and politically unfocussed way – a reflection of the way in which London's governance always – and now increasingly – lags behind its current sociological realities. The GLA and Mayor, the City of London Corporation, and many other pro-London organisations (London First etc.) can plead the case for more investment spend, but since those decisions will be made by central government – and every kilometre of new railway line has to be passed through parliament at Westminster – governments cannot be seen to favour London. Commentators, such as John Hall, while congratulating business groups for their input and contribution to London's planning and business policy, are still forced to complain about "procrastinations on Crossrail and other large schemes".[36] But this one-sided local corporatism is itself part of the political problem.

Of political virtue, we can start with the simple virtues of efficiency and competence in planning and delivery of new infrastructure. Londoners know to their cost this is absent. Social justice is another virtue. Cities are notorious for their unequal distribution of rewards.[37] Space is always at a premium, and living is always heavily dependent on the provision of services and the social environment. A global division of labour and its stratification intensifies inequality in the city. The in-built advantages and disadvantages of housing markets and the public goods, like schooling and the social and cultural environment that come with them, require muscular attention. Durkheim accepted that the modern division of labour made inequality inevitable, but he argued that social integration and cohesion could still be achieved through the fostering of a collective identity. The idea of a self-governing city provides the basis of such an identity. The Mayor's Office would seem to be very much aware of the need to construct a London identity, but lacking administrative powers embedded in the life of the city it is often reduced to propagandising London issues. Its favoured typographical rendition of LONDON, is a direct reference to the typography of Johnston and Pick's London underground map and signage. The nostalgia for the modernist cutting-edge aspects of the old LCC are understandable. London Transport, as it then was, was a vertically integrated administrative structure that could plan and deliver in an integrated way and impose a service ethos and etiquette. These powers are simply denied to the present Transport for London. The small addition of the London Extension Line, as a private enterprise, is a consortium of myriad of companies with little chance of unified vision, and further progress will be piecemeal. Rarely, these days, do you see elderly people on a London bus – they are an orthopaedic death trap as drivers accelerate and brake with no regard to their fragile passengers. A global city has no city walls and is subject to large migratory flows. For this reason a sense of place and style of everyday encounter becomes important. London may not be a permanent place of residence for many, but as a social entity it needs to impose its identity as durable and significant.

Democracy and political conflict are political virtues. The democratic deficit has already been mentioned. The London Assembly is not constitutionally designed as a democratic and active legislative chamber, and the Mayor's Office is granted only limited powers by central government. With democracy comes the articulation of social, cultural and economic interests, their debate, their resolution, and the accountability of decision making. Conflict, as Seymour Martin Lipset established in his classic book *Political Man*, is essential and functional for modern plural societies. The only real conflict apparent in the present set-up is between the local boroughs and the Mayor's Office, though it is not as intensive as it was in the GLC period. It is not a political virtue to try and diminish such conflict because the interests of boroughs and their constituencies will not necessarily align with pan-London strategies. Political conflict brings the articulation of different issues to the fore and through debate allows greater information to be debated. Machiavelli resolved republican city virtues in favour of the people's love of their city and its prestige and power. Today, we settle, in democratic theory, for citizen debate and its deliberated outcomes. What we have to guard against are the modern princes and the imposition of supervening political wills, which reflect decisionism more than their claim to objective strategy and plan.

In the same way, political conflict should be expected of and enabled between the interests of the 32 London boroughs and the larger commuter belt. Their fortunes and planning requirements are interlinked, but of course not the same. Any move to a London region would be as politically explosive as the extension of the GLC to the 32 boroughs, whose outlying more conservative and suburban boroughs objected strongly at the time. The interdependence is quite complex. London as a global city works through its agglomeration effects – being able to offer so much in the compact business centre of the city (i.e. the West End and the City of London). Yet this sophisticated and globally competitive capacity is serviced not only by a commuter belt but a 150 mile radius from which goods and services are imported on a daily basis. This creates acute tensions, at a local level, about land use, housing and transport provision, which local councils will chose to deal with as autonomous statutory powers. But there exists a sizeable common interest for thousands of local councils in relation to the behemoth of London. Through what legislative assembly are these issues treated? To an extent through the Westminster Parliament and Whitehall, but only through the prism of how the national planning guidelines are defined.

Conflicts of interest at GLA level and central government cannot be settled through political debate and dialogue because, as already noted, the Mayor and the GLA are structurally in no position to stand up to central government. Instead it is worth examining what had developed in its stead. It is a variant on a developing trend termed "urban regime" by urban sociologists and geographers. This was first picked up by analysts in the United States where city government was thought to operate along a political continuum from community participation to elite control. Was city government democratic or were cities ruled through non-elected elites? Urban regime analysis switches the question from "who governs?" to "what is the city agenda?". Where cities compete nationally, as in the United States, or internationally, there is an impetus for civic leaders, business sectors and their leaders, and city institutions to come together to formulate a strategy and profile for their city.[38] This is a case of sociological theory being applied – competition and trade between cities over command and control of world markets, as elaborated by Friedmann and others, then becomes the new policy consensus about how it is best achieved.

During the 1990s a network of business organisations (City of London Corporation, London First, London section of CBI, and the London Chamber of Commerce and Industry) worked with the London boroughs and their planning body, the London Planning Advisory Group, and the Government Office for London. There was considerable interest when Livingstone was elected mayor as to how he would approach this business-oriented network with its urban agenda of promoting London as a world city, seeking competitive advantage for the finance, banking and business sector. He had a history of supporting an alternative economic strategy while leading the GLC in the early 1980s. By the same token, he could be read as an economic interventionist – that civic governance should become directly involved in economic planning and decision-making. According to a number of academic commentators, who have closely followed Livingstone's record, he has committed the Mayor's Office to a pro-central business district strategy, and appointed leading business and City of London Corporation figures to key planning committees.[39]

The advantages of creating an urban regime are the Darwinian ones of efficiency and adaptability in a competitive world environment. The efficiency comes in having low transaction costs in reaching decisions, quickly. By contrast, democratic decision making is slower and has higher transaction costs. The rhetorical question that is posed is: would you prefer London to be a wealthier or a poorer city? Anyone who lived in London during the 1970s knows the answer to that question. In addition, officials in the Mayor's Office argue they can demand offsets from business and from government, most notably, they say, the policy of all new housing developments offering 50% affordable housing.[40]

The criticisms of London's new urban regime – leaving aside the obvious one that it is low on the democratic virtues of representation through elections, accountability and transparency – is that certain business sectors are excluded. If the central business district is favoured, what is happening to manufacturing in Brent, and office development in Bromley? Why are the "City fringes" subject to City pressure when the Isle of Dogs is still able to expand? Also the act setting up the GLA and the mayoralty stipulated the New Labour doctrine of the importance of community and social cohesion alongside that of competitiveness. Andy Thornley and colleagues have researched how the Mayor in the formulation period of the London Plan went out of his way to court civic forum groups as well as business, but that the role of the former were soon dispensed with. The democratic input to the London Plan, coming through the Deputy Mayor, Nicky Gavron, was sidelined in favour of selective business advice made directly to the Mayor.[41] Whatever the City of London Corporation (and it is core to the Mayor's business strategy) does, it does well. But it can hardly be envisaged that it will participate in London-wide social cohesion programmes, even though, as a driver of London as a global city, it has more effect on London's social division of labour than any other agent. Urban regime analysis, as the term implies, is not obviously compatible with the good intentions of third-way consensus building.

A further criticism can be mounted from the point of risk analysis. Should the Mayor's Office be so determinedly fronting up the financial and business interests of central London? We know from the dotcom bust of 2000, which led to the loss of 100,000 net jobs in London between 2000 and 2002,[42] and the stock exchange crash of 1987 that the virtual knowledge economy is subject to volatility and set-backs. The recent prosperity of the City of London has been driven by hedge funds, private equity ventures, and company flotations from abroad (Russia in particular). Is the Mayor's Office equipped to judge the robustness of this business to be promoted at the expense of the portfolio of London's other economic assets? Stephen Syrett argues that "there is only fragmented and partial evidence to support the view that governance forms have a significant impact on the extent of a city's global economic competitiveness".[43] Not least in this regard are the creative industries nestled into the inner city around the central business district for reasons of cultural capital. Insensitive and partisan spatial planning in favour of the City would not suggest a balanced approach to the still present multiple sectors of London's economy, which contribute just as much to London's status as a world city. Spontaneity, innovation, symbiosis and self-organisation are little understood. They have counted much for London's renaissance. Backing winners, as city policy, could disadvantage current, unnoticed innovative developments. Cities operate as much through 'ecologies of ignorance' and through 'known knowns'.[44]

In the framework of this article, my point is that we should not be surprised by the Mayor's strategy. The only way he can increase his statutorily limited powers is to align his policies with those of national government and with the leading edge of the national economy. It recognises that the Mayor's Office will gain most power through mediation and leverage. Livingstone has tried confrontation with the government over the Treasury preferred private public partnership for Transport for London. After failing at judicial review he has had to back down and reach an understanding with Whitehall. He can, and has, deployed populist rhetoric and sympathy against the government, but in a bruising encounter central government is the superior, and battle-hardened, player.

This extension of the Mayor and the GLA's powers are particularly required in the spatial planning for London's regional issues. The Spatial Integration Plan intimates an Abercrombie type regional planning role for the GLA. An imaginative plan has been formulated with four corridors running outwards from London. (Running eastwards, Thames Gateway; northwards, Hackney, the Lee Valley to Stansted and Cambridge; westwards, through Park Royal, Heathrow, to Reading and Basingstoke; and a southwards corridor through Croydon to the Crawley-Horsham area.) Although it is the Mayor's responsibility to prepare such a strategic plan, he has no statutory powers (or fiscal resources) to carry through the plan to development. Those powers lie with central government. But by acting as the leading strategic thinker, and in conformity with national policies, the Mayor's Office will come to assume a leading role. To some extent the Mayor is achieving this with the recent transfer of housing and regeneration funds from central government to the London

Development Agency.[45] This matters for London, because breaking out through the northern and eastern corridors would relieve the intense pressure on space and readjust the imbalance between London's poorer east side in comparison with its west.

However, the infrastructure and clean-up costs, and putting in place sustainable communities, is astronomically expensive – though not beyond the resources of a premier global city, which has to expand to maintain its world city advantages at a competitive level. The Government has to act first to make such funding available and hence the decision is accountable to national politics. Thames Gateway has been planned, or at least closely contemplated, but as yet hardly funded (and inadequate funding would result in a ribbon development of suburban shanty town – an urban form not lightly to be dismissed according to Peter Hall[46]). This brings us to the political context of the London Olympics. As an athletics nation, the UK could have probably lived without it. London itself had enough *grands projets* to be going on with. But the Olympics offered a ready-made solution for the Mayor and central government. The southern end of the northern corridor would now get the infrastructure spend, and the decision could be politically legitimated – this would not be for London alone but the whole country.

From a rational planning perspective this solution has a worrying number of perverse consequences. Winning, in some ways a lottery prize, throws all the planning and development agencies into immediate mode with huge opportunity costs for all other major developments. The two projects that have always come out as priorities since the 1980s, according to cost benefit analysis, are Crossrail and the Chelsea to Hackney underground line. Crossrail will not be built before the Olympics, and its future will not be unconnected to the overspend and whatever deficit results from the Games. Chelsea to Hackney (and extended up the Lee Valley) will be hard to re-launch as an idea. Thames Gateway could well face radical geographical abbreviation. With the kind of spend the Olympics will draw down over a six year period, an empowered regional planning board working since 1990 on six year cycles would be well on the way to transforming the London regional area – and working to reasoned and costed budgets. The recent news on the Olympics budget could be politically catastrophic. What seems to be happening is an accelerated urban regime – not accountable to any one authority, not transparent, and overriding normal planning procedures that acknowledge a measure of equity. The rationality of planning demands strict and accountable budgeting. The political climate for planning – always a difficult issue in a crowded isle – demands observance of public norms and protocol. What so far has been reported in the press is not encouraging in these two respects.[47]

Is There Another Way?
My analysis, just to summarise, is that a global city is part of, and contributor to, a complex social division of labour – one that does not lead to community and social cohesion but can provide the resource for underwriting these public and civic goods. From this stems the onus on global city government to be able to act as a countervailing force in terms of a city identity and the whole urban environment in which Londoners live their lives. The political analysis says that the GLA and Mayor set-up was flawed. In seeking to overcome the stasis of class based political parties at local level, a predominating role was given to the Mayor. In order to stop the Mayor upstaging national government, the powers of the GLA and Mayor were made subservient to central government and the relevant secretary of state. The rise of London as a premier global city demands a more honest appreciation of its regional and transnational importance.

The design of the GLA, which seems to have been drafted by a management consultancy and a think-tank (rather than commission with constitutional experts), was a fairly straight-forward reflection of recent political history. It would fill the gap left by the abolition of the GLC, advance a world city agenda, and favour consensus not political conflict. On the design of the GLC – to go back to the early 1960s – Pimlott and Rao quote a comment by Peter Hall. "The English have an extraordinary knack for devising pieces of administrative machinery for London that are admirably suited to the conditions of a quarter-century back."[48] Hall was complaining of the inability to think through the strategic planning needs of London and instead falling back into continuities of past administrative arrangements. Likewise, the think-tank commissioned to devise the GLA refused to learn any lessons from abroad – "national political cultures and legal systems vary, it is therefore misguided to hope to find ready-made solutions to London's problems abroad."[49]

Comparative analysis encourages conceptual thinking and it is worth mentally rehearsing models of regional governance that can deliver strategic needs. The defects of the present London system is that it aspires to give strategic capability to the GLA and Mayor without the administrative means, and that, if the extra political powers were granted to the Mayor, the legislative role of the GLA would have to be re-thought.

The North German city model of governance combines two interesting features. The leading cities are seats of regional government and the mayor is voted by the (elected) municipal council to lead the executive. Regional assemblies confer greater strategic power to the executive, which itself is democratically more beholden to the council that elects it – i.e. the mayor and *Magistrat* are chosen through indirect election.

The Madrid system, which no one appears to have considered, advances the regional principle to a capital city. London's governance is unequally shared by central government, advancing the political rights of a national capital city, and the GLA and Mayor reflecting in an attenuated form London's global and world city status. Madrid is an autonomous region of Spain which geographically takes in the surrounding 'counties' (in English terms). It has an elected regional parliament with its own president. Madrid also has an elected city council and mayor, both of which are directly elected. The city council and mayor are in charge of city wide functions which include education, local taxation, welfare services, policing, culture, and the environment. Members of the city council are appointed to head up the major 'ministries'. The city council has to work with the Madrid regional parliament on the strategic issues of their common region – both cities and countryside. Madrid, as the political capital of Spain, has the responsibility of leading a nation of autonomous regions.

The logic of the Madrid model is regionalism and a high degree of federalism. The London case is a victim of hundreds of years of a centralising dynastic and then national state, whereas Madrid is the beneficiary of the 1978 constitution which undid the centralising authoritarianism of the Franco regime. In this mental experiment the lesson to be worked on is how a dominant urban region is best governed within a national framework. In the UK, the logic of regionalism was articulated in the mid-1990s before the sub-regional/central business district/executive mayor model was introduced to London in 2000. There was a Commission for Regional Policy whose remit was: "To discuss how regional economic and social policy can be integrated within a democratically accountable regional government framework, building on Labour's commitment to devolve power to a Scottish Parliament and Welsh Assembly, and to regional government for England." The Regional Policy Commission, write Pimlott and Rao, "recommended the establishment of regional development agencies as the 'executive arms' of the regional assemblies, with responsibilities for economic development, regeneration and promotion of regional competitiveness and business efficiency. There was a strong preference for elected bodies in the place of a plethora of non-elected quangos."[50]

Such discussion might have a 'back to the future' feel about it, but against which it can be noted that much of the setting up of the GLA and Mayor had an air of short-term political pragmatism not unconnected to actual but transitory political personalities. What the Madrid model suggests is the acceptance of a London urban region whose governance should be more clearly demarcated from Westminster and Whitehall. And the trajectory of the London urban region is firmly integrated with trends in the global economy, just as Spanish regional autonomy only makes sense within the wider framework of the European Union.

Another look at regionalism will not appear on the agenda, until a new political conjuncture forms. Elements of that conjuncture would involve Scottish independence, the Olympic Games emptying the National Lottery, regional resentment at London's break-away economic success, and a reform movement within central government and its great ministries that recognizes that the nation-state framework and its centralising imperative are out of tune with globalisation. As Roland Robertson observed some time ago, globalisation is a movement that can re-invigorate the local, re-cast the regional, while diminishing the national in favour of the global.[51]

London is a major player in the process of globalisation and still has lessons to learn about governance issues. It also has opportunities to exercise political virtue in the global age. It is the pre-eminent city of European civilization, the possessor of the world's common language, and the holder of internationally accepted legal and commercial procedures. If, in some Hegelian sense, the centre of gravity of history has moved from nation to world cities, then this places London and its representatives in the front line of world history. The 'command and control' mantra of urban regime analysis then takes on a far wider significance – not an urban neo-imperialism but the start of a new urban civilization. The City of London and financial centres like it in Shanghai, New York, Tokyo, Singapore, and Frankfurt exist to facilitate the investment in the future (howsoever it is expressed in the financial language of income flows pertaining to financial instruments and assets). And in the language of finance, the future is made, putatively, risk free through the superiority of market information flows – the efficient market thesis, the use of balanced portfolios and offsetting, hedging devices.[52] In the global world switched to slow carbon roast the imperative now, and urgently, becomes investment in sustainability. Perhaps it will be the mayors of the great world cities who will broker the new world order, for they are responsible to urban electorates upon whom the stress of urban living now falls.

Notes

1   I would like to thank Sylvia Tarchova who provided invaluable research information for this article.

2   David Cameron, "Children wellbeing speech", Witney, 16 February, 2007.

3   Quoted in Mick Ryan, 2003, *Penal Policy and Political Culture in England and Wales*, Waterside Press, Winchester, p. 123.

4   Ibid. and Simon Hallsworth, 2006, *Punitive States: Punishment and the Economy of Violence*, Glasshouse, London.

5   Richard Sennett 2003, *Respect. The Formation of Character in an Age of Inequality*, Penguin, London.

6   Max Weber 1968 [orig. 1920], *Economy and Society*, Bedminster Press, New York, pp. 114-141.

7   See Peter Mandelson 2007, "The European Union in the Global Age" policy network, pp. 12-13.

8   Quoted by Steven Lukes, 1973 *Emile Durkheim, His Life and Work. A Historical and Critical Study*, Allen Lane, London, p. 154.

9   Karl Bücher 1901, *Industrial Evolution*, New York, H. Holt.

10 Peter Dicken 2003 (4th ed), *Global Shift: Transforming the World Economy*, London, Sage.

11 Quoted in Mark Abrahamson, 2004, *Global Cities*, Oxford, Oxford University Press, p. 11.

12 Saskia Sassen 1991, *The Global City. New York, London, Tokyo*, Princeton, Princeton University Press.

13 Stephen Syrett, "Governing the Global City: Economic Challenges and London's New Institutional Arrangements", *Local Government Studies*, 2006, 32, 3, p. 296. Buck, N., Gordon, I., Hall, P., Harloe, M. and Kleinman, M. 2002, *Working Capital: Life and Labour in Contemporary London*, Routledge, London, p. 141.

14 Oxford Economic Forecasting, 2006, p. 95.

15 "London's Place in the UK Economy, 2006-7", Oxford Economic Forecasting, 2007, London pp. 3-4, 43. The 2001 Census figures should probably be regarded as an underestimate, given the slackness with which the Census was carried out at enumerator level.

16 ibid, p. 12.

17 Syrett, "Governing the Global City", op.cit., pp. 297-8.

18 Chris Hamnett 2002, *Unequal City. London in the Global Arena*, Routledge, London.

19 Chris Hamnett, *Unequal City*, pp. 155-8, & 181.

20 Sennett, R. 2006, *The Culture of New Capitalism*, Yale University Press, New Haven.

21 Runciman, W.G. 1966, *Relative Deprivation and Social Justice*, London, Routledge & Kegan Paul.

22 Syrett, op.cit., p. 304.

23 Tony Travers, 2004 *The Politics of London. Governing an Ungovernable City*, Palgrave Macmillan, Basingstoke, p. 177.

24 Buck, N., Gordon, I., Hall, P,. Harloe, M. and Kleinman, M. 2002, *Working Capital: Life and Labour in Contemporary London*, Routledge, London, p. 195.

25 See Ben Pimlott and Nirmala Rao, *Governing London*, Oxford: Oxford University Press, 2002, pp. 16-19. They cite Douglas Yates tabulation of activism conjoined with low power resources, as providing only one option: the crusader. This does not accurately describe Livingstone's style which is closer to the entrepreneur model – the person who gets things done. According to Yates, this box is reserved for high power resources and high activism. It is a tribute to Ken Livingstone that he acts as if he did high power resources available. But this also relates to how Livingstone has broken out of the box by forming strategic alliances with central government, discussed below.

26 Martin Pilgrim, "London Regional Governance and the London Boroughs", *Local Government Studies*, 32, 3, 2006, pp. 226-7.

27 See Pilgrim, pp. 232-4.

28 Travers, T. 2004, *The Politics of London. Governing an Ungovernable City*, Palgrave Macmillan, Basingstoke, p. 205.

29 Syrett, op.cit., p. 306. Along with the new housing powers devolved to the mayor is the Barker Review on the reform of planning law and procedure. This will speed up local planning procedures in order to bring more housing developments on stream. Within the Review it is stated that "Community engagement should be front-loaded in the decision-making process to give people a voice over the principles of design and development." However this bullet-point is not expanded on, and it is left to developers to take into account community views. See www.barkerreview.org.uk, pp. 31 & 47.

30 Hackney in 2001-2004 had an average housing density of 104 units per hectare, compared with Bromley of 31. Planning permission densities averaged over 2004-2006 are 228 for Hackney and 51 for Bromley. "London Plan Annual Monitoring Report 3", February 2007, p. 25.

31 Rogers, R. and Power, A. 2002, *Cities for a Small Country*, Faber and Faber, London.

32 "London Plan Annual Monitoring Report 3," op. cit., pp. 5-6, 25, 57.

33 Bob Jessop and Rob Stones, "Old City and New Times", in *Global Finance and Urban Living. A Study of Metropolitan Change*, 1992, edited Leslie Budd and Sam Whimster, London, Routledge, p. 179.

34 *London's Place in the UK Economy*, 2006-07, Oxford Economic Forecasting, 2006, p. 39.

35 *London's Place*, p. 4

36 John Hall, 2006, "The Role of Business in London. Local and Regional Government: How it became Recognised as a Significant Player", *Local Government Studies*, 32, 3, p. 331.

37 Harvey, D. 1973, *Social Justice and the City*, Edward Arnold, London, pp. 96-118.

38 Urban regime analysis is applied to London by Andy Thornley, Yvonne Rydin, Kath Scanlon and Karen West in their article, "Business Privilege and the Strategic Planning Agenda of the Greater London Authority", *Urban Studies*, 42, 11, 2005, pp. 1947-1968.

39 See Thornley et al, op. cit.

40 Thornley et al, op. cit. p. 1963.

41 Pimlott and Rao, p. 164; Thornley et al, op. cit., p. 1958.

42 OEF, London's Place, p. 13.

43 Syrett, op. cit., p. 393.

44 The phrase "ecologies of ignorance" was coined by Niklas Luhmann. See Ash Amin and Nigel Thrift for its use in an urban context, 2002, *Cities. Reimagining the Urban*, Polity, Cambridge, p. 92.

45 ibid, pp. 301-3.

46 http://www.lse.ac.uk/collections/resurgentCity/Papers/peterhall.pdf

47 The seasoned journalist Max Hastings writes (*Observer*, 18 March 2007): "Blair and Jowell thought they could snatch glory for 'winning' the Games, then be long gone before the stupendous bills came in, the inevitable shambles unfolded. As it is, a scandal is already evident – and that is five years before we face the real-time misery of the event taking place in London, a city which never needed it."

48 Pimlott and Rao, p. 29.

49 Pimlott and Rao, p. 65.

50 Quoted Pimlott and Rao, p. 56.

51 For an update, see Roland Robertson, "Globalisation Theory 2000 +: Major Problematics" in *Handbook of Social Theory*, edited George Ritzer and Barry Smart, London, Sage, 2001, pp. 258-272.

52 See Joceyln Pixley's dismantling of a risk-free future in her *Emotions in Finance: Distrust and Uncertainty in Global Markets*, Cambridge, Cambridge University Press

Chapter 5

Geo-Politics, the 'War on Terror' and the Competitiveness of the City of London

Richard Woodward

> "If you want to hurt the government, hurt people at the same time, and you want to cause maximum disruption...where better to hit than at the financial centre?"
> James Hart, City of London Police Commissioner, August 2005[1]

On 16 September 1920 a horse-drawn wagon packed with dynamite and iron slugs exploded opposite the Wall Street offices of J P Morgan Company killing 30 people, injuring over 200 others and causing $2 million worth of damage. The perpetrator, Mario Buda, was a member of an anarchist group protesting at the detention of two of his comrades. This isolated incident was a harbinger of the 1990s when financial centres, institutions and markets became fashionable targets for terrorist conspirators. While many plots were foiled, the Provisional Irish Republican Army (IRA) committed a series of atrocities in the City of London in the 1990s[2] and in 1993 Islamic extremists detonated a bomb beneath the World Trade Center in the heart of New York's financial district. In the new millennium the financial system has become a vital battleground in the idiosyncratic 'war on terror'.

Following the destruction of the World Trade Center in September 2001, terrorists have struck India's pre-eminent financial district, Mumbai (August 2003), Turkish branches of HSBC bank (November 2003 and March 2006), and made credible threats to financial institutions in New York and London and financial centres throughout Asia and Oceania.[3]

The motivations for attacking financial targets are legion. First, financial institutions and the centres they inhabit constitute key nodes in the global financial structure upon which the wealth and power of nations largely depend.[4] For those bent on disfiguring icons of power and identity, financial centres have become prominent targets.[5] Second, the agglomeration of commercial and communications infrastructure in financial centres enables an enormous amount of damage and disruption to be caused in a single offensive. Costly repairs and rising insurance premiums may damage the long-term competitiveness of individual institutions or centres as a whole but this nothing compared with the interim disruption wrought by such an episode. Private financial markets have become the lifeblood of the global economy pervading everyday life to an unparalleled degree. In extreme circumstances, given the interconnectedness of financial institutions and the short-term nature of many transactions, the temporary (or even permanent) failure of key institutions, such as the four day hiatus on the New York Stock Exchange (NYSE) in September 2001 could prompt a wave of failures throughout the financial system. Indeed, as was alleged to be the case on September 11, the hope of pre-empting or profiting from financial crises and uncertainty maybe another motivation behind terrorist activity.[6] Equally political authorities are prosecuting their 'war on terror' via the financial system. By fortifying the security of financial centres and stopping the surreptitious siphoning of funds through the global financial system, governments hope to prevent terrorists from mounting future operations.

Notwithstanding the lingering menace posed by dissident splinter groups, the most immediate terrorist threat to the City of London seemed to recede following the announcement of the IRA ceasefire in July 1997. In some quarters it was suggested that the City police's preoccupation with terrorism had been supplanted by concerns about violence resulting from the consumption of alcohol and narcotics.[7] This optimistic outlook evaporated on 11 September 2001 since when, amidst talk of the inevitability of attacks and 'hostile reconnaissance' by terrorist suspects, the City has been on perpetual alert.[8]

This chapter argues that the events of 11 September were symptomatic of changing geo-political realities which have accentuated the terrorist threat to the City, but fears that terrorism jeopardises the City's competitiveness are unfounded. Despite the heightened threat, terrorism remains a relatively unimportant factor for the City's *competitive* position because it does not rank highly amongst the factors financial institutions and professionals take into account when making locational decisions and other financial centres are equally vulnerable to attack. A far greater danger, particularly given the hysteria whipped up by the Blair administration and the media,[9] is posed by an overzealous reaction that appreciably raises the costs of transacting business in the City, deters skilled labour by demonising foreigners and minority groups, undermines innovation, and detracts from more pressing issues such as the dilapidated transport infrastructure.

Geo-Political Change, Finance and Terror in the City
In its most abstract sense geo-politics examines "the links and causal relationships between political power and geographic

space".[10] Traditional approaches to geo-politics proceed from the premise that the world's geographic space is divided into hermetically sealed parcels of land each governed by a political power, the sovereign state. Equally the location, size and resources of these geographic spaces bestow power on states in the global political system. From this perspective the prime concern of geo-politics is to examine how geographic conferments affect *interstate* relationships and how interstate relationships contribute to the reconfiguration of geographic space. In recent years scholars have become increasingly dissatisfied with this straightforward correlation. Liberalisation and advances in communications technology have unleashed a torrent of forces that have rendered national boundaries increasingly porous, posing a serious challenge to the power of states and their capacity to govern their geographic space.[11] Moreover, the technological revolution "has been diffusing power away from governments and empowering individuals and groups to play roles in world politics – including wreaking massive destruction – that were once reserved for the governments of states".[12]

In other words, political power does not derive *exclusively* from control over a bounded territorial jurisdiction and is therefore not restricted to states. These so called "sovereignty free"[13] actors, including our two main protagonists, financial markets and terrorist groups, derive their political power from non-territorial sources. Consequently a full understanding of the causes and consequence of geo-political upheaval necessarily involves some consideration of non-state actors. Though this is not the place for a detailed discussion it is important to recognise the symbiosis between the realms of states and those of sovereignty free actors. It has long been accepted that transformations in interstate relationships affect the status of sovereignty free actors but it is readily apparent that sovereignty free actors can jolt interstate relationships. For instance, a terrorist attack on a major oil refinery might bring about shortages and sponsor a spike in prices supplementing, at least temporarily, the power of oil exporting states.[14]

Contemporary geo-political turmoil blended with the earlier rationale for assaulting financial centres has created formidable incentives to attack the City of London. Today, Islamic fundamentalists loosely associated with the nihilist philosophy of the Al-Qaeda movement are widely regarded as the likeliest source of a terrorist plot against the Square Mile. To an extent, Al-Qaeda's origins lie in the geo-political changes ushered in by the end of the Cold War. During the 1980s the US indirectly supported the Mujahadeen in Afghanistan against their Soviet aggressors. As the Cold War drew to a close the USSR withdrew from Afghanistan but already certain elements of the Mujahadeen, amongst them a group belonging to Osama Bin Laden that would eventually emerge as Al-Qaeda, were clamouring to export their operations to Islamic struggles worldwide. Released from the constraints imposed by Cold War enmities Islamic groups soon proved as pragmatic as their initial backers. Their hostility to the West was cemented during the first Gulf War in 1990. After Iraq's annexation of Kuwait, the Saudi Arabians had misgivings that they could be future victims of Iraqi expansionism. To forestall this Bin Laden offered to bolster Saudi forces with his own Mujahadeen. King Fahd rebutted his offer preferring instead to let US and allied troops use Saudi territory as a staging post from which they could expel Saddam Hussein from Kuwaiti territory. Bin Laden deemed this an act of treachery and, following his denunciation of the Saudi government, went into Sudanese exile from whence the Al-Qaeda movement germinated. It is generally agreed that the UK's close ideological and military affiliation with the US has made attacks on the UK more likely.

The globalisation of the capitalist creed is a frequently lauded outcome of the Cold War's cessation but has paradoxically improved the aptitude of terrorists to project their power. Technological progress already enabled them to adopt decentralised command structures making them awkward to trace but coupled with the open borders, demanded by neo-liberal proselytisers, terrorist organisations were permitted to marshal and move resources to orchestrate destruction at distance. Additionally, the widespread embrace of neo-liberal principles has placed financial markets at the centre of our everyday lives. The wealth of individuals, classes, firms, and nations is indelibly connected with the global financial system.

Given the previously noted association between wealth and power, financial markets are inviting targets for those seeking to maintain, alter or accelerate the geo-political trajectory. The City is an especially significant target because of its importance not only to the UK's economic health but to the global financial system as a whole. Conventional wisdom asserts that financial markets are placeless and that we are witnessing the 'end of geography'.[15] In reality, all financial transactions have to take place somewhere, the vast majority in financial centres falling within the geographical space, and hence the regulatory gaze, of a state. Financial centres are a key resource contributing to a state's standing and power in the international system even, as is the case with the City, when much of the centre is owned and controlled by foreign investors.

The City's contribution to the UK's economic wealth is unlikely to have escaped would-be aggressors. Financial services are the most vibrant and productive sector of the UK economy with the City alone accounting for 2.5% of GDP, employing 328,000 people and providing a sizable chunk of the UK's £20bn financial services exports.[16] Long-standing trepidation about the effects of terrorism on this mainstay of the UK economy[17] has been exacerbated by the ostensible 'Wimbledonisation' of the Square Mile. Since the Big Bang deregulation in 1986, many of the UK's venerable financial institutions have succumbed to foreign takeovers so that today more than half of the City's employment is provided by firms headquartered overseas.[18] There is a perception that in the bad times, such as a sustained bear market initiated by a terrorist attack, these overseas outposts will be the first to be sacrificed perhaps decimating the City.[19] A significant diminution of the

City would have severe negative repercussions for the UK
economy and might further impair the UK's ability to play a
meaningful role in global politics.

Finally, the highly internationalised nature of the City
exaggerates its potential contribution to the geo-political milieu.
In 2005, 54% of the UK's banking assets were held by foreign
banks and the UK financial sector had the biggest share of
international bank lending (20%) and international bank
borrowing (22%). The City also booked 43% of foreign equity
trades, undertook 31% of global foreign exchange trading, and
70% of the global trade in international bonds.[20] The global
distribution of wealth and power is intimately bound up with
decisions made by those working in the London's financial
markets. The ramifications of an onslaught against the City
would reverberate on geo-political relationships throughout the
globe precisely the reason why they make an excellent, and
some groups say a legitimate, target of terror.

Threat and Response
Conventional Attack
While the method was novel, the endeavour of the hijackers that
piloted their aircraft into the World Trade Center were
depressingly familiar: causing maximum damage and
disruption to the physical and financial infrastructure.
Deterring such incidents and ensuring robust systems are in
place should they occur, endures as the central focus of the
City's anti-terrorist authorities.

Beginning in the early 1990s a much vaunted 'ring of steel'
was thrown around the Square Mile followed later by an 'iron
collar' at the Docklands peninsula. These security cordons
ebbed and flowed alongside the terrorist threat but essentially
consist of checkpoints controlling the ingress and egress of
vehicles, elaborate surveillance schemes including public and
private CCTV and a digitised system recording vehicle number
plates, more overt policing, plus a variety of private initiatives
to fortify places of business.[21] The ring of steel is primarily a

mechanism to prevent terrorist acts by denying them access to their targets. However, the scale of the outrages executed in New York, the fact that the ring of steel would have done nothing to prevent an analogous episode in the City, and the widespread belief that some sort of attack was inevitable, forced the authorities to reappraise the durability of their emergency procedures.

Catastrophic loss of data and premises meant half of the businesses which closed temporarily following the atrocities in New York never reopened. Preparations for operational disruptions amongst London businesses were equally found wanting.[22] In 2002 the UK Financial Services Authority (FSA) estimated that 30 to 40% of regulated firms did not possess a disaster contingency plan.[23] Even the news that the 35 largest banks and financial institutions in the UK had adequate systems in place must be tempered by the London Chamber of Commerce's finding that a fifth of financial institutions with business continuity plans had not tested them for five years and that 83% of small and medium size enterprises in London have no contingency plans.[24]

Ultimately the responsibility for ensuring financial continuity rests individually and collectively with City institutions. Nevertheless, the tripartite authorities (the FSA, Bank of England and the Treasury) in concert with the private sector have instigated strategies to buttress the resilience of the UK finance sector by the publication of official guidance, encouraging the adoption of business continuity practices, enriching communications and facilitating market cooperation.[25] The general consensus is that City institutions have raised their game with regard to security and contingency planning and would be able to cope with a major operational disruption.[26] Levels of preparedness have been tested using marketwide exercises simulating a major operational disruption. The last exercise, involving 3000 people from 70 organisations, was held in November 2005 and revolved around a terrorist incident. The exercise seemed to demonstrate the sturdiness of the City's contingency plans but also yielded important insights regarding the need to liaise with third party suppliers and to further disperse recovery sites.[27]

Cyberterror and Weapons of Mass Disruption
Sources of operational disruption from terrorists are not limited to bomb blasts and missiles. Financial markets and life in advanced industrialised societies more generally are dependent on intricate networks of technology and communications. Governments are anxious that terrorists, thwarted by more orthodox counterterrorist instruments, will resort to computer hacking, viruses and other techniques to disable networks controlling essential infrastructure. These "weapons of mass disruption"[28] could also be deployed in conjunction with, or to facilitate, a conventional attack.[29] Where the IRA's attempt to immobilize the ring of steel in 1996 by detonating explosives at electricity substations was stymied, self-styled 'cyberterrorists' may succeed by corrupting related computer systems.[30]

Experts disagree about the exact threat posed by cyberterrorism. Proponents of the threat point to many examples and the fragility of poorly calibrated security systems. Between 1993 and 1996, several London institutions surrendered to extortionists threatening to obliterate their computer systems while some 40 other attempts were rebuffed.[31] In 2000 sympathisers of the Zapatista movement laid waste to the web sites of Mexican financial institutions while the US Department of Justice presents an extensive catalogue of crimes connected to computer systems and intellectual property.[32]

Sceptics cast doubts on the likelihood and efficacy of cyberterrorism. They suggest government agencies and private corporations have the resources to employ the staff needed to erect elaborate precautions to vanquish even a determined e-terrorist. That said, impressive external safeguards are pointless if gangs or individual saboteurs infiltrate an organisation with the intention of breaching security from the inside. For instance, the BBC has broadcast a 'mockumentary' portraying the fictional story of how a rogue trader with supposed terrorist connections prompted the collapse of a British investment bank and with it confidence in the British financial system.[33] The doubters dismissed the programme as a fantasy and pointed to the fact that the real culprit turned out to be the rogue trader's superior trying to eke out larger bonuses for himself and his staff. Nevertheless in her review of the programme Elaine Sternberg, a leading commentator on corporate governance issues, offers a less than glowing assessment of hiring procedures suggesting "'sleepers' might pose a danger of terrorism; all candidates should be carefully vetted...references obtained need to be both checked and understood; too often one or both elements are neglected".[34]

Reputational Attacks
Understandably, debates about terrorism in the City have been dominated by unease about spectacular strikes against material targets. Yet, an equally insidious dilemma arises from the use of London's markets as a conduit to launder money to support terrorist activity. There are countless reasons why corporations cluster in the City but underpinning them all is London's reputation for providing "an open, equitable and honest environment in which to conduct business".[35] The manipulation of the City's markets for nefarious purposes could dissolve this considerable competitive advantage.[36] The FSA's most recent Financial Risk Outlook cites terrorist finance amongst the 'priority risks' which "potentially poses significant danger to the reputation of UK financial markets".[37] In July 2006 the Economic Secretary to the Treasury, Ed Balls, revealed that 388 individuals and 181 entities are legally embargoed from raising, moving or using funds in the UK while 152 bank accounts containing £475,000 of suspected terrorist assets have been frozen.[38] This is certainly not evidence of an endemic problem but nevertheless, especially when considered in tandem with some of the high profile money laundering scandals of recent

years, does reveal that unlawful organisations have exploited the sheer scale of the City's financial markets to conceal criminal assets.

Action against terrorist financing stems from the broader international effort to clampdown on money laundering which began in earnest following the inauguration of the Financial Action Task Force (FATF) at the 1989 G7 Summit in Paris. Within a year the FATF published 40 Recommendations designed to tackle the scourge of money laundering. These measures, including the criminalisation of money laundering, measures for authenticating customer identities, reporting suspicious transactions and training frontline staff, were incorporated into the European Community's 1991 Money Laundering Directive and transposed into UK law by the 1993 Criminal Justice Act. From the outset doubts were raised about anaemic implementation and enforcement of the legislation and, by the turn of the century, the City's regulatory authorities stood accused of harbouring an archaic anti-money laundering (AML) regime.[39]

The 11 September attacks reinvigorated the international AML scene and catalysed a blizzard of initiatives to deny terrorists admission to the global financial system. The preliminary thrust came from the United Nations Security Council Resolution 1373 demanding *inter alia* that all member states criminalise terror funding, freeze terrorist assets, and prohibit the aiding and abetting terrorist groups.[40] These themes were subsequently taken up by FATF whose mandate was stretched to incorporate the development of standards to combat the financing of terrorism. The organisation announced 8 (and later a ninth) special recommendations on terrorist financing in October 2001 before setting about revising and updating the original 40 recommendations to take account of new money laundering techniques.[41]

In December 2001 the EU adopted its Second Money Laundering Directive expanding the scope of professions required to observe money laundering regulations, enlarging the numbers of crimes to which provisions applied and providing for the construction of financial intelligence units (FIUs) to render international cooperation more intensive and effective. In 2005 a Third Money Laundering Directive appeared reflecting the revisions to FATF's 40 Recommendations and bringing terrorist financing beneath the money laundering umbrella.[42] The IMF echoed the EU's call for the establishment of FIUs and from November 2002 brought much needed muscle to FATF's Recommendations on money laundering and terrorist financing by adding them to the list of international standards considered as components of their Financial Sector Assessment Program (FSAP).[43]

UK authorities moved with alacrity to enact the legislation required to meet fresh international obligations at the same time revitalising domestic AML initiatives.[44] Existing measures for countering terrorist finance contained in the Terrorism Act 2000 including criminalising the receipt or processing of funds connected to terrorism, creating obligations to report transactions suspected to relate to terrorism, and powers to confiscate terrorist assets were strengthened by the Anti Terrorism, Crime and Security Act 2001 and the Proceeds of Crime Act 2002. There has also been a renaissance amongst the mass of bodies dedicated to deterring, detecting, disrupting and defeating terrorist finance. The National Terrorist Financial Investigation Unit (NTFIU),[45] a previously unheralded division of the Special Branch dealing with terrorist finance, experienced a threefold expansion in staffing and significant additional funding to become the fastest growing section of the organisation.[46]

In a Parliamentary statement in October 2001, Chancellor of the Exchequer, Gordon Brown, announced the creation of a Terrorist Finance Unit within the National Criminal Intelligence Service (NCIS), the UK's FIU. Its task was to receive suspicious transaction reports (SARs) and to disseminate intelligence to other agencies devoted to preventing terrorist financing including Customs and Excise, the Inland Revenue, the police and the NTFIU. From April 2006 these functions have been subsumed by a new body, the Serious Organised Crime Agency (SOCA). Devising and enforcing money laundering rules for regulated firms is the preserve of the FSA as part of its statutory requirement to reduce financial crime. The FSA can bring criminal prosecutions against those found to have contravened these rules but the enforcement of primary money laundering legislation remains the responsibility of the Treasury and the Home Office. Yet, important though these initiatives undoubtedly are, the ultimate responsibility for preventing the use of the City's markets by terrorist financiers again lies with the private sector. The rules concocted by international agreements and government agencies need to be implemented by those on the front line, the staff of financial institutions. Strenuous efforts have been made to provide fora where the principal public and private stakeholders can convene to discuss the latest developments and share best practice incorporating seminars and conferences hosted by the FSA and taskforces and advisory groups chaired by the Treasury and the Home Office.

Despite the flurry of parliamentary activity, the veritable alphabet soup of bodies, and the plaudits heaped on the UK's AML and counter terrorist financing regime by the IMF,[47] the consensus amongst specialists is that London is still a haven for terrorists and money launderers.[48] Incredibly just months after the IMF's Michael Foot, the then Managing Director of the FSA's Deposit Takers and Markets Directorate, was quoted as saying "operation of procedures to combat the laundering of the proceeds of drugs and other crimes...is not satisfactory".[49] Meagre budgets and inadequate staffing of AML/terrorist finance organisations continue to impede implementation of regulations. Aspects of liberalised financial markets usually lauded as beneficial, namely their propensity for innovation and the ability for capital to flow to its most efficient use, pose additional dilemmas. The ingenuity of financial practitioners enables criminals to circumvent new procedures and to exploit fissures between the many bodies involved in the fight against laundering and terrorist finance. The open nature of financial borders means that the fight against terrorist finance is only as strong as the weakest links. Terrorist financiers can exploit loopholes in less stringently regulated jurisdictions and gain access to better regulated jurisdictions through correspondent banking relationships. The City is particularly vulnerable to these problems because of the highly internationalised nature of its business and the inventiveness of its workforce which is often extolled as one of its key competitive advantages.

Terrorism and Competitiveness in the City of London
The preceding paragraphs have at times painted a grim picture of the amplified likelihood of a terrorist catastrophe with terrorists running amok infiltrating and financing their fanaticism through London's financial institutions. Inevitably this has led to questions about the bearing of terrorism on the City's competitive position. In order for terrorism to have an impact on the City's competitiveness two preconditions have to be met. First, the patrons of financial centres must consider terrorism to be an important factor in determining the location of their business. Second, current and prospective customers must perceive that there is some differentiation between the City and its principal competitors in either the likelihood of terrorism or the costs of anti-terrorist measures. All other things being equal we would expect business to gravitate towards the financial centre which minimises terror at the lowest possible cost. The remainder of this chapter argues that terrorism is a minor issue in the competitiveness of London and other financial centres and that the real threat to the City is not terrorism per se but a disproportionate response to it. In other words, the cure may be worse than the disease.

Surveys of financial practitioners have consistently identified the foremost factors in the City's current and future competitiveness as accessibility to a skilled workforce, customers and international markets, the merits of the regulatory environment, the tax regime, quality of life, probity of the corporate environment, and the sensitivity of the government. In contrast, terrorism is viewed as an inconsequential matter which does not even figure amongst the Treasury's register of future challenges for UK financial services.[50] According to a MORI study carried out on behalf of the Corporation of London and the City of London Police, 57% of respondents said terrorism was a worry.[51] Importantly however, similar surveys suggest that terrorism is not an all encompassing fear amongst City dwellers. Fewer than one in ten of those canvassed considered the threat of terrorism on a daily basis or considered it a negative aspect of working in the City. An even smaller proportion of businesses (3%) judged it as a negative aspect of locating in the City.[52] Unsurprisingly apprehensions about terrorism peaked after the 7 July attacks on London's transport system with 59% of people believing the capital would be struck again within a year[53] but overall it is difficult to quibble with Z/Yen's conclusion that "terrorism risk [does not] seem strong in participants' perceptions of what matters"[54] and is a marginal influence on the City's competitiveness.

The City's competitive position is reinforced by the fact that its existing rivals (principally New York but also Paris and Frankfurt), are equally or more susceptible to terrorist attack and stigmatisation by association with terrorist money. As one London based New York banker comments:

> London is probably no more likely to get more bombs in the future than any other financial centre – indeed it's probably less likely than New York. Londoners seem pretty robust and seem to take terrorist attacks in their stride. As a foreigner I was amazed at how quickly London recovered [after the 7 July bombings][55]

Comparisons with New York are exceptionally pertinent because, as the world's only other "global financial centre",[56] it is the City's most direct competitor. Presently there seems limited scope for any additional global financial centres to emerge. The most likely candidates would seem to be Mumbai, whose predisposition to terrorism has been amply demonstrated, and Shanghai, whose suspected vulnerability has prompted the authorities to construct a large underground bunker to protect it.

A similar story emerges with regard to money laundering, including terrorist financing. HM Revenue and Customs estimate that £25bn is laundered in the UK annually[57] and, as the chapter previously indicated, experts have been unimpressed by various aspects of UK's AML/terrorist financing regime. Nevertheless, these defects need to be set in context. First, £25bn represents just a fraction of the £5,500bn transactions handled annually by UK banks alone.[58] Second, for all its shortcomings, the UK is something of a leader amongst laggards in the global fight against money launderers and terrorist financers. The UK has been in the vanguard implementing EU Directives and FATF recommendations ahead of its main competitors.[59] Paradoxically improving its reputation by slavishly adhering to international best practice could make the City a target for money launderers as money accepted there will have a tacitly international seal of approval. Prior to 11 September an almost pathological obsession with financial privacy and opposition from special interest groups hindered the development and application of anti-money laundering rules in New York. The passage of the Patriot Act in 2001 was supposed to alleviate these imperfections but officials on the ground say that incoherent implementation and the dilution of the original legislation have hampered its effectiveness.[60]

A second set of considerations surrounds whether recent anti-terrorist measures could be detrimental to the City's existing competitive advantages, especially those which practitioners feel will affect the City's competitiveness in the years ahead: the quality and cost of the regulatory regime, operational costs and the availability of a skilled and innovative workforce.[61] Industry surveys have repeatedly found that while it is highly regarded in terms of quality, the cost and intrusiveness of the regulatory system is one of the biggest concerns amongst City practitioners. For example, respondents to a survey commissioned by the Corporation of London in 2005 believed the regulatory environment constituted the second most important factor in a financial centre's competitive position with nine out of ten rating the City as good or excellent in this regard.[62] Yet, extravagant regulation was branded the biggest risk to the continued health of the financial sector in the Centre for the Study of Financial Innovation's (CSFI's) 2005 and 2006 Banking Banana Skins poll[63] while in December 2004 only 9% of those questioned by The Financial Services Practitioner Panel regarded costs of compliance as 'reasonable', 58% thought them 'excessive' and over two-fifths saw them as harmful to their business.[64] Consequently the additional burden resulting from tougher AML procedures has not found favour with City institutions.

The City's AML provisions are supposedly underpinned by 'risk based' principles concentrating rules and resources in those sectors judged to be the most vulnerable to money laundering activity.[65] This is designed to ensure a proportionate response which nullifies money laundering at the lowest possible cost. Unfortunately while it is almost universally agreed that the UK's mosaic of bodies provides for more rigorous AML provisions there is also a consensus that it is both more costly than in other jurisdictions but that it is no more effective.[66] Precise figures on money laundering are difficult to ascertain and distilling the subsidiary costs of counter terrorism regulations is impossible. Nevertheless with KPMG reporting a 61% rise in the costs of AML compliance amongst banks the perception is of escalating costs of transacting business in the City.[67]

The costs of AML compliance are exacerbated by the 'fear factor' which leads firms to invoke overly meticulous procedures for fear of being tarnished by sanctions for not complying with rules and guidelines. The resort to 'defensive reporting' by financial institutions could account for the tenfold expansion in suspicious transaction reports filed with the UK's FIU since 2001.[68] More worryingly from the perspective of City competitiveness, the perception is that costs have risen more sharply in the UK than elsewhere. AML costs as a proportion of GDP are one quarter higher in the UK than the US. Indeed 55% of those surveyed from the UK said that costs of AML requirements had gone up by more than half in the past five years compared with only 36% of overseas respondents who felt the same about their own jurisdiction.[69] Furthermore, financial institutions are unhappy that much of the burden has fallen upon them. There is a suspicion that the government is employing financial institutions as proxy AML agents instead of making the proper investment in public regulatory edifices.[70] In short, the City's AML framework is at the risk of providing the worst of both worlds: becoming a magnet for money launderers who believe the City is regarded in international circles as a leader in AML regulations but which are costly and ineffectively implemented.

Inevitably tougher AML provisions have raised the operational costs for companies located in London. This is aggravated by additional expenditure on security and property insurance. Important though these direct costs unquestionably are a more corrosive consequence is the climate of hostility and distrust which results from the obsession with terrorism. The City of London's greatest asset is its people. The availability of skilled personnel was recently ranked as the single most important factor determining the competitiveness of a financial centre with 98% scoring London as good or excellent in this respect.[71] Historically the City was populated by a self perpetuating oligarchy drawn from a narrow stratum of upper class British society. The occasional breaches by outsiders became a flood after the Big Bang of 1986 and today the upper echelons of the City are peppered with women, foreigners and ethnic minorities.[72] The City prides itself on its ability to attract and retain the most talented individuals whose capacity for ceaseless innovation is critical for London's competitiveness.

The City of London's Police Commissioner has spoken of the need to avoid turning London into a "kind of fortress that might frighten off investors".[73] He might also have pointed out that garrisoning the City might damage competitiveness by discouraging skilled labour, especially from overseas, from entering. Currently there is no widespread evidence of high skilled labour departing for other financial centres or companies struggling to recruit high calibre candidates because of fears about terrorism. Nevertheless, the shooting in July 2005 of Jean Charles de Menezes, a Brazilian immigrant mistakenly thought to be a terrorist suspect, will have done little to allay these fears.

Conclusion

With the revolution in communications technology meaning that the location of financial firms is no longer contingent on proximity to their markets some have forecast the imminent demise of large scale financial clusters. The threat of organised terrorist violence could only hasten this denouement spelling economic catastrophe for the many advanced industrialised states whose wellbeing has come to rest on the provision of financial services. Despite the many terrorist attacks on financial centres in recent years, and a sense that they are likely future targets, a mass exodus of firms from the world's financial conurbations is unlikely. For the moment the innate benefits of clustering including economies of scale and scope, the stimulus of likeminded people, sizable skilled workforces, and metropolitan lifestyles, far outweigh any fresh costs brought about actual or threatened terrorist attacks.[74]

Today, the City of London authorities are wrestling with the core dilemma of globalisation namely how to garner the benefits of open borders and open societies whilst minimising the risks associated with them. Paradoxically the openness that characterises the neo-liberal project revitalised the City in the 1980s but its restoration to the heart of the British economy and its lionisation as an artery of global capitalism have made it, along with financial centres generally, a leading target for terrorist groups. Public authorities and the private sector are rightly concerned about the destructive and reputational threats posed by terrorist organisations not only to the City's human and physical infrastructure but also its competitiveness and have elaborated a host of preventative measures in response. However, this chapter has argued that the real threat may not be terrorism per se but the disproportionate reaction to it. While the denizens of the City understandably exhibit misgivings about terrorism when compared to access to liquid markets, a skilled workforce and a superior regulatory environment it is a minor factor in the competitiveness of the Square Mile.

The events of the last two decades have also demonstrated that London's existing and future competitors are besmirched by terrorist finance and prone to physical attack. Moreover, new anti-terrorist measures now threaten to undermine London's traditional competitive advantages by raising operating costs, exacerbating discontent about the regulatory system, and fostering intolerance and xenophobia which could deter skilled workers from coming to the City.

In October 2006, in a chilling echo of Mario Buda, a British man pleaded guilty to conspiring to attack the IMF and World Bank buildings in Washington, the NYSE, Citigroup buildings in New York and the Prudential buildings in New Jersey using limousines packed with explosives. Together with attacks of 7 July 2005, reports that the UK is the "number one al-Qaeda target",[75] and bin Laden's stated intentions to attack economic interests this is a timely reminder of the ongoing threat to UK interests, especially the City of London. This chapter has not examined the possibility of the City being targeted either by weapons of mass destruction or a 'dirty bomb' which would contaminate the Square Mile and make it inoperative. Quite simply in the aftermath of a cataclysmic attack the health of the financial sector will be a trivial concern. Lastly, I would venture to suggest that the mindset of those employed in the financial sector needs to change. Financial practitioners and regulators regularly cite terrorism as a potential source of financial instability but nowhere do they cite financial instability or the growing inequality caused by financial markets as a cause of terrorism. Ultimately terrorism is not neutered by road blocks and CCTV but by ameliorating the sources of injustice that nourish it. So long as advanced industrialised countries are thought to be abusing the power conferred by financial markets so this will be used as a justification for targeting their financial centres with organised terrorist violence.

Notes

1   *Financial Times*. 2005, "City attack 'matter of time'", 10 August, p. 1.

2   Coaffee, J. 2004, "Recasting the "Ring of Steel": Designing Out Terrorism in the City of London?", in Graham, S. (ed.), *Cities, War and Terrorism: Towards an Urban Geopolitics*, Blackwell, Malden, pp. 278-9.

3   *Financial Times*. 2005, "Al-Qaeda to attack Asian city, says expert", 26 August, p. 1.

4   See Strange, S. 1988, *States and Markets*, Pinter, London, Chapter 5; Viner, J. 1948, "Power Versus Plenty as Objectives of Foreign Policy in the Seventeenth and Eighteenth Centuries", in World Politics, Vol. 1, No. 1, pp. 1-29.

5   *Financial Times*. 2001, "A post-modern conflict", 12 September, p. 21.

6   In the aftermath of September 11 reports circulated about suspicious trading activity in the shares of firms with offices in the World Trade Centre and other industries (such as insurance and aviation) which were likely to suffer as a consequence of the attacks, prompting the US Securities and Exchanges Commission to launch a probe. See BBC Online. 2001, "US launches terror trading probe", 3 October, available online at http://news.bbc.co.uk/1/hi/business/1576470.stm and Winer, J.M. & Roule, T.J. 2002, "Fighting Terrorist Finance", in *Survival*, Vol. 44, No. 3, p. 90. However, no hard evidence was ever produced and the story has been dismissed by some authorities on the subject, see Mathers, C. 2004, *Crime School: Money Laundering True Crime Meets the World of Business and Finance*, Firefly Books, New York, pp. 106-7.

7   Times. 2000, "Main threat in the City is drunken violence", 19 January, p. 4.

8   Financial Times. 2005, "City attack 'matter of time'", 10 August, p. 1.

9   In May 2004 the BBC sparked panic when it screened *Dirty War*, a mockumentary depicting the detonation of a 'dirty bomb' by terrorists in central London. Over 140 people complained to the BBC with more than half arguing that the fictional nature of the attack should have been made explicit. See BBC Online. 2004, "'Terror' Panorama sparks protests", 17 May, available online at http://news.bbc.co.uk/1/hi/entertainment/tv_and_radio/3722041.stm.

While it purported to provide a public service by informing people of what to do should such an incident occur it was denounced by the government as "alarmist and irresponsible". See BBC Online. 2004, "Terror programme 'irresponsible'", 15 May, available online at http://news.bbc.co.uk/1/hi/uk/3716785.stm (Accessed 21 August 2006).

10 Osterud, O. 1988, "The Uses and Abuses of Geopolitics", in *Journal of Peace Research*, Vol. 25, No. 2, p. 191.

11 The extent of the decline of the state remains one of the most vexed questions of political science. At one extreme are those that argue we now inhabit a 'borderless world' where the state is a relic that has been emptied of its power and legitimacy, see for example Ohmae, K. 1990, *Borderless World: Power and Strategy in the Interlinked Economy*, Collins, London, and Greider, W. 1997, *One World Ready or Not: The Manic Logic of Global Capitalism*, Penguin, London. At the other are those who argue that nothing has changed and that the decline of the state is a myth, see for example Weiss, L. 1998, *The Myth of the Powerless State: Governing the Economy in a Global Era*, Cambridge University Press, Cambridge; Waltz, K. 2002, "The continuity of international politics", in Booth, K. & Dunne, T. (eds.), *Worlds in Collision: Terror and the Future of the Global Order*, Palgrave, Basingstoke. These extreme views are widely held to be empirically and epistemologically suspect. The state's role is recognised as being in perpetual flux with a symbiotic relationship between it and global forces. See for example Held, D. et. al. 1999, *Global Transformations: Politics, Economics and Culture*, Polity, Cambridge.

12 Nye, J.S. 2002, *The Paradox of American Power: Why the World's Only Superpower Can't Go It Alone*, Oxford University Press, Oxford, p. x.

13 Rosenau, J. 1990, *Turbulence in World Politics*, Princeton University Press, Princeton.

14 This point is illustrative only. Following the oil crisis of 1973 advanced industrialised countries created the International Energy Agency housed the OECD to coordinate measures in times of oil shortage and to ensure states have appropriate stockpiles.

15 O'Brien, R. 1992, *Global Financial Integration: The End of Geography*, Pinter, London.

16 International Financial Services London. 2006, *International Financial Markets in the UK*, available online at http://www.ifsl.org.uk/uploads/RP_IFM_2006_04.pdf (Accessed 4 August 2006); HM Treasury. 2005, *The UK financial services sector: Rising to the challenges and opportunities of globalisation*, HMSO, London, pp. 14-5.

17 See Coaffee, J. 2004, "Recasting the "Ring of Steel": Designing Out Terrorism in the City of London?", op cit, p. 285.

18 Roberts, R. 2004, *The City: A Guide to London's Global Financial Centre*, Profile Books, London, p. 289.

19 See Augar, P. 2000, *The Death of Gentlemanly Capitalism: The Rise and Fall of London's Investment Banks*, Penguin, London.

20 These figures are drawn from International Financial Services London. 2006, op cit.

21 On the evolution of the ring of steel see Coaffee, J. 2004, "Recasting the "Ring of Steel": Designing Out Terrorism in the City of London", op cit and Coaffee, J. 2004, "Rings of Steel, Rings of Concrete and Rings of Confidence: Designing out Terrorism in Central London pre and post September 11", in *International Journal of Urban and Regional Research*, Vol. 28, No. 1, pp. 201-11.

22 BBC Online. 2005, "City a target, police chief fears", 10 August, available online at http://news.bbc.co.uk/1/hi/business/4137068.stm (Accessed 8 August 2006).

23 BBC Online. 2002, "Terror attack: How would the City cope?", 10 September, available online at http://news.bbc.co.uk/1/hi/business/2230760.stm (Accessed 7 August 2006).

24 London Chamber of Commerce and Industry. 2003, *Disaster Recovery: Business Tips for Survival*, available online at http://www.londonprepared.gov.uk/business/lcc_disaster_recovery.pdf (Accessed 7 August 2006).

25 See Financial Sector Continuity, available online at http://www.fsc.gov.uk/home.asp?catid=7, (Accessed 7 August 2006) and HM Treasury. 2003, *The financial system and major operational disruption*, HMSO, London.

26 *Financial Times*. 2006, "A Year On: City better prepared to deal with another attack, says retiring police chief", 1 July, p. 4.

27 See Financial Sector Continuity. 2005, *Resilience Benchmarking Project Discussion Paper December 2005*, available online at http://www.fsc.gov.uk/upload/public/Files/9/Web%20-%20Res%20Bench%20Report%2020051214.pdf (Accessed 8 August 2006); KPMG. 2006, *UK Financial Sector Market-wide Exercise 2005: Executive Summary*, available online at http://www.fsc.gov.uk/upload/public/Files/15/MWE%20executive%20summary%2006.pdf (Accessed 27 July 2006).

28 Homer-Dixon, T. 2002, "The Rise of Complex Terrorism", in *Foreign Policy*, No. 128, pp. 54-5.

29 *Guardian*. 2002, "Cyber hype", 5 December, p. 1.

30 Kochan, N. 2005, *The Washing Machine: How Money Laundering and Terrorist Financing Soils Us*, Thomson, Mason, pp. 275-7.

31 *Sunday Times*. 1996, "City surrenders to £400m gangs", 2 June, p. 1.

32 US Department of Justice. 2006, *Computer Crime and Intellectual Property Section*, available online at http://www.usdoj.gov/criminal/cybercrime/index.html (Accessed 10 August 2006).

33 The BBC's 'Man Who Broke Britain' was broadcast on 9 December 2004.

34 Sternberg, E. 2004, "The Terror of Finance: The Man Who Broke Britain", available online at http://www.socialaffairsunit.org.uk/blog/archives/000258.php (Accessed 27 July 2006).

35 Michael Snyder, Chairman Policy and Resources Committee, Corporation of London quoted in Z/Yen Limited. 2005, *Anti-Money Laundering Requirements: Costs, Benefits and Perceptions*, Corporation of London, London, p. 4; see also HM Treasury. 2004, *Anti-Money Laundering Strategy*, available online at http://www.hm-treasury.gov.uk/media/D57/97/D579755E-BCDC-D4B3-19632628BD485787.pdf, p. 13 (Accessed 1 August 2006).

36 HM Treasury. 2004, op cit, p. 13.

37 Financial Services Authority. 2006, *Financial Risk Outlook 2006*, available online at http://www.fsa.gov.uk/pubs/plan/financial_risk_outlook_2006.pdf (Accessed 8 August 2006), pp. 5, 92-3 (my emphasis).

38 United Kingdom Parliament. 2006, *House of Commons Hansard Written Answers for 24 July 2006*, available online at http://www.publications.parliament.uk/pa/cm200506/cmhansrd/cm060725/text/60725w2060.htm, (Accessed 8 August 2006), Column 1388W; See also BBC Online. 2006, "'Not enough' terror money frozen", 4 August, available online at http://news.bbc.co.uk/1/hi/uk_politics/5244330.stm (Accessed 8 August 2006).

39 See for example Kochan, N. 2005, op cit, p. 254; Lilley, P. 2003, *Dirty Dealing: The Untold Truth about Global Money Laundering, International Crime and Terrorism (2nd edition)*, Kogan Page, London, pp. 168-9.

40 United Nations Security Council. 2001, *United Nations Security Council Resolution 1373 (2001)*, S/RES/1373 (2001), available online at http://daccessdds.un.org/doc/UNDOC/GEN/N01/557/43/PDF/N0155743.pdf?OpenElement (Accessed 8 August 2006).

41 Financial Action Task Force. 2004, *Special Recommendations on Terrorist Financing*, available online at http://www.fatf-gafi.org/dataoecd/8/17/34849466.pdf (Accessed 8 August 2006); Financial Action Task Force. 2004, *The Forty Recommendations*, available online at http://www.fatf-gafi.org/document/28/0,2340,en_32250379_32236930_33658140_1_1_1_1,00.html#40recs (Accessed 8 August 2006).

42 European Union. 2005, *Directive 2005/60/EC of the European Parliament and of the Council*, 26 October, available online at http://eur-lex.europa.eu/LexUriServ/site/en/oj/2005/l_309/l_30920051125en00150036.pdf (Accessed 8 August 2006).

43 See International Monetary Fund. 2006, *Financial Sector Assessment Program*, available online at http://www.imf.org/external/np/fsap/fsap.asp (Accessed 9 August 2006).

44 HM Treasury. 2004, op cit, Chapter 4.

45 Previously known as the Financial Investigation and Special Access Unit.

46 HM Treasury. 2002, *Combating the financing of terrorism: A report on UK action*, HMSO, London, p. 14, 18; Robinson, J. 2003, *The Sink: Terror, Crime and Dirty Money in the Offshore World*, Constable, London, pp. 303-4.

47 International Monetary Fund. 2003, *United Kingdom: Financial System Stability Assessment including Reports on the Observance of Standards and Codes on the following topics: Banking Supervision, Insurance Supervision, Securities Regulation, Payments Systems, Monetary and Financial Policy Transparency, Securities Settlement Systems, and Anti-Money Laundering and Countering Terrorist Financing*, available online at http://www.imf.org/external/pubs/ft/scr/2003/cr0346.pdf (Accessed 10 August 2006), pp. 98-108.

48 Lilley, P. 2003, op cit, pp. 235-6; Kochan, N. 2005, op cit, Chapter 14; Montebourg, A. 2000, *Rapport D'information Depose en Application de article 145 Du Reglement Par La Mission D'information Commune Sur Les Obstabcles Au Controle et A La Represion De La Delinquance Financiere et Du Blanchiment Des Capitaux en Europe (1) No. 2311*, March 30, Assemblee Nationale, Paris.

49 *Observer*. 2005, "How the City has become hooked on hot money", 5 June, p. 3 (Business).

50 Z/Yen Limited. 2005, *The Competitive Position of London as a Global Financial Centre*, Corporation of London, London, pp. 18-49; HM Treasury. 2005, *The UK financial services sector*, op cit, Ch. 4. Corporation of London. 2003, *Sizing up the City – London's Ranking as a Financial Centre*, Corporation of London, London, pp. 12-33; Roberts, R. 2004, op cit, pp. 18-9.

51 Corporation of London and City of London Police. 2005, *Survey of City Workers Summary Report*, available online at https://www.corpoflondon.gov.uk/consultations/files/workers%20panel%201st%20survey%20summary%20report%20for%20web(1).pdf (Accessed 11 August 2006), p. 6.

52 A City of London Police survey quoted by Coaffee, J. 2004, "Recasting the "Ring of Steel": Designing Out Terrorism in the City of London?", op cit, p. 295; Chiumento Consultants. 2003, *Facing the future in the City*, Chiumento Consultancy, London.

53 *Economist*. 2005, "Learning to live with it; Terrorism", Vol. 376, No. 8437 30 July, pp. 28-9

54 Z/Yen Limited. 2005, *The Competitive Position of London as a Global Financial Centre*, op cit, p. 16.

55 Ibid p. 42.

56 On the distinguishing features of global financial centres see Sassen, S. 1999, "Global Financial Centres", in *Foreign Affairs*, Vol. 78, No. 1, pp. 75-87.

57 Z/Yen Limited. 2005, *Anti-Money Laundering Requirements*, op cit, p. 15.

58 Ibid, p.16.

59 HM Treasury. 2004, op cit, p. 7; HM Treasury. 2005, *The UK financial services sector*, op cit, p. 38.

117

60 Kochan, N. 2005, op cit, Chapter 12.
61 Z/Yen Limited. 2005, *The Competitive Position of London as a Global Financial Centre*, op cit, p. 52.
62 Ibid, p. 21.
63 Centre for the Study of Financial Innovation. 2005, *Banking Banana Skins*, CFSI, London. Centre for the Study of Financial Innovation. 2006, *Banking Banana Skins*, CFSI, London.
64 Financial Services Practitioner Panel. 2004, *Third Survey of the FSA's Regulatory Performance December 2004*, available online at http://www.fs-pp.org.uk/docs/surveys/2004performance_report.pdf (Accessed 19 August 2006), pp. 32-7. See also Corporation of London. 2003, *Sizing up the City – London's Ranking as a Financial Centre*, op cit, pp. 15-6.
65 HM Treasury. 2004, *Anti-Money Laundering Strategy*, op cit, p. 23.
66 Z/Yen Limited. 2005, *Anti-Money Laundering Requirements*, op cit, pp. 4-5, 29.
67 KPMG. 2004, *Global Anti-Money Laundering Survey 2004: How Banks are Facing Up to the Challenge*, available online at http://www.kpmg.co.uk/master/pubs.cfm?currentpage=17&keyword=&searchwords=# (Accessed 1 August 2006), p. 9.
68 On the rising number of SARs see BBC Online. 2001, "Laundering reports reach record high", op cit; United Kingdom Parliament. 2004, *House of Commons Hansard Written Answers for 16 March*, available online at http://www.publications.parliament.uk/pa/cm200304/cmhansrd/vo040316/text/40316w05.htm (Accessed 1 August 2006); Z/Yen Limited. 2005, *Anti-Money Laundering Requirements*, op cit, p. 44.
69 Ibid, p. 32-3.
70 Kochan, N. 2005, op cit, p. 256.
71 Z/Yen Limited. 2005, *The Competitive Position of London as a Global Financial Centre*, op cit, p. 7, 18. See also HM Treasury. 2005, *The UK financial services sector*, op cit, p. 50.
72 Thompson, P. 1997, "The Pyrrhic Victory of Gentlemanly Capitalism: The Financial Elite of the City of London, 1945-90", in *Journal of Contemporary History*, Vol. 32, No. 3, pp. 283-304. Thompson, P. 1997, "The Pyrrhic Victory of Gentlemanly Capitalism: The Financial Elite of the City of London, 1945-90, Part 2", in *Journal of Contemporary History*, Vol. 32, No. 4, pp. 427-40. Thrift, N. and Leyshon, A. 1994, "A phantom state? The de-traditionalization of money, the international financial system and international financial centres", in *Political Geography*, Vol. 13, No. 4, pp. 299-327. Kynaston, D. 2002, *The City of London: Volume IV A Club No More 1945-2000*, Pimlico, London.
73 Financial Times. 2002, "Police warn about cutting corners in the Square Mile", 24 June, p. 4.
74 See Roberts, R. 2004, op cit, pp. 18-9, 293; HM Treasury. 2005, *The UK financial services sector*, op cit, p. 29.

75 BBC Online. 2006, "UK 'number one al-Qaeda target", 19 October, available online at http://news.bbc.co.uk/1/hi/uk/6065460.stm (Accessed 19 October 2006).

Further Reading

Augar, P. 2000, *The Death of Gentlemanly Capitalism: The Rise and Fall of London's Investment Banks*, Penguin, London.

Centre for the Study of Financial Innovation. 2006, *Banking Banana Skins*, CFSI, London.

Chiumento Consultants. 2003, *Facing the future in the City*, Chiumento Consultancy, London.

Coaffee, J. 2004, "Recasting the 'Ring of Steel': Designing Out Terrorism in the City of London", in Graham, S. (ed.), *Cities, War and Terrorism: Towards an Urban Geopolitics*, Blackwell, Malden.

Coaffee, J. 2004, "Rings of Steel, Rings of Concrete and Rings of Confidence: Designing out Terrorism in Central London pre and post September 11", in *International Journal of Urban and Regional Research*, Vol. 28, No. 1.

Corporation of London. 2003, *Sizing up the City – London's Ranking as a Financial Centre*, Corporation of London, London.

Economist. 2005, "Learning to live with it; Terrorism", Vol. 376, No. 8437 30 July.

Financial Action Task Force. 2004, *The Forty Recommendations*.

Financial Action Task Force. 2004, *Special Recommendations on Terrorist Financing*.

Financial Sector Continuity. 2005, *Resilience Benchmarking Project Discussion Paper December 2005*.

Financial Services Authority. 2006, *Financial Risk Outlook 2006*.

Financial Services Practitioner Panel. 2004, *Third Survey of the FSA's Regulatory Performance December 2004*.

Greider, W. 1997, *One World Ready or Not: The Manic Logic of Global Capitalism*, Penguin, London.

Held, D. et. al. 1999, *Global Transformations: Politics, Economics and Culture*, Polity, Cambridge.

HM Treasury. 2002, *Combating the financing of terrorism: A report on UK action*, HMSO, London.

HM Treasury. 2003, *The financial system and major operational disruption*, HMSO, London.

HM Treasury. 2004, *Anti-Money Laundering Strategy*.

HM Treasury. 2005, *The UK financial services sector: Rising to the challenges and opportunities of globalisation*, HMSO, London.

Homer-Dixon, T. 2002, "The Rise of Complex Terrorism", in *Foreign Policy*, No. 128.

International Financial Services London. 2006, *International Financial Markets in the UK*.

International Monetary Fund. 2003, *United Kingdom: Financial System Stability Assessment including Reports on the Observance of Standards and Codes on the following topics: Banking Supervision, Insurance Supervision, Securities Regulation, Payments Systems, Monetary and Financial Policy Transparency, Securities Settlement Systems, and Anti-Money Laundering and Countering Terrorist Financing*.

International Monetary Fund. 2006, *Financial Sector Assessment Program*.

Kochan, N. 2005, *The Washing Machine: How Money Laundering and Terrorist Financing Soils Us*, Thomson, Mason.

KPMG. 2004, *Global Anti-Money Laundering Survey 2004: How Banks are Facing Up to the Challenge*.

KPMG. 2006, *UK Financial Sector Market-wide Exercise 2005: Executive Summary*.

Kynaston, D. 2002, *The City of London: Volume IV A Club No More 1945-2000*, Pimlico, London.

Lilley, P. 2003, *Dirty Dealing: The Untold Truth about Global Money Laundering, International Crime and Terrorism (2nd edition)*, Kogan Page, London.

Mathers, C. 2004, *Crime School: Money Laundering True Crime Meets the World of Business and Finance*, Firefly Books, New York.

Montebourg, A. 2000, *Rapport D'information Depose en Application de article 145 Du Reglement Par La Mission D'information Commune Sur Les Obstabcles Au Controle et A La Represion De La Delinquance Financiere et Du Blanchiment Des Capitaux en Europe (1) No. 2311*, March 30, Assemblee Nationale, Paris.

Nye, J.S. 2002, *The Paradox of American Power: Why the World's Only Superpower Can't Go It Alone*, Oxford University Press, Oxford.

O'Brien, R. 1992, *Global Financial Integration: The End of Geography*, Pinter, London.

Ohmae, K. 1990, *Borderless World: Power and Strategy in the Interlinked Economy*, Collins, London.

Osterud, O. 1988, "The Uses and Abuses of Geopolitics", in *Journal of Peace Research*, Vol. 25, No. 2.

Roberts, R. 2004, *The City: A Guide to London's Global Financial Centre*, Profile Books, London.

Robinson, J. 2003, *The Sink: Terror, Crime and Dirty Money in the Offshore World*, Constable, London.

Rosenau, J. 1990, *Turbulence in World Politics*, Princeton University Press, Princeton.

Sassen, S. 1999, "Global Financial Centres", in *Foreign Affairs*, Vol. 78, No. 1.

Strange, S. 1988, *States and Markets*, Pinter, London.

Thompson, P. 1997, "The Pyrrhic Victory of Gentlemanly Capitalism: The

Financial Elite of the City of London, 1945-90", in *Journal of Contemporary History*, Vol. 32, No. 3.

Thompson, P. 1997, "The Pyrrhic Victory of Gentlemanly Capitalism: The Financial Elite of the City of London, 1945-90, Part 2", in *Journal of Contemporary History*, Vol. 32, No. 4.

Thrift, N. and Leyshon, A. 1994, "A phantom state? The de-traditionalization of money, the international financial system and international financial centres", in *Political Geography*, Vol. 13, No. 4.

Times. 2000, "Main threat in the City is drunken violence", 19 January.

Viner, J. 1948, "Power Versus Plenty as Objectives of Foreign Policy in the Seventeenth and Eighteenth Centuries", in *World Politics*, Vol. 1, No. 1.

Waltz, K. 2002, "The continuity of international politics", in Booth, K. & Dunne, T. (eds.), *Worlds in Collision: Terror and the Future of the Global Order*, Palgrave, Basingstoke.

Weiss, L. 1998, *The Myth of the Powerless State: Governing the Economy in a Global Era*, Cambridge University Press, Cambridge.

Winer, J.M. & Roule, T.J. 2002, "Fighting Terrorist Finance", in *Survival*, Vol. 44, No. 3.

THE GEO-POLITICS OF THE CITY

Chapter 6

European Supra-National Bonds: What (Political) Risks Lie Ahead?

Lauren M. Phillips

The advent of the Euro helped to reduce currency risks across less creditworthy member states, thereby dramatically realigning the borrowing premium of countries with less strong macroeconomic fundamentals or smaller economies.[1] The alignment of European bonds has in fact been so complete that Pagano and bon Thadden argue that the market can credibly be conceived as a single entity.[2] Encouraged by this trend and the dual-track integration of currency markets and financial services, both political economists and financiers have argued that further gains could be realised by unifying European bond markets. The benefits of increasing integration and joint issuance are said to be increased liquidity and reduction of transaction costs, which could make European sovereign bonds more important vis-à-vis other international credits such as US Treasuries.[3] Politically, such a move is also favoured by advocates of European integration, as it would provide a powerful mechanism for financing pan-European programmes and thereby transferring more fiscal responsibility to the supra-national level.

While the transactional benefits of integrated European bond markets have been well explored, there has been less attention paid to how such bonds would be received by the financial markets and in particular their likely impact on two inter-related variables: perceived creditworthiness and the perception of political risk. It is unclear whether such joint bonds would be seen as exceptionally credible – a risk shared jointly amongst several of the world's largest and most creditworthy economies – and thereby enjoy the highest possible rating, such as the bonds issued by the World Bank which are guaranteed by all of its members,[4] or whether the bonds would be lacking in credibility due to uncertainty about the ongoing and multi-track European "project" and the credibility of smaller / more indebted countries.[5] A related concern is how the market would price political risk in such bonds. Political risk could either be evaluated exclusively at the supra-national level – essentially a judgement about the European "project" – or it could be the aggregation of all underlying political risks across member states.[6] For example, riots in Budapest could conceivably be reflected as a risk premium or volatility in such a bond if Hungary helped to guarantee it or benefited from the bond's proceeds.

This chapter speculates about some of the likely implications on credibility and political risk of joint European Bonds utilising theory primarily developed to discuss similar issues in the context of emerging market sovereign bonds. An empirical analysis of the impact of political variables demonstrates that European bond markets are not immune from them (as some assert), and therefore that it is not unreasonable to expect that new pan-European instruments would be similarly affected by the nature of the polities that they represent. The analysis suggests that integrated European bond markets would be positively received by traders and analysts, as the diffusion of power amongst political actors is rewarded with a decrease in risk premium. This is in contrast to evidence on emerging markets where a move from autocracy to democracy (diffusion of power amongst a greater number of actors) increases credibility only to a point, after which point credibility declines, suggesting a parabolic relationship. However, the empirical evidence also suggests that some caution is advisable: fractionalisation amongst political actors increases the perception of risk in European bonds, and therefore in order to reduce risk, joint sovereign bonds would require a high level of political buy in and support from a large number of national and supra-national politicians and policy makers for the bonds to be viewed as credible.

The chapter is structured as follows. First, a review of the theory of sovereign borrowing and credibility is provided, focusing on the role of politics in determining creditworthiness. It is suggested that the diffusion of political power amongst a number of "veto players," actors with power to influence the policy process, has an impact on the credibility of a country, as does the extent to which such veto players are cohesive and hold similar ideas about the ultimate path of policy. Section three undertakes a series of regressions to determine what the impact of political institutional variables are on the risk premiums of European sovereign bonds over the recent years. The final section argues that the implications on creditworthiness and political risk of further unified European bond markets are expected to be largely positive, and suggests that further research should be done to determine what the impact of political variables are on the perception of political risk on a daily basis – that is to say, what role political information plays in generating market volatility.

Sovereign Borrowing, Credibility and Politics

Sovereign borrowing is distinguished from corporate borrowing primarily by the role that politics plays in the process of debt issuance and repayment, and therefore by the impact of politics on creditworthiness. Credibility is a complex concept, and in the case of sovereign borrowers, it is linked to reputation of repayment established over a long period of time – years, decades or even centuries.[7] Credibility has two components: the market perceptions of a country's (objective) ability to service its debt obligations (measured against a set of liquidity and solvency variables) and a far more subjective judgement about a country's willingness to service its debt obligations.[8] Willingness to repay is critical because it is difficult if not impossible to collateralise given the values of modern day debt stocks (50-100% of GDP for most European economies) and because previous means of enforcing repayment ("gun-boat diplomacy") is no longer an acceptable practice. Litigation to enforce payment is difficult and costly – nothing akin to national level corporate bankruptcy court exists at the international state-to-state level.[9] As such, the repayment of sovereign debt is inextricably linked to a government's willingness to continue paying its obligations and interest.

Given this theoretical link, a number of political economists have investigated what sorts of arrangements of political systems and institutional settings are more likely to lead governments to repay their debts. A seminal piece on this topic investigates the variation in creditworthiness between Britain and France in the early modern era, and hypotheses that the check the British parliament posed on the Monarch's borrowing habits resulted in higher levels of creditworthiness than in France, where the Monarch borrowed without constraint, and therefore defaulted more often.[10] This finding led to a theoretical insight: checks and balances – or an increased number of "veto players" – in a given political economy should increase creditworthiness. Democratic systems should be more creditworthy than autocratic systems.[11]

The term veto players was coined by Tsebelis, who has written extensively on the topic.[12] They are defined as "individual or collective actors whose agreement is necessary for a change of the status quo."[13] Three characteristics of veto players are thought to be important: their sheer number, the degree to which multiple veto players exhibit internal cohesion (or its opposite, fractionalisation) and the degree to which the policy preferences of such veto players diverge (how polarised they are). He argues that while a given number of veto players bring policy stability to a given polity (by making any single rule harder to alter or introduce given the number of people it must be approved by), an excess of veto players can lead to regime instability in presidential systems and government instability in parliamentary democracies.[14] Thus, there might be a turning point in which too many veto players make a country unstable, and thereby be detrimental to perception of creditworthiness.

In fact, research on emerging market democracies, who are active borrowers in the international sovereign debt markets, has demonstrated that there might be a U-shaped or parabolic relationship between creditworthiness and veto players. While countries gain credibility from moving from an autocratic system to a democratic one,[15] too many veto players might be bad for financial market stability.[16]

While there is little question about the current levels of credibility of European countries (who have not defaulted for an extensive period of time and generally enjoy very high credit ratings), it is unclear what the unification of European risk in joint sovereign bonds would do to this credibility. Applying the insights from the literature reviewed above to European sovereign bonds provides two alternative hypotheses. On the one hand, it is possible that the pricing of such bonds would be based on the stability of the issuing entity – for example the European Central Bank – and thereby overlook the layers of authority complicating policy decisions underneath such bonds. The other alternative is that the bonds could be perceived as high risk because of the layered authority represented in their issuance – local, provincial, national and supra-national veto players are salient in determining the policies that govern their creditworthiness (willingness to pay). They might therefore pay a relatively high political premium, regardless of underlying economic strength (ability to pay).

Prior to investigating the likelihood of either of these two hypotheses, a more fundamental point requires investigation. Since the theories discussed above have been developed with historical European cases and emerging market borrowers in mind, it is not necessarily obvious that modern European governments' sovereign bonds are priced and trade on the basis of their political institutions. In fact, the literature on this is conflicted. While at least one notable work finds explicitly that financial markets do not respond to policy and politics in advanced capitalist economies,[17] studies looking more specifically at the reaction of financial markets in European countries to political events have found that there is a market reaction. Bernhard and Leblang, whose work forms part of a small cohort of scholars interested in the effects of political variables on financial market performance,[18] investigated the impact of Austrian cabinet formation in 1999 on the performance of the stock market and sovereign bonds and found that while bond markets remained relatively calm during this period, they did adjust to the news, suggesting that political information is salient for sovereign bond pricing in European economies.[19] Similar results have been found for the impact of presidential elections on US equity markets.[20]

If European bond markets, and in particular the price at which such countries can borrow money, are affected by political variables and the distribution of power (veto players), then the opposing hypotheses about the impact of pan-European bonds can be investigated. This is the objective of the coming section.

Empirical investigation of politics and borrowing in the EU
The purpose of this section is to determine whether European

sovereign bonds at present are priced in part on their political institutional arrangements. This requires building an econometric model which determines whether bond yields are explained by both political and economic variables. The model in turn provides some predictions about how investors would respond to European supra-national bonds.

The determinants of interest rate differentials for European bond pricing have been well explored in a wide-ranging literature, with most research focusing on the relationship between yield spreads and public indebtedness and debt service.[21] Liquidity and currency denomination (whether countries borrow in their own currencies or foreign currencies) have also been identified as important. In fact Bernoth et al find that the difference between the yield on German bonds and other EU members is correlated to three fiscal variables – the debt to GDP ratio, the deficit to GDP ratio and the debt service to revenue ratio – and results vary based on whether or not countries are members of EMU.[22] The results are also sensitive to the liquidity of a given country's bond market – measured as total issuance of sovereign debt.

As mentioned earlier, with one notable exception, there is almost no literature which has looked at the impact of political variables on European bond pricing. Nonetheless, there is a strong theoretical reason to believe that more permanent institutional features of European political systems might impact the price at which European governments are able to borrow, and additionally the volatility of their bond markets (a claim which is not investigated here). Thus, the following section tests empirically the impact of institutional political variables on predicting the differential between yields of European sovereign bonds.

The Test

The regressions use a short (three year) time series from 2000 to 2002 for 20 European countries – both new and older member states.[23,24] The dependent variable is the average annual yield for a national bond of long (10 year) maturity, as provided by the

European Commission's statistical branch, Eurostat. All tests in this section were also run with an alternative dependent variable – the difference between a given country's yield on its 10 year bonds and the German yield, as the German bond is generally perceived to be the benchmark for European borrowing. Results were almost identical from a statistical standpoint. Significance levels for macroeconomic and political variables were identical, as were the direction and general size of coefficients. R-squared were also similar across the regressions. As such, results are not reported.

Annual periodicity is used instead of higher frequency data for several reasons. First, annual data is better at tracking the long run effects of macroeconomic and political variables on yield whereas higher frequency data (daily, weekly or monthly) is better for capturing the impact of specific events on yields. As neither macroeconomic results nor political institutional measurements change with great frequency (macroeconomic variables data is available for most accounts on a monthly basis though is more reliable on a quarterly basis; political institutional variables are only available annually), regressing highly volatile yields against static independent variables is likely to provide biased results. Indeed, most of the variation would likely be explained by a lagged dependent variable rather than a series of independent variables. High frequency data in which lagged variables are not included often have problems with auto-regression and autocorrelation.[25]

Since all bonds are of a similar maturity, variation in the yield should be primarily attributable to differences in perceived creditworthiness rather than maturity. These yields are regressed against a vector of macro-prudential variables and a vector of political institutional variables. These variables are discussed in turn.

Economic Variables
All economic variables are taken from the Eurostat database to ensure consistency of measurement across countries and

variables.[26] They include: real GDP growth, which is not lagged as bonds tend to respond in real time to changes in projections and economic variable results (GDPG); the percentage of total government debt to GDP (DebtGDP); the current account balance measured as a percentage of GDP (Cabal); the fiscal balance measured as a percentage of GDP (Fiscbal); the total interest paid in a given year, measured as a percentage of GDP (IntPaid); the annual change in the consumer price index (CPI); and a variable designed to measure the total liquidity of the bond market for the given country which is the total amount of government debt in millions of euros (Liquid).

The three fiscal variables – debt to GDP, fiscal balance and interest paid – are consistent with the Bernoth et al study,[27] and the liquidity variable is reproduced. As government revenue figures and debt service numbers were not readily available, interest payments as a percentage of GDP is used instead. The additional variables – the current account balance and the consumer price index – are often used in models of emerging market debt[28] and are therefore thought to hold some potential importance for European bonds.

Political Variables

As explained above, we are interested in measuring the extent to which the dispersion of political authority in a given political system impacts its credibility – or to see whether centralisation of power results in credibility gains. Following Tsbelis, three variables are measured. All variables are taken from a large comparative dataset designed by Beck et al of the World Bank called the Database of Political Institutions, or DPI.[29,30] The first is the number of checks and balances in a given political system, measured as the number of actors which have the right to veto legislation, law, etc (CB). A squared term of this variable is also tested for relevance – to see whether extreme dispersion of authority is marked by declining credibility (CBSQ). The second variable measures the fractionalisation of two different multiple veto players, the legislature and the government.[31] Both variables measure the probability that any two representatives chosen in a random draw would be of different parties, thereby explaining mathematically not only how many parties are represented in a given legislature or government, but also the relative size and importance of each constituent party (Legfrac & Govtfrac). Finally, the polarisation of preferences between veto players is measured. The polarisation variable available in the DPI measures the greatest distance in stated economic policy preferences (categorised as left, right and centre) between up to four political parties in the country and the president / executive in non-parliamentary systems (Polar).

Dummy Variable

Finally, to help control for the fact that countries might receive borrowing benefits from their membership in the Euro, a dummy variable coded 1 for EMU members and 0 for those outside of the euro zone is introduced (Euro). This is similar to the metric used in Bernoth et al.

Model Specification

Lenders analyse the value of European sovereign bonds and the risk of debt default based on two constraints: the country's economic ability to pay its debt obligations, and the perceived political willingness to pay those same obligations, which in turn is dependent upon its political institutions and particularly the distribution of power within a polity. The model, which looks to see the significance of political institutional variables against Thus:

$$y_{it} = \alpha + \sum_{j=1}^{j} \beta_{jit} P_{jit} + \sum_{j=1}^{j} \phi_{jit} E_{jit} + D_{it} + \varepsilon_{it}$$

where y_{it} are yields for country i's bonds over time t; P is a vector of political variables for countries over time t, E is a vector of macro-prudential variables over time and D_{it} is the dummy variable measuring whether countries are a member of the euro zone. Coefficients for each type of variable are represented by β, θ and δ, respectively and ε_{it} is a stochastic disturbance term. Yields and political and economic variables were collected into a balanced panel, and pool regression techniques were employed. Given the yearly nature of the data, it is not necessary to employ modelling techniques which are perhaps more suited to high frequency financial market data, such as ARCH models or regime switching models. Thus, a simple linear regression model was employed. However, the initial model demonstrated significant group-wise het-eroskedasticy and therefore a panel corrected standard error model was used.[32]

Results
Regressions were run step-by-step, introducing economic variables first (including the liquidity metric), and then adding political variables. This was done both to ensure that variables were not significantly correlated and to see what the explanatory power of the economic model alone was. The first regression shown in Table 1 below includes all economic variables, but given the high correlation between 1) the debt to GDP ratio and interest payments (0.88) and 2) between the fiscal balance and current account balance (0.72), these variables were added to the equation one by one in regressions 2 and 3.

Liquidity proves to be consistently insignificant in all of the regressions and is later dropped. The amount of interest paid appears to be highly insignificant (see regression 3), and the fiscal balance proves not to be significant when regressed against spreads without the interaction of the current account balance (see regression 4). In contrast, the debt to GDP level, current account balance and CPI are all highly significant (at the 1% level), and have the predicted coefficients. Increases in the debt to GDP level increase yields, an improved current account position decreases yield, and an increased inflation rate increases yield. The results for these variables are shown in regression five (the simplified economic model) where insignificant variables and highly correlated variables dropped. It is worth noting that the most significant variable appears to be the CPI, as measured by the size of its coefficient, which does a significant amount of the explaining of yield variation.

Table 1: European sovereign bond yields against selected macroeconomic variables

Linear Regression using Panel Corrected Standard Errors Model

Dependent Variable = Yield

	Regression Estimates				
	No. 1	No. 2	No. 3	No. 4	No. 5
DebtGDP	3.42 (0.010)	0.62 (0.00)	--	0.67 (0.00)	0.67 (0.00)
Intpaid	45.02 (0.034)	--	-1.40 (0.74)	--	--
Cabal	-1.80 (0.559)	-4.42 (0.01)	-4.28 (0.00)	--	-4.51 (0.00)
Fiscbal	-3.34 (0.511)	--	--	-4.85 (0.14)	--
CPI	32.27 (0.01)	38.76	39.14 (0.00)	38.6 (0.00)	39.16
(0.00)					
Liquid	0.00 (0.64)	0.00 (0.60)	0.00 (0.27)	0.00 (0.36)	--
Constant	5.26 (0.00)	4.89 (0.00)	4.57 (0.00)	4.94 (0.00)	4.88 (0.00)
R^2	0.568	0.532	0.523	0.526	0.532
N	60	60	60	60	60

Above: Results in each column show coefficients (p value)

Once these results were formulated, the institutional political variables were added to the simplified regression, along with the euro dummy. The R^2 of the combined equations is significantly higher than the R^2 of the regressions which include economic variables alone. As checks and balances and checks and balances squared are almost perfectly correlated (0.98), they are entered into the regression estimates separately, as are legislative and government fractionalisation, whose pair-wise correlation is 0.86.

All of the institutional political variables and the euro dummy variable are significant, at the 5% level.[33] Polarisation, however, has a coefficient which is not in the predicted direction. Rather than increasing risk (yield), increases in polarisation appear to decrease the yield. This may be because in such situations, the probability of the status quo remaining the same increases due to blocks in the legislature. However, as it is the least important based on the size of its coefficient, the result is thought to be less important than that of the other two political variables. Increased checks and balances decrease yields, as does checks and balances squared (and to the fourth exponential), demonstrating that there are not negative impacts of increased dispersion of political power on bond yields in the European Union. In contrast, legislative and government fractionalisation increase yield, suggesting that fractionalised leadership and governance has a negative impact on creditworthiness. Of the three political variables, legislative fractionalisation has the strongest coefficient. Euro membership increases credibility by decreasing yield, which also would be expected.

There are also some impacts on the salience of the macroeconomic variables by introducing the political institutional variables. While the current account balance and inflation rate remain highly significant, the debt / GDP level decreases in explanatory power, falling below the 10% significance threshold, except when government fractionalisation is included instead of legislative fractionalisation when the variable remains significant.[34] This is potentially because the variable demonstrates a relatively strong (though acceptable) pair-wise correlation against checks and balances (0.41).

Table 2: European sovereign bond yields against selected macroeconomic and political variables

Linear Regression using Panel Corrected Standard Errors Model.
Dependent Variable = Yield

	Regression Estimates		
	No. 6	No. 7	No. 8
DebtGDP	0.24 (0.23)	0.22 (0.21)	0.39 (0.00)
Cabal	-2.83 (0.06)	-2.65 (0.08)	-5.43 (0.00)
CPI	30.91 (0.00)	30.65 (0.00)	28.85 (0.00)
CB	-0.19 (0.07)	--	-0.16 (0.07)
CBSQ	--	-0.03 (0.02)	--
Legfrac	2.69 (0.05)	2.81 (0.04)	--
Govtfrac	--	--	1.63 (0.00)
Polar	-0.28 (0.01)	-0.29 (0.01)	-0.36 (0.00)
Euro	-1.12 (0.00)	-1.14 (0.00)	-1.11 (0.00)
Constant	4.76 (0.00)	4.38 (0.00)	6.22 (0.00)
R^2	0.666	0.670	0.686
N	60	60	60

Above: Results show Coefficients (P Value)

Interpreting the Results for the Unification of the European Bond Market

These findings confirm that European bond yields are partially explained by reference to their underlying political characteristics, and in particular, the dispersion of power and authority within each polity. The results – that increases in checks and balances are positive for credibility whereas increases in government and legislative fractionalisation negatively impact credibility – provides some scope for analysing the competing hypothesis presented earlier. If European supra-national bonds were to be issued, there would likely be little political premium applied on the basis of an increasing number of veto players. Layered institutions – where veto players are present at various levels of the policy cycle – appear to have a positive rather than negative impact on European credibility. This is potentially because of insulation from the impact of any particular veto player. However, the fact that government and legislative fractionalisation has a negative impact on credibility suggests that there is a significant risk that, as European governance fractionalises to accommodate a variety of national and international parties, there would be credibility losses. This would probably be the case in particular if the European Parliament had a strong role in allocation of expenditure from bond proceeds, as there fractionalisation is high. If in contrast issuance and allocation of proceeds were completed centrally – by the European Central Bank or by the President or Commission – the risk premium paid on such bonds would likely be lower.

This empirical test overlooks however another consequence of politics on sovereign bond performance. Political news and events play a large role in determining the daily movement in bond prices, as demonstrated in a number of studies cited earlier. Further tests (e.g. econometric event studies) would be needed to gauge what the impact of layered authority would be on the bond markets' daily response to political information using high frequency data. This might change some of the implications provided in the paragraph above.

Conclusions

Given the context of increasing financial integration in the European Union, this chapter has briefly suggested how supra-national European bonds might be received by investors and traders. It has argued that the distribution of power and authority across a polity has a strong impact on its credibility, and as such, bond pricing in the European Union, as in other areas, reflects in part these underlying political characteristics. Supra-national European bonds, were they to be issued, might be perceived as highly creditworthy and of minimal political risk, or might rather be seen as highly risky given the multiple layers of government which underwrite such bonds.

The empirical analysis has shown that the average yields on European bonds are better explained with both macroeconomic and political variables. This is a rather important finding in and of itself given previous research which has suggested a weak link between European financial market performance and political variables. The findings also suggest that a pan European bond would not necessarily be penalised for multi-level governance, and that strong buy-in and leadership from European institutions could minimise the impact of fractionalised government on the price of European bonds. These findings are important to bear in mind as the discussion on European financial integration continues, and in particular in the light of overwhelmingly positive transaction cost benefits from the further integration of the European bond market.

Notes

1   Bronk, R. "Commitment and Credibility: EU Conditionality and Interim Gains," *LSE European Institute Working Paper Series*, No. 2 December 2002.

2   Pagano, M. & von Thadden, E. 2004, "The European Bond Markets Under EMU" *Centre for Studies in Economics and Finance Working Paper*, No. 126, Fisciano, Italy.

3   Ibid; Baele, L. et al, 2004, "Measuring Financial Integration in the Euro Area" *European Central Bank Occasional Paper Series*, No. 14, Frankfurt, Germany. ; Dunne, P et al, 2006, "European Government Bond Markets: Transparency, Liquidity and Efficiency" *Centre for Economic and Policy Research Commisioned Paper*, May.

4   The World Bank's lending to middle income countries through the International Bank for Reconstruction and Development (IBRD), one of five World Bank divisions, is financed by issuance of bonds on the international capital markets. These bonds enjoy an AAA credit rating.

5   This is an especially salient question given the current pessimistic mood about further European integration after the rejection in 2005 of the European Constitution in France and the Netherlands.

6   A similar question was asked when Venezuela and Argentina announced in mid 2006 their intention to issue a "joint" sovereign bond, which would be the first of its kind particularly in emerging markets. See the *Financial Times* story at http://www.ft.com/cms/s/475b87de-0f6f-11db-ad3d-0000779e2340.html.

7   Tomz, M. 2001, "How Do Reputations Form: New and Seasoned Borrowers in International Capital Markets" at the *2001 Annual Meeting of the American Political Science Association*, San Francisco, 30 August to 2 September.

Reinhart, C. and Rogoff, K. et al. 2003, "Debt Intolerance" *Brookings Papers on Economic Activity*, Vol. 2003, No. 1.

8   For example models of debt spreads, creditworthiness and default see Eaton, J. and Gersovitz, M. 1981, "Debt with Potential Repudiation: Theoretical and Empirical Analysis" *Review of Economic Studies*, Vol. 74, No. 4, pp. 289-309. Bulow, J. and Rogoff, K. 1989, "A Constant Recontracting Model of Sovereign Debt" *Journal of Political Economy*, Vol. 97, No.1, pp. 155-177. Fishlow, A. 1989, "Conditionality and Willingness to Pay: Some Parallels from the 1890's" *The International Debt Crisis in Historical Perspective*, Eichengreen, B. and Lindert, P. eds, MIT Press, Cambridge, Mass.

9   Drazen, A. 2000, *Political Economy in Macroeconomics*, Princeton University Press, New Jersey, p. 587.

10 North, D. Weingast, B. 1989, "Constitutions and Commitment: The Evolution of Institutions Governing Public Choice in 17th Century England" *The Journal of Economic History*,Vol. 49, No. 4, pp. 803-832.

11 For an extensive review of formal models of credibility under varying political and economic conditions see Drazen, A. 2007, op cit, pp. 166-215.

12 For an extensive review of formal models of credibility under varying political and economic conditions see Tseblis, G. 2002, *Veto Players: How Political Institutions Work*, Princeton University Press, New Jersey.

13 Ibid, p. 19.

14 Ibid

15 Rodríguez, J. & Santiso, J. 2005, "Banking on Democracy: The Political Economy of International Bank Flows in Emerging Markets," Presented at the Tenth Annual Meeting of the Latin American and Caribbean Economic Association, Paris: 28 – 29 October; and see literature arguing a similar benefit in attracting foreign direct investment to emerging market democracies, e.g. Rodrik, D. 1996, "Labor Standards in International Trade: Do they Matter and What Do We Do About Them?" in Lawrence et al. ed. *Emerging Agenda for Global Trade: High Stakes for Developing Countries*, Johns Hopkins University Press, Baltimore; Harms, P & Usrsprung, H. 2002, "Do Civil and Political Repression Really Boost Foreign Direct Investment?" *Economic Inquiry*, vol. 40, no. 14: 651-663.

16 MacIntyre, A. 2001, "Institutions and Investors: The Politics of the Economic Crisis in Southeast Asia," *International Organization*, Vol. 55, no. 1: 81-122; Phillips, L. 2006, *Political Risk in Emerging Markets: Democracy, sovereign debt and financial market volatility in Brazil and Mexico*, PhD Dissertation, London School of Economics and Political Science, Department of International Relations.

17 Mosley, L. 2003, *Global Capital and National Governments*, Cambridge University Press, Cambridge.

18 See for example Bernhard, W. and Leblang, D. 2000, "The Politics of

Speculative Attacks in Industrial Democracies," *International Organization*, Vol. 54, no. 2: 291-324; Pantzalis, C. & Strangeland, D. et al. 2000, "Political Elections and the Resolution of Uncertainty: The International Evidence," *Journal of Banking and Finance*, Vol. 24: 1575-1604; Hays, J. & Freeman, J. et al. 2001, "Democratization and Globalization in Emerging Market Countries: An Econometric Study," Presented at the 2001 Annual Meeting of the American Political Science Association, San Francisco, 30 August – 2 September; Bernhard, W. and Leblang, D. 2002, "Democratic Processes, Political Risk and Foreign Exchange Markets," *American Journal of Political Science*, Vol. 46, no. 2: 316-333; Schamis, H. and Way, C. 2003, "Political Cycles and Exchange Rate-Based Stabilization," *World Politics*, Vol. 56, no. 1; Block, S. A. & Vaaler, P. M. 2004, "The Price of Democracy: Sovereign Risk Ratings, Bond Spreads and Political Business Cycles in Developing Countries," *Journal of International Money and Finance*, Vol. 23, no. 6: 917-946.

19 Bernhard, W. & Leblang, D. 2004, "Parliamentary Politics and Financial Markets," Available on http://www.socsci.duke.edu/ssri/papers/bernhard.pdf.

20 Roberts, B. 1990, "Political Institutions, Policy Expectations and the 1980 Election: A Financial Market Perspective," *American Journal of Political Science*, Vol. 34, no. 2: 289-310.

21 For an overview of some studies see Bernoth, K. et al 2004, "Sovereign Risk Premia in the European Government Bond Market," European Central Bank Working Paper Series, no. 369: Frankfurt, Germany.

22 Ibid.

23 The countries included in the analysis are: Austria, Belgium, Cyprus, Czech Republic, Denmark, Finland, France, Germany, Greece, Hungary, Ireland, Italy, Malta, Netherlands, Poland, Portugal, Slovak Republic, Spain, Sweden and the United Kingdom. Full data was not available for the other five Member States.

24 The relatively short nature of the dataset has to do with the fact that the political variables were only available until 2002. There were data limitations on some macroeconomic variables prior to 2000 – spotty reporting from a number of countries on key inputs would have resulted in an unbalanced panel.

25 Masson, P. R. & Chakravarty, S. et al. 2003, "The normal, the fat-tailed and the contagious: modelling changes in emerging market bond spreads," CSED Working Paper, no. 32, Brookings Institution: Washington, DC; Kittel, B. & Winner, H. 2005, "How reliable is pooled analysis in political economy? The globalization-welfare state nexus revisited," *European Journal of Political Research*, Vol. 44: 269-293.

26 Available online at http://epp.eurostat.ec.europa.eu

27 Bernoth et al. 2004, op cit.

28 Edwards, S. 1984, "LDC Foreign Borrowing and Default Risk: An Empirical Investigation, 1976-1980," *The American Economic Review*, Vol. 74, no. 4: 726-734; Min, H. 1998, "Determinants of Emerging Bond Spreads: Do Economic Fundamentals Matter?," World Bank Working Paper, no. 1899, World Bank: Washington DC; Ferrucci, G. 2003, "Empirical Determinants of Emerging Market Economies: Sovereign Bond Spreads" Bank of England Working Paper: London.

29 Beck, T et al 2001, "New Tools and New Tests in Comparative Political Economy: The Database of Political Institutions," *The World Bank Economic Review*, Vol. 15, no. 1: 165-176.

30 The original dataset runs until 2000 – I was able to obtain data for 2001 and 2002 by requesting the updated dataset from the authors which will be made public shortly.

31 As all countries in the dataset are parliamentary democracies, the fractionalisation of the government refers to the fractionalisation of the government coalition, if the government is made of multiple parties. In countries, like the UK, where the government is a single party, fractionalisation is 0.

32 Other tests – e.g. multicollinearity and stationarity – demonstrated that the regressions were robust.

33 Checks and balances is significant at the 10% level, while checks and balances squared is significant at the 5% level.

34 This is interesting because the pair wise correlation between debt to GDP and these two variables is almost identical and very low: 0.06 and 0.06, respectively.

Chapter 7

Managing Chaos: An Examination of FX Policy in the UK from Bretton Woods to Tiger Woods

Alex Brassey

Can chaos be managed? This paper discusses the question of who, if anyone should be or could be in control of a country's currency. The implications of Foreign Exchange (FX) policy fall well beyond the City's dealers and international bank dealing rooms. It affects every man woman and child in an economy and in many different ways. The following discussion will explore how FX policy has profound effects on interest rates affecting savings, mortgages and corporate debt as well as other macroeconomic variables such as the balance of payments, inflation, employment and overall economic growth. FX policy not only has a profound impact on the monetary side of an economy but also, as our European partners in the Euro are experiencing, it also has a significant impact on fiscal policy (government spending and taxation).

This paper will lay out how UK FX policy has previously been formulated as well as considering the current and future possibilities. One might think that given the central role of FX in determining all aspects of a country's economic performance, governments would take a keen interest in ensuring that FX policy was well formulated. As this paper will argue, UK FX policy and FX market regulation has been a showcase of mismanagement and sometimes ignorance.

The FX market buys and sells around £1,000,000,000,000 per day.[1] It is unrivalled in its depth and liquidity. A sharp movement in currency values can create or destroy a country's economic future for decades. FX policy, in short, is very important and an understanding of the economic and political implications is vital for policy makers and others who wish to express a view on geo-politics and international economics.

The following discussion will be divided into five sections. Firstly I will lay out the basic economics behind FX policy in general terms. The second section will look at some historical trends in major currencies, namely Sterling (STG) and US Dollar (USD) from Bretton Woods (1944). I will briefly discuss the events of the Plaza and Louvre Accords of 1985 and 1987, which produced profound changes in direction for the USD.

The third section will examine the failings of UK Government FX policy, in particular the humiliating collapse of STG from the European Monetary System (EMS) and the transfer of several billion STG worth of UK wealth into the hands of wealthy investors including the infamous George Sorros who voluntarily transferred around USD1 billion of UK taxpayers money to the Hungarian economy. I will explain how sharp movements of FX are often a double edged sword notably leading to the renaming of "Black Wednesday" to "White Wednesday", 16th September 1992. (The day Britain left the European Exchange Rate Mechanism.)This section will also examine the changing nature of UK FX policy through the EMS crisis. Finally I will examine some of the major trends in international FX. This will include the 'Dollar Dilemma' faced by the economies of China and Japan and the problems the international community faces given the fact that virtually all commodities including oil, gold and agricultural produce are priced in US Dollars.

This paper will draw from my personal experience as FX Dealer at Barclays Global Markets (now Barclays Capital), Senior Dealer at Sakura Bank (now Sumitomo Mitsui Financial Group), Director of Foreign Exchange at Lehman Brothers and Assistant Vice President, Treasury Division at Citibank in London – the world's largest FX dealing room.

The final section will tentatively discuss a number of options and dilemmas faced by our current batch of policy makers and attempt to draw conclusions from the lessons of the past.

FX and Economics

Macroeconomics considers the behaviour of the whole of an economy. It is principally concerned with economy-wide phenomena such as balance of payments, unemployment, inflation and economic growth. The value of a country's currency exerts a significant influence on each of these macroeconomic variables. This section will take each variable in turn and explain how changes in the exchange rate affect the variable.

A key term in economics is the Latin expression 'ceteris paribus' which roughly translates as 'all things being equal'. When economists want to consider the impact of changing one variable in their economic model they will employ the term "ceteris paribus" in order to demonstrate how the change in one element, (for the purposes of this paper we will be considering a change in the FX rate) affects the other variables holding all other things constant. Of course, in the real word it is never the case that all other things remain equal.

(i) The Balance of Payments

The balance of payments broadly speaking is a measure of the total payments one country makes to others, including the price of imports and outflow of capital including gold minus the total

145

receipts it receives from foreign countries including the price of exports and the inflow of capital including gold.

FX plays an important role in this process. Assume that STG suddenly doubles in value against USD. This would immediately halve the costs of all goods and services we buy from the United States. Economic theory – in line with common sense – suggests that UK demand for US goods would increase, given that their goods and services have halved in price for the UK consumer.

As the price of imported goods and services from the US falls and demand increases, similarly, US demand for UK goods and services would decrease as the price increases.

It is important to understand that the implications of this are manifold. The immediate reaction of individuals to a 'devaluation' or 'depreciation' of their currency is typically one of disapprobation. It is seen as a 'bad' thing. However, from this example, it should be noted that a 'weaker' currency could be perceived as a major benefit.

Note from the example above that an increase in the value of STG leads to an increase of our imports (of foreign goods) and a decrease of our exports to other countries. The movements of FX hold all other relevant variables as constant. In other words issues of quality, competitiveness, speed of delivery and other non-price factors are set aside. Ceteris paribus, an increase in the value of a country's currency will lead to a worsening of their balance of payments situation. They will, in short, buy more from overseas than then sell, as a result of the FX movement.

(ii) Unemployment and Economic Growth
The implications that stem from changes in demand for a country's goods and services are widespread. In this example where STG doubles against the USD, we can now see that US manufacturers will be able to export into the UK market more easily as a result of their price advantage. The question is what will be the impact on our exporters into the US market? Clearly,

they will have a choice to make. Either they could reduce their prices to cope with the change in FX or alternatively they could increase the USD price at which they sell their goods. The former scenario would result in lower profits; the latter scenario would result in reductions in demand for their goods.

As STG increases in value, therefore, it is fair to say that exports are likely to fall. In the longer term, this will result in job losses in UK manufacturing and a slowing of economic growth. As unemployment increases, benefits from the state to those who have become unemployed would increase leading to either an eventual increase in taxation or a reduction of government expenditure on other projects. This again will lead to a slow down in the general economy as economic activity further slows down.

(iii) Inflation
The inflationary effects of a significant increase in the value of STG are favourable. If STG rises, it makes imports of raw materials from other countries cheaper. This would include all commodities which are priced in USD, such as oil, gold, non-ferrous metals and agricultural produce. As our import costs fall, this allows manufacturers to reduce their consumer prices to people within the UK and also provides them with the capacity to reduce export prices to other countries.

Stabilisation
Stabilisation is critical in FX theory for a number of reasons. When we look at the theoretical economic implications above, it is clear we are looking at a dynamic picture, i.e. the situation is constantly in a state of change. As one variable changes it affects all other variables.

The principle of stabilisation in respect of FX relates to how the value of a country's currency will rebalance as other macroeconomic variable change. In the example, STG rises; this leads to a rise in imports, a fall in exports, an increase in unemployment, a fall in inflation, an increase in taxation and a

147

slowdown of UK economic growth. The appropriate Bank of England response to this set of circumstances would be to reduce interest rates.

A reduction of interest rates would lead, ceteris paribus, to a fall in the value of STG leading to a partial or full reversal of the macroeconomic movements stated above. This process is known as the stabilisation process. In other words it is possible for the movement of FX rates to fix the problems they cause.

It is also possible for FX rates to fix problems they have not caused. FX given its potential to impact on all areas of macroeconomic policy is a valuable and powerful tool for policy makers in an open economic model.

A Brief History of STG From 1944

In the late stages of the Second World War, all 44 Allied Nations met in Bretton Woods, New Hampshire to determine a post-war economic and monetary regime. It was here that the UK government agreed that STG would fix its value against the USD (which was convertible into gold until the collapse of the system in 1971) within a tight +/-1% band. The IMF and the World Bank were also established at this time at Bretton Woods.[2]

Operating under the Bretton Woods system since 1959, the Wilson government of 1966 responded to downward pressure on STG, by tightening exchange controls. These restrictions, which lasted until 1970 included banning tourists from taking more than £50 out of the UK.[3] The pressure on STG eventually led to a 14.3% devaluation to USD2.41 in late 1967. To which Wilson famously appeared on television to proclaim that 'the pound in your pocket' was not worth less.

During the late 1960s and early 1970s another new financial development in the form of the Euromarkets was also causing pressure on international currencies, leading to a fragmentation of fixed rate agreements. In essence, financial market dealers were striking agreements outside of the national jurisdiction to which the currency was originated. In other words, French banks, for example, would be prepared to take USD deposits from the Russian government and provide them with USD based facilities – all the time remaining outside the jurisdiction of the US government. The motivation to do this was essentially political given the heightened tensions of the cold war. The French banks were able to profit from USD deposits whilst at the same time the Russians could avoid having their assets frozen by the US government.

The phenomenon of the offshore market presented serious challenges to direct exchange controls as a mechanism to control currency movements. The independence of the offshore markets led to the abandonment of the UK government to fix its market rate and as a result STG began floating against other currencies in the early 1970s.[4]

In 1976 following a number of years of macroeconomic problems in the UK, a report from the IMF was leaked. It stated that in their view STG's value against the USD should be around the STG1:USD1.5 level. STG crashed and the UK government was forced to borrow around £2.3 billion to shore up domestic fiscal problems as a result of general economic mismanagement and industrial relations difficulties.

The end of the 1970s brought a change of government and with it a complete change of macroeconomic philosophy, (if not policy, since Labour Chancellor Dennis Healy had uncere-moniously given birth to British monetarism in 1976). Monetarism, espoused by Milton Friedman and the Chicago school had profoundly influenced US economic policy – later described as 'Reganonomics'.[5] The central plank of monetarism lay in its attempts to control inflation by targeting the money supply.

The monetarists viewed inflation as being essentially, a monetary phenomenon and claimed that prices rose as a result of 'too much money chasing too few goods'. This suggested that the solution to the problem meant either reducing the money supply or improving productivity and other 'supply-side' variables within the macro economy. Thatcher, influenced by Friedman, Joseph[6] and other neo-classical economists including

149

Patrick Minford and Alan Walters[7] decided to pursue the dual goals of supply-side economics and money supply targeting.

The fall-out of relaxing labour markets in the UK led to a rapid increase in unemployment as firms shed jobs. Unions became increasingly powerless to counter firms streamlining their labour force as a result of the numerous pieces of employment and union legislation delivered over the period 1979 – 1992.[8]

The initial effect of these moves on STG was positive. STG reached above STG1/USD2 in the early part of the 1980's but fell back to a low of STG1/USD1.05 in 1985. Movements in interest rates predominantly determined exchange rate movements at this time. As the government targeted the money supply by increasing interest rates, the value of STG rose. The increase in interest rates led to a severe economic contraction over the period 1979 – 1981 leading to a recession with around 3 million unemployed.[9] The increased value of STG, resulting from higher interest rates also made UK exports significantly more expensive for the rest of the world and exacerbated the effects of the manufacturing led recession.

UK Interest rates fell, resulting in a fall in STG to the low levels seen in 1985.[10] It should be noted, however, that the value of STG is not just the result of UK economic and FX policy. It is also the result of the economic policies of foreign governments.

Since the inception of Bretton Woods, the USD has been the singularly most important currency in the world. STG's influence has waned with the disintegration of the empire and commonwealth. Today, virtually all commodities are denominated in USD including oil, gold and other precious metals, agricultural produce and non-ferrous metals.

The collapse of the gold standard, which essentially fixed the values of currencies to gold, occurred in the early 1970's. Major currencies floated against one another once again and the market determined the value. The spectre of a 'fiduciary monetary system' arguably led to inflationary pressures in a number of industrial economies as governments around the world printed money with relative impunity. The previous commitment to control money supply relative to the amount of gold in reserves had led to a fairly strict system of monetary discipline and the well-documented pressures of stagflation in the late 1970's emerged within a short time.

The decline of STG relative to the USD and in fact virtually all major world currencies reached a peak in 1985 – at a time when a new regime of international currency co-operation was emerging. It was clear by the early 1980's that control over currency values had become a matter for the market to determine. Currency speculation increased aided by the plethora of new financial derivative products. Increasingly companies with international exposure were using derivatives to hedge out risk from overseas earnings, but more worryingly a number of firms were using the currency derivatives markets to increase risk.[11] One firm, Allied Lyons, lost more than $270 million in 1991 on currency speculation alone.

Plaza and Louvre

One of the uncontroversial downsides to market led price discovery is the problem of 'overshoot'. Overshoots occur when a long-term trend develops and then accelerates leading to speculative positions being taken to gain a financial advantage, regardless of underlying or fundamental value. Common examples of this include the South Sea Bubble of 1720, the Wall Street Crash of 1929 or more recently the dot com boom of 1999-2001. Overshoot also occurs in currency markets.

Governments recognised that an overshoot had occurred in 1985 as the value of the USD began to cause serious macroeconomic risks to the world. On September 22 1985 in the Plaza Hotel, New York, the G5 (biggest industrialised nations): US, UK, Germany (West), Japan and France met up to discuss how they could influence the international value of the USD. It was clear from this meeting that all governments recognised they had to change national economic strategy using both fiscal and monetary tools to affect a change.[12]

Arguably, this meeting demonstrated that policy makers were

151

beginning to realise that real macroeconomic change would lead to changes in financial markets. Previously government had been in a position to dictate value, now they could only influence value through their actions. The Plaza Accord objectives of a managed depreciation of the USD were successfully met. Over the following two years the USD fell by around 50% against the Yen and Deutche Mark. This was achieved without causing financial panic that accompanied other market led devaluations of previous and future years.[13]

The immediate concerted central bank sales of USD which ran to around USD10 billion, would not have had such a sustained impact but for the reversal and implementation of substantial speculative currency positions which aided the USD's fall.

History has shown that any successful currency management programme under the aegis of a floating exchange rate must be reflected by the relevant economy performing in a symbiotic manner. The 1985 Plaza Accord was successful due to the increasing size of the US current account deficit that had reached 3.5% of GDP. The US population's appetite for foreign goods had been aided by the high value of the USD and by 1985 began to look unsustainable. In addition to this, the US government needed to be able to recover from a serious recession that had started with the tight monetary regime imposed on the US by Paul Volker, Chairman of the Federal Reserve. The high value of the USD had made US industry uncompetitive in the global markets which in turn had both worsened the recession leading to the twin deficit problem of budget and trade. The structural elements of the US trade deficit is something to which I return in the next sections and arguably poses the greatest risks to world financial stability.

In 1987, the G6 (G5 + Canada) met at the Louvre in Paris.[14] The aim of the meeting had been to stop the successful decline of the USD that had begun with the implementation of the Plaza Accord two years earlier.[15] The communiqués that emanated from Paris however were unsuccessful as the world continued to worry about the twin deficits of the US. It took until December of 1987 – following a collapse of world equity markets – before the USD began to recover some of its value.

Plaza and Louvre taught international governments and financial market participants that direct interventions in currency markets were futile. Currency values were determined by underlying causes; they were not the cause themselves unless the government deliberately forced a rate of exchange on its value. In the long term, however, this strategy has repeatedly proved to be unworkable. Currency markets have the potential to alleviate a macroeconomic problem provided that the government signals a change in its appropriate use of fiscal and monetary tools. This occurs when the markets recognise a real change is likely to occur and positions are taken accordingly.

It is often stated that the currency markets themselves, or rather the 'speculators' are somehow responsible for causing underlying problems within the economy. This view is false. Speculators react to underlying problems – it is the policy makers that cause them.

The next section takes a look at the European Exchange Rate Mechanism (ERM) and specifically the UK's experience. Norman Lamont, the then Chancellor of the Exchequer, presided over the embarrassing rejection of STG from the ERM in the Autumn of 1992. This episode highlights, more than any other, the gaps in the regulators' understanding of currency markets and the reality of a world which operates in accordance with the price discovery via the price mechanism.

The ERM and EMS

In 1979 an agreement was reached between several European countries to attempt to stabilise their respective exchange rates. The motivation for this agreement lay in the wider attempt to control inflation and exchange rate volatility. EMS was part of a bigger scheme to eventually move towards European Monetary Union that led to the introduction of the Euro in 1999 and appeared as notes and coins in member countries in 2001.

153

The ERM was based on a strictly managed exchange rate system whereby member currencies were able to 'float' within narrow margins. Each country's currency was permitted to float within a margin of 2.25% on either side of a bilateral rate – with the notable exception of the Italian lira which operated within a margin of 6%.

From an operational perspective, the margins would be enforced by respective national authorities who agreed to directly intervene in the markets to influence rates by buying and selling their own currencies. Intervention was to take the form of national central bank assistance, by informal agreement, by other European central banks.

The European project has always been something of a difficult political issue for Britain, ever since it joined the EEC in 1973 following a referendum presented to the UK population. Despite the Conservative government, led by Edward Heath, achieving a two to one majority, there have always been voices of dissent within the party in respect of the UK moving closer to our European partners. There was also hostility towards Europe in the Labour Party until the late 1980's.

The UK's progression to the wider project of monetary union began to look more certain with the UK's entry to the ERM in 1990. The benefits and disadvantages of greater European integration, in particular membership of monetary union, are discussed at length elsewhere.[16] However, STG's fate was decided on 16th September 1992.

Many commentators, including the National Institute of Economic and Social Research, believed that the original entry rate of STG into the ERM has been miscalculated.[17] The UK's entry came following a backdrop of experimental monetarist inspired macroeconomic policies. In the late 1980's the then Chancellor of the Exchequer, Nigel Lawson presided over an inflationary strategy that essentially revolved around tracking the DEM. In the 1987 budget Lawson slashed fiscal policy reducing higher rates and lower rates of tax, coupled with significant cuts in interest rates which had risen in order to tackle inflation. The new strategy of encouraging STG to track the DEM at a fairly high rate should, ceteris paribus, led to lower inflation in the UK given the lower prices achievable by UK importers for goods and services such as oil. Lawson was subsequently criticised for relying on interest rates too much by the former Prime Minister Edward Heath who suggested that Lawson was a one club golfer:

> As the Chancellor knows, he is my favourite one-club golfer. On the last occasion, he made a splendid drive from the tee. Enormous reductions in taxation were widely hailed. He now finds himself in a bunker, and he is discovering how difficult it is to get out of a bunker with the wooden club with which he drove off. All I ask is that he should now reconsider his bag of clubs and perhaps embrace a few more.[18]

The STG strategy failed on a number of counts. Firstly, the low interest rates and fiscal stimulus eventually created an inflationary boom which was not restrained by higher STG rates. Secondly, the relatively higher value of STG made UK exporters uncompetitive relative to other world suppliers.

Alan Walters, who was Prime Minister Margaret Thatcher's chief economic adviser, clashed with Lawson over the ERM strategy, calling the ERM a half baked system. Lawson resigned, recognising that he has lost the support of his prime minister. However, following Lawson's replacement with John Major, backed up by the pro-European Foreign Secretary Douglas Hurd the Conservative government joined ERM in 1990 with STG set at DEM2.95. This rate led right-wing Tory MP Norman Tebbit to rename the ERM as an 'eternal recession mechanism'[19] reflecting the view that the UK would face difficulties in the world markets resulting from such a high rate. The Government, however, insisted that the entry band was appropriate. Within 18 months STG began to fall to the lower end of the band as more and more speculators joined in selling anticipating either a collapse of STG or a revaluation. The balance of payments deficits returned by UK plc were simply too great to sustain their parity levels.

The inevitable happened on 16 September 1992. Precipitated by the Bank of England being given a killer punch by the infamous speculator George Sorros through his hedge fund, Quantum, Sorros took out a short-term loan, reputedly of around STG5 billion. He exchanged this sum for DEM at the lower band rate of around DEM2.78. As the Bank of England simply ran out of available foreign currency funds to continue supporting STG, the Treasury attempted to assist the UK's efforts by increasing interest rates during the day initially from 10% to 12%. The market smelt the panic from government and the selling pressure continued throughout the day. The Treasury signalled to the Bank of England to increase interest rates again to 15% but by this time the markets knew that the measure was a last desperate attempt by officials and politicians who had lost control of STG to understand what was happening.

Private sector economists[20] pointed to the inevitability of STG failure in the ERM given the fact that the Bundesbank, the German Central Bank, had been pursuing an anti-inflationary monetary strategy from the start of the 1990's. The Germans had been concerned with inflation relating to unification and their tighter monetary stance began to place great strain on other currencies in the ERM. The UK on the other hand had been having difficulties with the twin deficit problems of trade and budget – signalling the need for divergent monetary positions.

The UK clearing banks began to shift huge sums of money into money market instruments to take advantage of these artificially raised rates. These corporations and individuals, however, were the paupers at the feast. The UK Government was leaking taxpayers' money.

At 7pm that evening a dishevelled and embarrassed Norman Lamont walked on to the street outside the Treasury, flanked by future Conservative leader David Cameron, then a Special Adviser to the Treasury, to announce that the UK was no longer a member of the ERM. Interest rates were to remain at 12% and

STG went into freefall.

In the aftermath of Black Wednesday, later known as White Wednesday in some quarters, given the obvious trading advantages the UK gleaned from the debacle, STG eventually fell below DEM2.20 in the spring of 1995. Monetarists led by Milton Friedman and Alan Walters insisted that STG's unceremonious exit from the ERM was not only an inevitable consequence of membership, but ultimately would prove to be good for the long-term interests of the economy.

The performance of the UK economy following 16 September 1992 shows that Friedman and Walters were probably correct. Figures from the OECD indicate that between 1996 and 2005 UK GDP grew at an annualised rate of 2.7% verses 1.3% in Germany and 2% in Euroland overall. The long-term economic damage may have been mitigated, but the short-term financial misadventure cost the UK billions.

A Treasury report published in 1997 on the events of 16 September 1992 indicated that it had cost taxpayers more than STG3.3 billion, a transfer of wealth directly into the hands of speculators and banks. Sorros' Quantum fund made around STG650 million – large sums of this were subsequently donated under his charitable foundation to public institutions in Hungry his native country.

The Financial Times reported:

> The trading losses in August and September were estimated at £800m, but the main loss to taxpayers arose because the devaluation could have made them a profit. The papers show that if the government had maintained $24bn foreign currency reserves and the pound had fallen by the same amount, the UK would have made a £2.4bn profit on sterling's devaluation.[21]

Chinese Torture?
'He who cannot agree with his enemies is controlled by them'
Ancient Chinese Proverb

FX policy makers, under the guise of the G8 have been recently putting pressure on the Chinese government to allow a more flexible approach to exchange rate setting. The debate, that also shadows discussions of the value of the Yen during the 1990's, revolves around the issue that the value of a currency has a direct bearing on the competitiveness of its exports. The economics behind the debate is fairly simple. If the value of a currency increases in value relative to other currencies it, de facto, increases the cost of its exports to other countries. Similarly, if the value of a currency decreases in value relative to other currencies, it makes the cost of exports to other countries less expensive. Given that a primary consideration for purchasing decisions is cost, the value of a county's currency has a direct bearing on its competitiveness in the global market.

The Chinese, like the Japanese before them, are fully aware of the implications of this relationship and as a result have pursued a policy of manipulating or fixing the Yuan's value at a rate that allows its exporters to compete in the global market.

Classical economics suggests that as a country increases its exports, their currency should, ceteris paribus, appreciate as the foreign purchasers have to buy the exporters' currency prior to purchasing their goods or services. As exports grow, the demand for a country's currency should increase its value making exports gradually more expensive. Eventually, so the theory suggests, the price of a country's exports become so expensive that other countries should be able to compete on price with a major exporting country, such that there is a redress in the balance of trade until the exchange rate re-bases back to its former level.

Neo-classical economics suggests that ultimately the principle of price (currency) driven competition would be a futile method of improving a country's competitiveness such that other factors would come into play that were not exchange rate driven. The model then proposes that supply-side factors such as quality, marketing, product, research and development issues would, and should, ultimately determine the long term success of a country's ability to compete in the global market.

The model, however, does not seem to work in practice. The US had a current account deficit equal to USD218 billion in the second quarter of 2006.[22] By contrast the Chinese and Japanese recorded surpluses in excess of USD160 billion in 2006.[23]

This apparent conundrum can be solved with a glance at the foreign currency reserves of both countries. In September of 2006 Japan held around USD880 billion of foreign currency reserves with China holding in excess of USD1 trillion at the same time.

The neo-classical model seems to have broken down on the basis that the Chinese and Japanese governments are preventing the exchange rate from doing its 'stabilisation work'. In other words as foreigners come in to buy Yuan and Yen, exchanging Euros STG and USD, the Chinese and Japanese governments buy up this foreign currency to prevent an appreciation of their currencies – sustaining the price (currency) advantage afforded to their exporters.

The Chinese and the Japanese are now the two largest holders of US government debt. A good proportion of their foreign currency reserves are therefore paradoxically funding US federal government expenditure and allowing the second Bush administration to afford the tax cuts that have been put in place over the last few years. This was due to the fact that had the Japanese and Chinese not purchased US government debt, the US would have had to increase interest rates to fund their deficit making increases in US budget spending significantly more difficult both economically and politically.

The 'Dollar Dilemma' therefore could be presented to the Japanese and the Chinese. They have the choice either to:

1. Allow their currency to appreciate against the USD. This would have two central negative consequences:
   a. The Yuan and Yen value of their foreign exchange reserves would fall in direct proportion to their own currency's appreciation.

b. The cost of the goods and services that they export would become more expensive and less desirable for overseas buyers – namely the US consumer. This could potentially reduce their economic growth rates and cause domestic unemployment.

2. Maintain a policy of restricted movement of their currency (China) or consistently intervene in the FX markets to keep the value of the USD strong relative to the Yen (Japan). This would have two central negative consequences:

a. The foreign exchange reserves of both countries would continue to grow making an eventual appreciation progressively more expensive in terms of its macroeconomic consequences and ultimate value of its foreign currency reserves.

b. Both governments will face increasing calls from the international community to address their current account surpluses and may face the ultimate sanction of increasing quotas and tariffs on their exported goods to the US and EU as has already been threatened at G8 level.

It would seem that both options are fairly unpalatable to China and Japan, hence the dilemma. The position of the US government is clear: they would like to see the markets determine the appropriate level of currency rate. Economists argue that a sustained appreciation of the Yen and in particular the Yuan would have limited effects on the US economy in terms of its net exporting position. This, however, is contrary to the prima facie situation as discussed above.

Conclusion and Suggestions

There exists today a series of internationally significant challenges in the way the worldwide FX system operates. It is likely that the build up of FX reserves in the East will continue until the political will of the West reaches breaking point. It is hard to see when or indeed if this will happen in the foreseeable future given the political intransigence of Chinese politicians on this issue.

The UK government's record of FX management does not bode well for other countries attempting to manipulate currency rates against the will of the markets with the possible exception of China. It would seem that regulators and central bankers are often quick to blame speculators and other market participants for the ills brought on nation states as a result of adverse currency movements. It is my view that FX movements, however, are a consequence rather than a cause of macroeconomic deficiency. The people engaged in 'playing the markets' neither seek, nor are able to sustain, long term movements in FX rates. They are simply driven by fear and, more often than not, greed. If there is a situation in which a market operates effectively under Adam Smith's invisible hand[24] it would be the FX market. Governments may choose to ignore the perils of attempting to stem the natural flow of free FX movements. However, they are merely delaying and augmenting the inevitable rather than abating or preventing it.

There have, over the years, been many attempts and suggestions to regulate FX flow. These have included exchange controls, fixed exchange rates and recommendations such as the Tobin Tax.[25] I would argue that, given the recent experience of governmental attempts to manipulate rates, the result would eventually be failure.

It was F.A. Hayek who championed the cause of the free market.[26] The classical economist explained how the principles of economic efficiency are best achieved when the market mechanism is allowed to operate freely. Hayek also suggests that the kinds of people one is likely to end up with in charge are precisely the kinds of people who should not be there. In the case of the FX markets, it might be said that Hayek has been proved correct in his analysis time and time again. Governmental ineptitude is the hallmark of any historical analysis in regards to FX policy.

Despite my argument that the FX markets ought to operate

without sustained governmental intervention, it is my view that there are potential systemic risks endemic in the way FX participants transact. The FX market itself is not currently regulated by the UK Government. Under the Financial Services and Markets Act 2000, the Financial Services Authority of the UK (FSA) is empowered to ensure a number of primary objectives. One of these objectives is:

'To ensure market confidence: Maintaining confidence in the financial system.'[27]

The FSA, however, takes no responsibility for regulating the FX mechanism. The world's largest FX electronic broker (EBS), recently acquired by the regulated broker ICAP[28] is responsible for transacting $145 billion per day. Until its acquisition, this firm operated outside of the UK regulatory framework. The Bank of England, HM Treasury and the FSA all deny any responsibility for the EBS operating mechanism.

The UK government has given up attempting to influence the exchange rate. It is my view, however, that it should not give up in attempting to ensure that the system itself is safe and secure. That would seem, at least, to be a primary objective if it is to comply with its statutory duty to maintain confidence in the financial system.

The UK government appears to have learned that using the one club golfing technique as practiced by Lawson to influence both inflation and the exchange rate is ultimately doomed to failure. It is high time, however, that they should look to use the full range of powers and resources of government to tighten potential systemic difficulties and learn to play international economics with more clubs – who knows they may find they could play as well as Tiger Woods.

Notes

1   Bank of England, FX Joint Standing Committee, 2006.
2   www.archive.treasury.gov.uk/press/1999/p168_99
3   www.bankofengland.co.uk/statistics/abstract/sectionc
4   hm-treasury.gov.uk/media/359/2F/adnorfolk_exec_96.pdf
5   www.friedmanfoundation.org
6   Joseph, K. 1976, *Monetarism Is Not Enough*, CPS, London.
7   http://oll.libertyfund.org/Home3/HTML.php?recordID=0517.21
8   Employment Act 1980, 1982, 1988, 1990; Trades Union Act 1984
9   www.hrmguide.co.uk/jobmarket/unemployment.htm
10 http://www.bankofengland.co.uk/statistics/abstract/ab1t22_1.xls
11 www.sjsu.edu/faculty/watkins/
12 www.economist.com/research/Economics/alphabetic.cfm
13 Asian currencies crisis 1998, Mexico, Argentina, Rubble etc. see:
    www.umich.edu/~iinet/journal/vol5no2/lim.htm
14 www.g7.utoronto.ca/finance/fm870222.htm+louvre+accord&hl
    =en&gl=uk&ct=clnk&cd=2
15 www.morganstanley.com/GEFdata/digests/
16 www.hm.treasury.gov.uk/documents/international_issues/the_euro/
    assessment/report/
17 http://www.niesr.ac.uk/
18 http://www.publications.parliament.uk/pa/cm198889/cmhansrd/
    1989-03-20/Debate-2.html
19 http://politics.guardian.co.uk/foi/comment/0,,1409637,00.html
20 Cobham, D., 'Inevitable Disappointment? The ERM as the Framework for UK
    Monetary Policy 1990-92', International Review of Applied Economics, 1997
    Vol 11 (2)
21 Financial Times, 10th February 2005
22 http://www.cia.gov/cia/publications/factbook/rankorder/2187rank.html
23 http://en.wikipedia.org/wiki/Foreign_exchange_reserves
24 Smith, A. 1982, *The Wealth of Nations*, Penguin, London.
25 A suggestion from the Economist James Tobin which proposed taxing FX
    transactions to discourage speculation.
26 Hayek, F.A. 2001, *The Road to Serfdom*, Routledge, London.
27 http://www.fsa.gov.uk/Pages/about/aims/statutory/index.shtml
28 Daily Telegraph, 26th January, 2006

Chapter 8

Is the Global Economy Sustainable?

Güler Aras & David Crowther

Most corporations in the world are currently trying to distance themselves from the excesses and misbehaviours which have been manifest in recent years by those which have been symbolised as *rogue* corporations.[1] Many would consider that these corporations have however behaved no differently to most others and have merely been found out. Nevertheless the distancing of the rogues from the rest has led to a tremendous resurgence of interest in behaviour which has been classified as Corporate Social Responsibility (CSR). So, corporations are busy repackaging their behaviour as CSR and redesignating their spinmasters as Directors of CSR, for there is much evidence that little has changed in corporate behaviour except for this repackaging – the power of the semiotic being far more potent in the modern world than the power of actual action, and also obviating the need for such action. Crowther & Rayman-Bacchus[2] have argued that the corporate excesses, which are starting to become disclosed and which are affecting large numbers of people, have raised an awareness of the social behaviours of corporations. This is one reason why the issue of corporate social responsibility has become a much more prominent feature of the corporate landscape. There are other factors which have helped raise this issue to prominence and Topal & Crowther[3] maintain that a concern with the effects of bioengineering and genetic modifications of nature is also an issue which is arising general concern. At a different level of analysis Crowther[4] has argued that the availability of the World Wide Web has facilitated the dissemination of information and has enabled more pressure to be brought upon corporations by their various stakeholders. But, Wheeler & Elkington[5] talk about the end of the corporate environmental report due to the fact that historically this report has not engaged stakeholders and it appears to be the development of truly interactive (cybernetic) corporate sustainability and communications delivered via the internet and other channels.

Another point of view, about the diffusion of information and its impact,[6] was presented by Unerman & Bennette.[7] They explain the difficulties in identifying all stakeholders that are affected by a corporation's activity. All these perspectives, therefore raise the question as to what exactly CSR is, how it can manifest and what exactly can be considered to be corporate social responsibility. According to the EU:

> ...CSR is a concept whereby companies integrate social and environmental concerns in their business operations and in their interaction with their stakeholders on a voluntary basis.[8]

From these various writings about CSR we can infer that the social enterprise is not a new definition and has resonance with earlier ideas such as those of Dahl,[9] who stated:

> ....every large corporation should be thought of as a social enterprise; that is an entity whose existence and decisions can be justified insofar as they serve public or social purposes.

Shaw[10] explains that the principal characteristics of a social enterprise are:

i   the orientation, "...directly involved in producing goods and providing services to the market, making an operating surplus..."
ii   the aim, "...explicit social aims (job creation, training or provision local services), strong social values and mission (commitment to local capacity building), accountable to their members and wider community for their social, environmental and economic impact.[11] The profits are to their stakeholders or for benefit the community."
iii and the ownership, "...autonomous organizations with loose governance and participation of stakeholders in the ownership structure."

All definitions – and there are many – seem to have a commonality in that they are based upon a concern with more than profitability and returns to shareholders. Indeed involving other stakeholders, and considering them in decision-making is a central platform of CSR. The broadest definition of corporate social responsibility is concerned with what is – or should be – the relationship between the global corporation, governments of countries and individual citizens. For example, the OECD has studied investment in weak governance zones.[12] More locally, the concept of CSR is concerned with the relationship between a corporation and the local community in which it resides or operates. One such case was Timberland, which logged 44,000 community service hours during the three-year period and US recognition[13] for its commitment to social responsibility.[14] Another concept of CSR is concerned with the relationship between a corporation and its stakeholders. In this situation, activity could be focused on employees.[15] The corporation develops its codes of conduct that could make some progress in improving labour rules and process, but the scope is limited and it is unclear if they can make a significant impact without the help of Governments with law-enforcement. These efforts are likely to benefit only a small segment of the target workforce.[16]

For the authors all of these definitions are pertinent and represent a dimension of the issue. A parallel debate is taking place in the arena of ethics as to whether corporations should be controlled through increased regulation or whether the ethical base of citizenship has been lost and needs replacing before socially responsible behaviour will ensue. For example, Fülöp et al.[17] state that people in Hungary often comment that ethics in the Hungarian economic life is a delusion rather than a reality.[18] However this debate is represented it seems that it is concerned with some sort of social contract between corporations and society.

For corporations however, within the broad concept of CSR there are three real issues which focus their attention at the moment: sustainability, corporate governance and the harmonisation of accounting standards. All are issues which are global in their impact and must be considered in the context of globalisation. We will look at each in turn, although it will become apparent that they are all interrelated within the broader concept of corporate social responsibility.

A Focus on Sustainability

Over recent years there has been a focus in corporate activity upon the concept of corporate social responsibility (CSR) and one of its central platforms, the notion of sustainability. Indeed many corporations, which ten years ago produced environmental reports, renamed them CSR reports and now produce sustainability reports. And one of the latest terms is that of sustainable development. One of the effects of persuading that corporate activity is sustainable is that the cost of capital for the firm is reduced as investors are led into thinking that the level of risk involved in their investment is lower than it actually is. One part of our argument therefore is that methodologies for the evaluation of risk are deficient because of the misrepresentation of the concept of sustainability; moreover this affects the short-term as well as the longer-term. The issues we discuss will affect assessments of risk and our argument is that a better evaluation by investment analysts will itself lead to better managerial decision making.

The globalisation debate which is taking place in the present can be viewed dialectically as an opposition between the proponents of an unregulated market and the opponents of such untrammelled capitalism. Few would dispute that in the present the proponents of an unregulated world – carefully packaged in the pejorative term of the free market – have the ascendancy. Thus the dominant ideology of the modern western world is that of the free market which, if unregulated, maximises economic wealth and optimises its distribution, according to its proponents. Consequently there is increasing pressure upon governments around the world to throw off the shackles of regulation so that we may all benefit from the prosperity which ensues from the free market. Omitted (whether by ignorance or by design) from the discourse of ideological pressure is the fact that a completely unregulated free market only operates effectively in a situation of perfect competition – in other words never! The opponents of an unregulated world are more difficult to categorise as they represent a diverse collection of people and interests without a great deal of commonality except for their opposition to the dismantling of regulation and the ascendancy of global capitalism. Discourse between the two groups tends to be confrontational and often violent: indeed it is problematic to describe it as discourse as most of both sides are not particularly interested in talking, preferring instead to seek dominance for their view. On the face of it therefore it would seem problematic to describe these differing views as dialectical as there seems little scope for any synthesis to emerge. One aspect of the synthesis which has developed however is encapsulated in the concept of corporate social responsibility.

For a few years now the concept of corporate social responsibility has gained prominence to such an extent that it seems ubiquitous in popular media and is gaining increasing attention around the world among business people, media people and academics from a wide range of disciplines. There are probably many reasons[19] for the attention given to this phenomenon not least of which is the corporate excesses which continue to become manifest in various parts of the world. These have left an indelible impression among people that all is not well with the corporate world and that there are problems which need to be addressed. Such incidents are too common to recount but have left the financial markets in a state of uncertainty and have left ordinary people wondering if such a thing as honesty in business exists anymore.

More recently the language used in business has mutated again and the concept of CSR is being replaced by the language of sustainability. Such language must be considered semiotically[20] as a way of creating the impression of actual sustainability. Using such analysis then, the signification is about inclusion within the selected audience for the corporate reports on the assumption that those included understand the signification in a common way with the authors. This is based upon an assumed understanding of the code of signification used in describing corporate activity in this way. As Sapir[21] states:

> ...we respond to gestures with an extreme alertness and, one might almost say, in accordance with an elaborate and secret code that is written nowhere, known by none and understood by all.

It is comfortable to assume a shared signification based upon a shared understanding of the language used; this shared signification may however be fictitious. An alternative – arguably more sinister – interpretation would be to view the language of the statements concerning sustainability to be made in the Orwellian[22] sense of being used as a device for corrupting thought as an instrument to prevent thought about the various alternative realities of the organisation's activity. However one views these interpretations is to a large extent dependent on one's views of sustainability.

Is Sustainability Sustainable?

A growing number of writers over the last quarter of a century have recognised that the activities of an organisation impact upon the external environment and have suggested that such an organisation should therefore be accountable to a wider audience than simply its shareholders. Such a suggestion probably first arose in the 1970s[23] and a concern with a wider view of company performance is taken by some writers who evince concern with the social performance of a business, as a member of society at large. This concern was stated by Ackerman[24] who argued that big business was recognising the need to adapt to a new social climate of community accountability, but that the orientation of business to financial results was inhibiting social responsiveness.

McDonald and Puxty[25] on the other hand maintain that companies are no longer the instruments of shareholders alone but exist within society and so therefore have responsibilities to that society, and that there is therefore a shift towards the greater accountability of companies to all participants. Implicit in this concern with the effects of the actions of an organisation on its external environment is the recognition that it is not just the owners of the organisation who have a concern with the activities of that organisation.

Additionally there are a wide variety of other stakeholders who justifiably have a concern with, and are affected by, those activities. Those other stakeholders have not just an interest in the activities of the firm but also a degree of influence over the shaping of those activities. This influence is so significant that it can be argued that the power and influence of these stakeholders is such that it amounts to quasi-ownership of the organisation. Indeed Gray, Owen and Maunders[26] challenge the traditional role of accounting in reporting results and consider that, rather than an ownership approach to accountability, a stakeholder approach, recognising the wide stakeholder community, is needed.[27] Moreover Rubenstein[28] goes further and argues that there is a need for a new social contract between a business and its stakeholders.

Central to this social contract is a concern for the future which has become manifest through the term sustainability. This term sustainability has become ubiquitous both within the discourse of globalisation and within the discourse of corporate performance. Sustainability is of course a controversial issue and there are many definitions of what is meant by the term. At the broadest definitions sustainability is concerned with the effect which action taken in the present has upon the options available in the future.[29] If resources are used in the present then they are no longer available for use in the future, and this is of particular concern if the resources are finite. Thus raw materials of an extractive nature, such as coal, iron or oil, are finite in quantity and once used are unavailable for future use. At some point in the future therefore alternatives will be needed to fulfil the functions currently provided by these resources. This may be at some point in the relatively distant future but of more immediate concern is the fact that as resources become depleted then the cost of acquiring the remaining resources tends to increase, and hence the operational costs of organisations tend to increase.[30]

Sustainability therefore implies that society must use no more of a resource than can be regenerated. This can be defined in terms of the carrying capacity of the ecosystem[31] and described with input – output models of resource consumption. Thus the paper industry for example has a policy of replanting trees to replace those harvested and this has the effect of retaining costs in the present rather than temporally externalising them. Similarly motor vehicle manufacturers such as Volkswagen have a policy of making their cars almost totally recyclable. Viewing an organisation as part of a wider social and economic system implies that these effects must be taken into account, not just for the measurement of costs and value created in the present but also for the future of the business itself.

Such concerns are pertinent at a macro level of society as a whole, or at the level of the nation state but are equally relevant at the micro level of the corporation, the aspect of sustainability with which we are concerned in this work. At this level, measures of sustainability would consider the rate at which resources are consumed by the organisation in relation to the rate at which resources can be regenerated. Unsustainable operations can be accommodated for either by developing sustainable operations or by planning for a future lacking in resources currently required. In practice organisations mostly tend to aim towards less unsustainability by increasing efficiency in the way in which resources are utilised. An example would be an energy efficiency programme.

Sustainability is a controversial topic because it means different things to different people. Nevertheless there is a growing awareness (or diminishing naivety) that one is, indeed, involved in a battle about what sustainability means and, crucially, the extent (if at all) it can be delivered by MNCs in the easy manner they promise (United Nations Commission on Environment and Development).[32] The starting point must be taken as the Brundtland Report[33] because there is explicit agreement with that Report and because the definition of sustainability in there is pertinent and widely accepted. Equally, the Brundtland Report is part of a policy landscape being explicitly fought over by the United Nations, Nation States and big business through the vehicles of the WBCSD and ICC.[34]

There is a further confusion surrounding the concept of sustainability: for the purist sustainability implies nothing more than stasis – the ability to continue in an unchanged manner – but often it is taken to imply development in a sustainable manner[35] and the terms sustainability and sustainable development are for many viewed as synonymous. Ever since the Brundtland Report was produced by the World Commission on Environment and Development in 1987 there has been a continual debates concerning development[36] and this has added to the confusion between sustainability and sustainable development. For us we take the definition as being concerned with stasis; at the corporate level if development is possible

173

without jeopardising that stasis then this is a bonus rather than a constituent part of that sustainability.

Most analysis of sustainability[37] only recognises a two-dimensional approach of the environmental and the social. A few[38] recognise a third dimension which is related to organisation behaviour. We argue that restricting analysis to such dimensions is deficient. One problem is the fact that the dominant assumption by researchers is based upon the incompatibility of optimising, for a corporation, both financial performance and social / environmental performance. In other words financial performance and social / environmental performance are seen as being in conflict with each other through this dichotomisation.[39] Consequently most work in the area of corporate sustainability does not recognise the need for acknowledging the importance of financial performance as an essential aspect of sustainability and therefore fails to undertake financial analysis alongside – and integrated with – other forms of analysis for this research.[40] We argue that this is an essential aspect of corporate sustainability and therefore adds a further dimension to the analysis of sustainability. Furthermore we argue that the third dimension sometimes recognised as organisational behaviour needs to actually comprise a much broader concept of corporate culture. There are therefore 4 aspects of sustainability which need to be recognised and analysed, namely:

- Societal influence, which we define as a measure of the impact that society makes upon the corporation in terms of the social contract and stakeholder influence;
- Environmental impact, which we define as the effect of the actions of the corporation upon its geophysical environment;
- Organisational culture, which we define as the relationship between the corporation and its internal stakeholders, particularly employees, and all aspects of that relationship; and
- Finance, which we define in terms of an adequate return for the level of risk undertaken.

These four must be considered as the key dimensions of sustainability, all of which are equally important. Our analysis is therefore considerably broader – and more complete – than that of others. Furthermore we consider that these four aspects can be resolved into a two-dimensional matrix along the polarities of internal versus external focus and short term versus long term focus, which together represent a complete representation of organisational performance this can be represented as the model below:

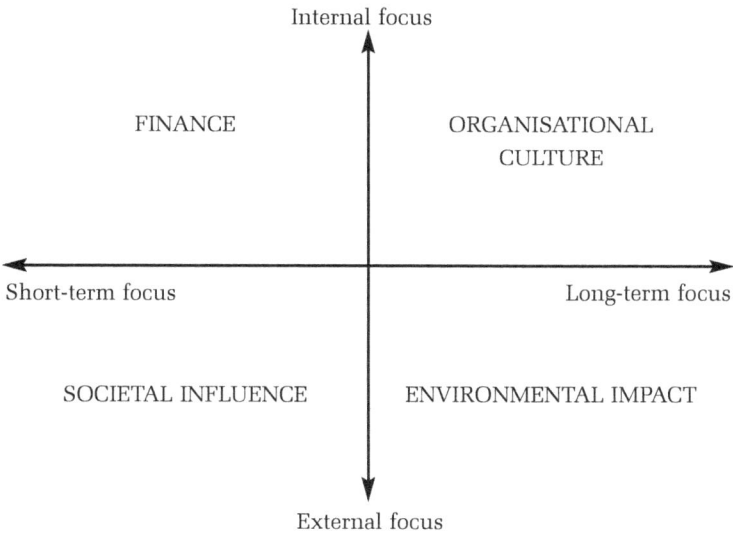

Internal focus

FINANCE   ORGANISATIONAL
                                              CULTURE

Short-term focus   Long-term focus

SOCIETAL INFLUENCE   ENVIRONMENTAL IMPACT

External focus

Fig 1: Model of corporate sustainability

This model provides both a representation of organisation performance and a basis for any evaluation of corporate sustainability.

In order to achieve sustainable development[41] it is first necessary to achieve sustainability and there are a number of elements to this. What is important for sustainability is not just addressing each of these elements individually but also paying attention to maintaining the balance between them. It is the maintenance of this balance which is the most challenging – but also the most essential – aspect of managing sustainability. There are a number of elements which must be addressed but these can be grouped together into four major elements, which map exactly onto the model for evaluating sustainability outlined earlier. These four major elements of sustainability therefore are:

- Maintaining economic activity, which must be the central raison d'etre of corporate activity and the principle reason for organising corporate activity. This of course maps onto the finance aspect.
- Conservation of the environment, which is essential for maintaining the options available to future generations. This maps onto the environmental impact aspect.
- Ensuring social justice, which will include such activities as the elimination of poverty, ensuring protection of human rights, the promotion of universal education and the facilitation of world peace. This maps onto the societal influence aspect.
- Developing spiritual and cultural values, which is where corporate and societal values align in the individual and where all of the other elements are promoted or negated; sadly at present they are mostly negated.[42] This maps onto the organisational culture aspect.

Often theorists attempt to prioritise these but our argument is that it is the balancing of them equitably which is essential to developing sustainability, and hence we maintain that most considerations of the concept are unworkably simplistic. It can therefore be seen that the representation of corporate activity is considerably more complex than simply managing the stakeholder versus shareholder dichotomisation which is ever present in organisational theory.

Is Success Sustainable?

The definition of success for an organisation is often multiple and involves much more than profit maximisation. Indeed profit maximisation in a long-term perspective can involve very different behaviour to that of a short-term perspective. Often the approach taken is that of satisficing – the balancing of the long-term with the short-term and the balancing of the expectations of all stakeholders. These, in combination with a desire for growth – now often called sustainable development – and for survival form the objectives of an organisation and a mix of these in the form of a balanced scorecard will be the objectives of an organisation and its definition of success will be dependence upon meeting these objectives.

Of course for any firm which is successful, according to its definition of success, then the matter of maintaining that success becomes important. Here we argue that only by recognising – and addressing – the four aspects of sustainability outlined earlier is it possible for a form to maintain its success. In other words the sustainability of success is dependent upon recognising and addressing the components of sustainability. Here the creation of the semiotic without action will be insufficient and there are many firms which have adopted the rhetoric and created this semiotic without taking action. For these firms any success achieved can only be ephemeral.

The Global Economy and International Institutions

The phenomenon known as globalisation is a multidimensional process involving economic, political, social and cultural change. However the most important discussion about globalisation is related to the economic effect it has upon countries. Globalisation in the economic and financial markets is a recognised international fact in the 21st century for all countries. The globalisation process has dynamic, critical and inevitable consequences for institutions, business and the environment, especially for developing countries. Because of this, globalisation is the main issue for some "important" international institutions and some associations such as International Monetary Fund (IMF), World Bank, United Nations (UN), World Trade Organization (WTO) and the Bank for International Settlement (BIS); as well as for the anti-capitalist protest movement. For example one of the international organizations – the IMF – has identified six key principles that should strengthen the framework for the global economy.[43] These are:

1 The issue of international interdependence must be given greater priority within national policy,
2 International cooperation should not replace national self-responsibility,
3 Globalisation urgently requires solidarity,
4 The ecological threat to the planet knows no national boundaries,
5 We need recognised rules of the game or a level playing field, for participation in Globalisation,
6 We should regard the diversity of experiences and cultures as part of the wealth of our planet.

As can be seen these principles cover national politics, ecological and environmental issues, wealth distributions and international corporate behaviour, sharing experiences and roles of main players of this process. One of the main questions is whether globalisation is inevitable and will have the same effect or not for all countries and markets. And does globalisation causes less independence for countries? According to all literature, research and experiences it looks as if that not only is it an inevitable fact but also that it is having a strong effect on all countries. Therefore, in another publication, the IMF has also identified the following four key principles for strengthening the process of globalisation:[44]

1 All countries need to have trust that their voices will be heard,
2 There must be trust that each country will live up to its own responsibility,

3 International decision making should be seen to respect national and local responsibility, religious, culture and traditions, and

4 A global economy needs global ethics, reflecting respect for human rights.

These key principles indicated that globalisation has needed some basic rules such as solidarity, respect, and responsibility for each nation's value, and global ethics, for all actors in this process. Another issue is co-operation, solidarity, sharing experience and decisions which also will affect the dependency of nations.

On the other hand, some writers mention that, as international institutions, the IMF and the World Bank – which are describing financial architecture – have been working hard to improve the life of millions or billions of people in the world over the last 50 years or so.[45] And the call for a new international financial architecture by the IMF as well as the World Bank is a step in the right direction. However, this call is not going to change the fortunes of many developing countries and give them the ability to improve the underlying causes of their financial inability to deal with their economic and social or environmental problems.[46]

Financial Markets and Globalisation
The liberalisation of trade in financial assets is often called financial globalisation. In neoclassical models, financial globalisation generates major economic benefits: in particular the theory holds that it enables investors worldwide to share risks better, it allows capital to flow where its productivity is highest, and it provides countries an opportunity to reap the benefits of their respective comparative advantages.[47] Globalisation is clearly an important influence on financial markets. Globalisation of financial markets affects assets and debts securities, bank loans and deposits, titles to land and physical capital. Trade in these assets and debt is much easier

to globalise than trade in commodities and labour. Indeed, their globalisation has progressed most rapidly because nothing is involved in financial transactions beyond exchanging pieces of paper or making entries in electronic ledgers. The communications revolution makes these transactions easy, fast and cheap. No physical frontiers have to be crossed by financial assets. The only barriers to financial transactions are national regulations.[48] However, it can be seen that regulation is not enough to regulate and control international transactions and capital flows in developing countries and transitional economies.

Conventional wisdom suggests that an integration of national financial markets facilitates financial flows from rich countries to poor countries, thereby accelerating development in those poor countries. According to this view the globalisation of financial markets helps to reduce the inequality of nations. There is, however, a widely held belief that poor countries are unable to compete in an integrated financial market against rich countries, which can offer financial security to lenders in an imperfect world.[49] The expected benefit from the development of financial market integration and financial asset movements is creating the prospect of a more efficient worldwide allocation of savings and investment than was possible in the past. However, the impact of this globalisation on financial markets in developing and transitional economies can be very severe and destructive. Imperfectly competitive financial markets[50] can react perversely to adverse economic shocks, which can be spread to other countries with a contagious effect. One of the main causes of financial shock and crisis is capital flows, especially portfolio investments, for developing countries which have unregulated markets and unsound financial systems. These countries are wide open for international financial shocks; therefore we can say that financial globalisation carries with it large risks.

Financial stability and market discipline are the main factors required to combat the inevitable, and most of the time, uncontrolled effects of globalisation. Therefore, until market discipline becomes more effective in ensuring sound financial systems, closer regulatory oversight will be key to increasing the benefits and limiting the risks of globalisation. To achieve this goal, policy makers in developed and developing countries, as well as supervisory and regulatory bodies (such as the Basle Committee of Banking Supervisors) and international financial institutions (such as the IMF and the World Bank) are taking steps to enhance financial system soundness in the new environment.[51]

It is clear that globalisation is a growing influence on financial markets and for all the reasons mentioned, it is necessitating global standards and regulations for international trading and for corporations. If the world is going to be (almost) only one federation we will have need of international rules and standards such as international bank regulations, international accounting standards and trade regulations. And also achieving true financial globalisation would require a global financial institution that can play a central coordinating and regulatory role.[52]

Globalisation, Market Misbehaviour and Financial Crises

Contagions and crises are the downside of financial globalisation. The economic and financial crises of the 1990s give an indication that financial globalisation is not always beneficial to all, and that it can potentially lead to serious disorder and high cost in terms of bank failures, corporate bankruptcies, stock market turbulence, depletion of foreign exchange reserves, currency depreciation and increased fiscal burden. A unique characteristic of globalised financial markets is the sudden reversal of capital flows when market perception regarding the creditworthiness of the borrowing entity changes.

The probability of a randomly selected country experiencing a crisis has doubled since 1973. To avoid recurrences of such scenarios, policy makers must strive to make their financial systems deep, broad and resilient. They must address financial weaknesses that make financial structures vulnerable to

181

external shocks. This needs to be achieved both at national and global levels.[53]

There are of course benefits to go alongside the problems. Thus the integration of financial markets has also improved access to the pool of global savings for many developing countries. Many countries have been able to borrow more and hence grow faster than otherwise possible, while generating higher yields for international investors and giving them the opportunity to reduce risk though portfolio diversification. Thus the process of financial market integration and associated increase in international financial mobility has been viewed as a welcome development by many.[54] For this reason globalisation has increased the speed of market reactions in the financial markets of developing countries. These countries, which tend not to have sufficient market rules and regulations, are clearly open for the external effects which come from capital flows and portfolio investment. In terms of the increasing volume of international trade and portfolio investment, globalisation causes markets to misbehave in these emerging countries. For example, one of the main causes of the Asian crisis lies in the rapidly increasing globalisation and the unregulated market conditions. In 1997 the annual average net private capital flows in developing countries was $285 billion. If you compare net capital flows in earlier and later years then for example, in 1982 was $57 billion while in 2003 it was $167 billion – a rapid increase followed by a sharp decrease in capital flows in these developing countries after the crisis.

As we know, globalisation caused a series of financial crises in last century. These show us that developing countries need to have a set of preconditions in place in order to benefit from financial globalisation, and to avoid an increased probability of a currency or banking crisis.

Globalisation, Homogenisation and Convergence

Thus we can see that the world is getting smaller through globalisation and mediums such as the internet are bringing people closer together; indeed ITC (Information and Communication Technology) will eventually change the way organisations operate and society itself will also change. As the world shrinks different cultures are coming into contact with each other. This is having an effect on different areas of life and business is no exception. As Solomon and Solomon state, "International harmonisation is now common in all areas of business".[55]

When cultures meet it is the dominant culture that prevails; thus for example Solomon and Solomon[56] highlight concerns that the Anglo – American model of corporate governance, is becoming more prevalent internationally than others. It could be argued on a number of levels that this is not the best way forward as countries have their own individuality. As Cornelius[57] states, if all countries were the same it would erase the competitive advantage that some countries have over others. At the same time there are organisations such as the OECD which are promoting a need for a basic global standard of corporate governance.

One of the main issues, therefore, which has been exercising the minds of business managers, accountants and auditors, investment manages and government officials – again all over the world – is that of corporate governance. Often companies main target is to became global – while at the same time remaining sustainable – as a means to get competitive power. But the most important question is concerned with what will be a firms' route to becoming global and what will be necessary in order to get global competitive power. There is more then one answer to this question and there are a variety of routes for a company to achieve this.

Probably since the mid-1980s, corporate governance has attracted a great deal of attention. Early impetus was provided by Anglo-American codes of good corporate governance.[58] Stimulated by institutional investors, other countries in the developed as well as in the emerging markets established an adapted version of these codes for their own companies. Supranational authorities like the OECD and the World Bank did not remain passive and developed their own set of standard principles and recommendations. This type of self-regulation was chosen above a set of legal standards.[59] After big corporate scandals, corporate governance has become central to most companies. It is understandable that investor protection has become a much more important issue for all financial markets after the tremendous firm failures and scandals. Investors are demanding that companies implement rigorous corporate governance principles in order to achieve better returns on their investment and to reduce agency costs. Most of the time investors are ready to pay more for companies to have good governance standards. Similarly a company's corporate governance report is one of the main tools for investor decisions. It is for these reasons companies cannot ignore the pressure for good governance from shareholders, potential investors and other market actors.

On the other hand banking credit risk measurement regulations are requiring new rules for a company's credit evaluations. New international bank capital adequacy assessment methods (Basel II) necessitate that credit evaluation rules are elaborately concerned with operational risk which covers corporate governance principles. In this respect corporate governance will be one of the most important indicators for measuring risk. Another issue is related to firm credibility and riskiness. If the firm needs a high rating score then it will have to be pay attention for corporate governance rules also. Credit rating agencies analyse corporate governance practices along with other corporate indicators. Even though corporate governance principles have always been important for getting good rating scores for large and publicly-held companies, they are also becoming much more important for investors, potential investors, creditors and governments. Because of all of these factors, corporate governance receives high priority on the agenda of policymakers, financial institutions, investors, companies and academics. This is one of the main indicators that the link between corporate governance and actual performance is still open for discussion. In the literature a number of studies have investigated the relation between corporate governance mechanisms and performance.[60] Most of the studies show mixed result without a clear cut relationship. Based on these results, we can say that corporate governance matters to a company's performance, market value and credibility, and therefore that company has to apply corporate governance principles. But the most important point is that corporate governance is the only means for companies to achieve corporate goals and strategies. Therefore companies have to improve their strategy and effective route to implementation of governance principles. Companies have to investigate what their corporate governance policies and practices need to be.

Since corporate governance can be highly influential for firm performance, firms must know what the corporate governance principles are; and how applying these principals will improve strategy. In practice there are four principles of good corporate governance, which are:

• Transparency
• Accountability
• Responsibility
• Fairness

All these principles are related with the firm's corporate social responsibility.

Globalisation and Accounting
The tools of accountancy are its accounting and financial models. Accountancy has its work cut out to continue developing GAAP[61] models for external reporting that can be applied universally across the world and this work is in hand. Models for the production of internal financial information are much less well developed and standardised. Less progress is

being made here partly because of strong resistance by corporate managers, often on the grounds that more transparency would erode their competitive advantage. Better internal financial management models must be devised. They must be coherent with external financial information models if they are to achieve the level transparency needed to monitor and control the changing intentions of corporate mangers. There may be a case for more standardisation and possible regulation of these models.

As far as external financial information models are concerned then progress is being made to improve accounting worldwide and up-date it to increase its relevance in the "global village" in which we now all live. New international accounting standards have been introduced from 1 January 2005.[62] The aim is to harmonise accounting practices across the world which is crucial to providing a regulatory environment to monitor and control international activities, especially those of multi-national companies, who can exploit gaps in different accounting regimes to their own advantages. There is a wide variety of practices world-wide making harmonisation a challenge requiring compromises at national level to move towards world-wide standardisation. If successful, external accounting reports across the world will become more universal, comprehensible and transparent. Accounting as a profession will be more uniform across the world with the possibility of more ready transferability of accounting skills. To achieve international harmonisation the focus must be, at least initially, on eroding differences rather than expanding the overall scope of regulation and conforming to the international standard may also reduce flexibility at national level. For these reasons it may be that innovative solutions for the improvement of internal financial management information will emerge from sources other than the international standard setting process.[63]

Fundamental to the management of an organisation is the need to separate the core cost of generating income on an on-going basis from all other costs. Both the trading account and the cost of sales used in GAAP models purport to make this distinction but in fact do not do so. Separating core and discretionary costs would provide better financial management information to managers than if the GAAP model is used on its own. There is a possibility of using of value based models to overcome the weaknesses of GAAP models for the provision of relevant and useful financial management information. The main recommendation of value based management is to separate operating and investing activities,[64] which more or less correlate to core and discretionary costs. The purpose is to classify expenditure transactions according to the characteristics of the return on that expenditure.[65] Operating transactions have a quick return whilst investing transactions have a longer term return cycle. This theme is continued with the further classification to value streams[66] Baggaley & Maskell[67] also recognised on the basis of different characteristics of return on expenditure. As yet, few organisations currently apply value based models for day to day management, but those that do, also continue to use GAAP models. It is important that individual organisations develop alternative solutions to improving their financial management information because it is vital potential source of competitive advantage.

There is no compulsion on organisations to use GAAP models as the basis of their internal financial management information. When an organisation does use GAAP as the basis of its financial management information it will be able to monitor the impact of management on external reporting. Internal and external financial information can be reconciled readily and this alignment will ensure a high level of transparency.[68] The lack of regulation over the use of models for internal use gives managers a degree of discretion which they can exploit to "fudge" the links between the internal and the external information. In this way, their activities are not transparent. Auditors and stakeholders are unable to unlock the information for their purposes and the accountability trail is broken. Managers often justify such actions on the grounds of competitive advantage. One solution might be to develop GAAP models to fully support financial management information requirements as well as external reporting and regulate their use. This would ensure greater transparency but may have consequences on the competitive position of the organisation and this issue would need to be addressed in some way.

Just as slow has been the harmonisation of the rules that determine economic activity throughout the world which originally varied from country to country. Where there has been a high degree of world-wide standardisation there have been opportunities to develop world wide channels of communication and trade. The information profession, for example, has benefited from a high level of standardisation of technical rules which has allowed the 'www' to develop. The benefits of a world-wide level playing field are not universally accepted as the erosion of national specialities can be eroded along with conformation with global standards. The accountancy profession, lagging behind, has failed to achieve a high degree of harmonisation across the world, and managers of organisations have exploited the loop-holes thus created with as much attention as any other lucrative source of business. Whether or not harmonisation is ultimately good or bad, the process of harmonisation has increased complexity in the short-term. There is still a long way to go, but partial harmonisation is worse than either of both extremes. Accelerating the pace of harmonisation to a situation where complexity starts to reduce will be a major factor in accountancy becoming a more useful tool once again for monitoring and influencing organisational behaviour.

Conclusions

There are a number of issues which come out of our review of the current issues affecting corporate activity. In one respect it can all be considered to be issues implicated within corporate social responsibility, arguably the biggest issue affecting economic society at the present time. A different level of analysis would however suggest that the main issue is concerned with identifying and managing risk and the effects of globalisation. Another analysis would suggest that the key issue is concerned with transparency of corporate activity. All the evidence shows that these issues are increasing in importance and are being tackled by corporations through their corporate governance procedures, through their accounting policies and through their activities designed to foster sustainability. Our argument therefore is that these issues are inevitably intertwined and our prognosis is that the demand from stakeholders for increasing information will continue to result in increasing transparency of corporate activity, as a means of addressing the other key issues.

Notes

1   Enron is of course the best known of these but there are many more examples of corporations exhibiting bad behaviour, although probably not on the same enormous scale.

2   Crowther, D. and Rayman-Bacchus, L. 2004, "Perspectives on Corporate Social Responsibility" in Crowther, D. and Rayman-Bacchus, L. *Perspectives on Corporate Social Responsibility*, Ashgate, Aldershot, pp 1-17.

3   Topal, R. and Crowther, D. 2004, "Bioengineering and Corporate Social Responsibility" in Crowther, D. and Rayman-Bacchus, L. (eds), *Perspectives on Corporate Social Responsibility*, Ashgate, Aldershot. pp. 186-201.

4   Crowther, D. 2000, *Social and Environmental Accounting*, Financial Times Prentice Hall, London; Crowther, D. 2002(a), "The Psychoanalysis of On-line Reporting" in Holmes, L., Grieco, M. and Hosking, D. (eds) *Organising in the Information Age*, Ashgate, Aldershot, pp. 130-148; Crowther, D. 2002(b), "Psychoanalysis and Auditing" in Clegg, S. (ed), *Paradoxical New Directions in Management and Organization Theory*, J Benjamins, Amsterdam, pp. 227-246.

5   Wheeler, D. and Elkington, J. 2001, "The End of the Corporate Environmental Report? Or the Advent of Cybernetic Sustainability, Reporting and Communication" *Business Strategy and the Environment*, 10 (1), Jan/Feb: 1-14.

6   Unerman, J. and Bennett, M. 2004, "Increased Stakeholder Dialogue and the Internet: Towards Greater Corporate Accountability or Reinforcing Capitalist Hegemony?" *Accounting, Organizations and Society*, 29 (7), 685-707. They explain the interactive ways that the financial report could exist. For them: ...it is not possible to ascertain from the web forum (i.e. it is a mechanism to ensure movement towards inter subjective acceptance by all stakeholders of

the corporate responsibilities recognised) the extent to which postings have actually affected corporate decisions.

7   Ibid, pp. 687-707.

8   European Commission, 2002, *Corporate Social Responsibility: A Business Contribution to Sustainable Development*. COM, 347 final. Official publications of the European Commission, July 2,Brussels.

9   Dahl, R. 1972, "A Prelude to Corporate Reform" *Business and Society Review*, Spring: 17-23

10 Shaw, E. 2004, "Marketing in the Social Enterprise Context" *Qualitative Market Research: An International Journal*, 7 (3): 194-205.

11 An empirical study concerning the operational reporting of corporate natural assets (i.e., habitats, fauna and flora) can be seen in Jones, M. 2003, "Accounting for Biodiversity: Operationalising Environmental Accounting" *Accounting, Auditing and Accountability Journal*, 16 (5): 762-789.

12 Following the external inputs invitation, till 28 February 2005, the concept is that: "... in some investment environments, public authorities are unwilling or unable to protect rights (including property rights) and to provide basic public services (e.g. social programmes, infrastructure development and prudential surveillance). These "government failures" lead to broader failures in political, economic and civic institutions that the project refers to as "weak governance"." Organization for Economic Cooperation and Development (OECD). 2005, *Conducting Business with Integrity in Weak Governance Zones: Invitation for Public Comment*, OECD, Paris.

13 Recognition included a corporate conscience award from the council on economic priorities and public accolades from Presidents Bush and Clinton, see Austin J, Leonard, H. and Quinn J. 2004, "Timberland: Commerce and Justice" *Harvard Business School*, 9-305-002, December.

14 Ibid.

15 Parker, L. 1977, "The Accounting Responsibility towards Corporate Financial Reporting to Employees." *Accounting Education*, 17 (2): 62-83.

16 See for example OECD reports published in 2000 and Scherrer, C. and Greven, T. 2001, *Global Rules for Trade: Codes of Conduct, Social Labelling, Workers' Rights Clauses*, Verlag Westfälisches Dampfboot, Münster.

17 Fülöp, G., Hisrich, R. and Szegedi, K. 2000, "Business Ethics and Social Responsibility in Transition Economies". *Journal of Management Development*, 19 (1): 5-31.

18 Similarly an Islamic perspective on CSR can be found in Rizk, R. 2005, "The Islamic Perspective to Corporate Social Responsibility" in Crowther, D. and Jatana, R. (eds), *The International Dimension of Corporate Social Responsibility* Vol 2, ICFAI University Press, Hyderabad. pp 1-34; and on business ethics in Pomezanz, F. 2004, "Ethics: Toward Globalisation" *Managerial Auditing Journal*, 19 (1): 8-14.

19 Crowther, D. and Ortiz-Martinez, E. 2006, "The Abdication of Responsibility: Corporate Social Responsibility, Public Administration and the Globalising Agenda" in Crowther, D. and Caliyurt, K. T. (eds), *Globalisation and Social Responsibility*, Cambridge Scholars Press, Newcastle, pp. 253-275.

20 Barthes, R. 1973, *Mythologies*, trans. A Lavers; Harper Collins, London.

21 Sapir, E. 1949, "The Unconscious Patterning of Behaviour in Society" in Mendelbaum, D. G. (ed), *Selected Writings of Edward Sapir*; University of California Press, Berkley, Ca.

22 Orwell, G. 1970, *Collected Essays, Journalism and Letters* Vol. 4,Penguin, Harmondsworth;

23 Although philosophers such as Robert Owen were expounding those views more than a century earlier.

24 Ackerman, R. W. 1975, *The Social Challenge to Business*, Harvard University Press, Cambridge, Ma..

25 McDonald, D. and Puxty, A. G. 1979, "An Inducement - contribution Approach to Corporate Financial Reporting" *Accounting, Organizations and Society*, 4 (1/2), 53-65.

26 Gray, R. Owen, D. and Maunders, K. 1987, *Corporate Social Reporting: Accounting and Accountability*, Prentice-Hall, London.

27 The benefits of incorporating stakeholders into a model of performance measurement and accountability have however been extensively criticised. See for example Freedman, R. E. and Reed, D. L. 1983, "Stockholders and Stakeholders: a New Perspective on Corporate Governance" *California Management Review*; Vol XXV No 3 pp 88-106; Sternberg, E. 1997, "The Defects of Stakeholder Theory" *Corporate Governance: An International Review*, 6 (3), 151-163; Sternberg, E. 1998, *Corporate Governance: Accountability in the Marketplace*, IEA, London; and Hutton, W. 1997, *Stakeholding and its Critics*; London; IEA Health and Welfare Unit; for details of this ongoing discourse.

28 Rubenstein, D. B. 1992, "Bridging the Gap between Green Accounting and Black Ink" *Accounting Organizations and Society*, 17 (5), 501-508.

29 Crowther, D. 2002 (c), *A Social Critique of Corporate Reporting*, Ashgate, Aldershot.

30 Similarly once an animal or plant species becomes extinct then the benefits of that species to the environment can no longer be accrued. In view of the fact that many pharmaceuticals are currently being developed from plant species still being discovered this may be significant for the future.

31 Hawken, P. 1993, *The Ecology of Commerce*, Weidenfeld and Nicholson, London.

32 Schmidheiny, S. 1992, *Changing Course*, MIT Press, New York.

33 WCED (World Commission on Environment and Development),1987, *Our Common Future* (The Brundtland Report), Oxford University Press; Oxford.

34 Beder, S. 1997, *Global Spin: The corporate assault on environmentalism*, Green Books, London; Mayhew, N. 1997, "Fading to Grey: the use and abuse of corporate executives' 'representational power'" in R. Welford (ed), *Hijacking Environmentalism: Corporate response to sustainable development*, Earthscan, London, pp 63-95
   Gray, R. H. and Bebbington, K. J. 2001, *Accounting for the Environment*, Sage, London.

35 Marsden, C. 2000, "The New Corporate Citizenship of Big Business: Part of the Solution to Sustainability" *Business and Society Review*, 105 (1), 9-25; Hart, S. L. and Milstein, M. B. 2003, "Creating Sustainable Value" *Academy of Management Executive*, 17 (2), 56-67.

36 Chambers, R. 1994, "The Origins and Practice of Participatory Rural Appraisal" *World Development*, 22 (7), 953-969; Pretty, J.N.1995, "Participatory Learning for Sustainable Agriculture" *World Development*, 23 (8), 1247-1263.

37 Dyllick, T. and Hockerts, K. 2002, "Beyond the Business Case for Corporate Sustainability" *Business Strategy and the Environment*, 11, 130-14.

38 Spangenberg, J. H. 2004, "Reconciling Sustainability and Growth: Criteria, Indicators, Policy" *Sustainable Development*, 12, 76-84.

39 Crowther, D. 2002(c), op cit.

40 Of course the fact that many researchers do not have the skills to undertake such detailed financial analysis even if they considered it to be important might be a significant reason for this.

41 Many authors continue to assume both the possibility and desirability of sustainable development, hence our mentioning of it. For us however the achievement of sustainability is both a necessary precondition and sufficient in itself.

42 Davila Gomez, A. M. and Crowther, D. 2007, in Davila Gomez, A. M.and Crowther, D. (eds), *Ethics Psyche and Social Responsibility*, Ashgate, Aldershot. (forthcoming); Crowther, D. and Davila-Gomez, A.M. 2006 (a), "Is lying the best way of telling the truth" *Social Responsibility Journal*, Vol. 1, No. 3 and 4, pp. 128-141; Crowther, D. and Davila-Gomez, A.M.(2006 (b), "Stress in the Back Office", in *Proceedings of India - the Processing Office of the World*, Kochi, January 2006, pp.27-38; Crowther, D. and Davila-Gomez, A.M. 2006 (c), "I Will if You Will: Risk, Feelings and Emotion in the Workplace" in Crowther, D. and Caliyurt, T.K., (eds.), *Globalisation and Social Responsibility*, Cambridge Scholars Press, Newcastle, UK, pp. 163-184.

43 International Monetary Fund, 2002 (a), *Strengthening the Framework for the Global Economy*, IMF, Washington DC, USA.

44 International Monetary Fund, 2002 (b), *Working for a Better Globalisation*, IMF, Washington DC, USA.

45 Moshirian, F. 2003, "Globalisation and Financial Market Integration" *Journal*

of Multinational Financial Management, Vol.13 pp. 289-302.

46 Moshirian, F. 2002, "New International Financial Architecture" *Journal of Multinational Financial Management*, Vol. 12, pp. 273-/284.

47 Stulz, R M. 2005, "The Limits of Financial Globalisation" *The Journal of Finance*, Vol. LX, No. 4, pp. 1595-1638.

48 Tobin, J.2000, "Financial Globalisation" *World Development* Vol. 28, No.6 pp. 1101-1104.

49 Matsuyama, K. 2004, "Financial Markets Globalisations, Symmetry-Breaking and Endogenous Inequality of Nations", *Econometrica*, Vol. 72, No.3, pp. 853-884.

50 It is frequently ignored that a completely unregulated free market only operates effectively in a situation of perfect competition – in other words never. It is simply a construct in theoretical economics.

51 Knight, M. 1998,"Developing Countries and the Globalisation of Financial Markets", *World Development*, Vol.26, No.7, pp. 1185-1200.

52 Arestis, P, Santonu, B. and Sushanta, M. 2005, "Financial Globalisation: the Need for a Single Currency and a Global Central Bank" *Journal of Post Keynesian Economics*, 27 (3), 507-531.

53 Das, D K. 2006, "Globalization in the World of Finance: An Analytical History" *Global Economy Journal* Vol.6, No. 1.

54 Park, J H.2002, "Globalisation of Financial Markets and the Asian Crisis: Some Lessons for Third World Developing Countries", *Journal of Third World Studies*, Vol. 19, No. 2, pp. 141.

55 Solomon, J. and Solomon, A. 2004, *Corporate Governance and Accountability*, John Wiley and Sons, London.

56 Ibid.

57 Cornelius, N. Wallace, J. 2005, "An Analysis of Corporate Social Responsibility, Corporate Identity and Ethics Teaching in Business Schools" *Journal of Business Ethics*.

58 An example is the Cadbury Report.

59 Van den Berghe, L. 2001, "Beyond Corporate Governance" *European Business Forum*, Issue 5, Spring .

60 Agrawal, A. and Knoeber, C. R. 1996, "Firm Performance and Mechanisms to Control Agency Problems between Managers and Shareholders" *Journal of Financial and Quantitative Analysis*, 31(3), 377–398; Dalton, D.R.. Daily, C. M. Ellstrand, A.E. and Johnson. J.L., 1998, "Meta-analytic Reviews of Board Composition, Leadership Structure, and Financial Performance" *Strategic Management Journal*, Vol. 19, No. 3, March, pp. 269-290; Bhagat, S. and Black, B. 1999, "The Uncertain Relationship between Board Composition and Firm Performance" *The Business Lawyer*, 54 (3), 921-963; Coles, J. W. McWilliams, V. B. and Sen, N. 2001, "An Examination of the Relationship of Governance Mechanisms to Performance" *Journal of Management*, 7, 23-50;

Gompers, P. A., Ishii, J.L. and Metrick, A. 2001, "Corporate Governance and Equity Prices" *National Bureau of Economic Research*, Working Paper 8449; Patterson, J. 2002, "The Patterson Report: Corporate Governance and Corporate Performance Research" downloadable at: http://www.thecorporatelibrary.com/study/patterson.asp; Heracleous L. 2001, "What is the impact of Corporate Governance on Organizational   Performance?", *Conference Paper*, Blackwell Publishing; Demsetz, H. and Villalonga, B. 2002, "Ownership Structure and Corporate Performance", *Journal of Corporate Finance*, 7, 209–233; Bhagat, S. and Jefferies R. H. 2002, *The Econometrics of Corporate Governance Studies*; MIT Press, Cambridge, Ma; Becht, M. Bolton, P. and Roell, A. 2002, "Corporate Governance and Control" *Working Paper*, ECGI; Millstein, I.M. and MacAvoy, P.W. 2003, "The Active Board of Directors and Performance of the Large Publicly Traded Corporation" *Columbia Law Review*, Vol. 8, No. 5, 1998, pp. 1283-1322 in Journal of General Management Vol. 28 No. 3 Spring 2003; Bøhren, Ø. and Ødegaard, B. A. 2004, "Governance and Performance Revisited" 2003 Meeting of the European Finance Association.

61 Generally Accepted Accounting Practice

62 Deloitte, 2004, 'Summaries of International Financial Reporting Standards (IRFS)'. Downloadable at www.iasplus.com/standard/standard/htm

63 Eastburn, S. 2000, "Better Financial Planning with Balance Sheet Modelling" *The Journal Of Bank Cost and Management Accounting*, 13 (2), p. 20-27.

64 Copeland, T. Koller, T. and Murrin, J. 2000, *Valuation: Measuring and Managing the Value of Companies*, McKinsey and Co, London.

65 Return on expenditure is not the traditional ratio, return on investment ROI. Instead it is used loosely to describe the streams of future cash flows that relate to the expenditure.

66 Also known as lines of business.

67 Baggaley, B. and Maskell, B. 2003, "Value Stream Management for Lean Companies: Part 1" *Journal of Cost Management*, 17 (2).

68 Adler, P. and Borys, B. 1996, "Two Types of Bureaucracy: Enabling and Coercive" *Administrative Science Quarterly* 41 (1), 61-90; Ahrens, T. and Chapman, C. 2004, "Accounting for Flexibility and Efficiency: A Field Study of Management Control Systems in a Restaurant Chain" *Contemporary Accounting Research*, 21 (2).

Chapter 9

India and China: Emergence of the Elephant and the Dragon

Swati Raju

India and China have come a long way from the 1950s to emerge as Asia's giants, witnessing rapid growth in their economies. During 2000-04 China experienced growth at an average of 9.4% per year and India an average of 6.2% per year (India grew at 8.2% in 2003-04 and 7.5% in 2004-05). In 2006, China's growth was in the region of 9.1% and India's at 8.4%.[1] Although political structures in India and China are different, initially both were autarkic and adopted similar strategies to development – planned economies with emphasis on industri-alisation. With the initiation of reforms in China in 1978 (on the back of turmoil after the Cultural Revolution and the death of Mao) and in India in 1991 (subsequent to a serious macroeconomic and balance of payments crisis) both countries have been proactive about the integration of their domestic economies with the world economy and are vying for larger shares in world exports and external capital flows. A comparative analysis of China and India, in this essay, focuses on and juxtaposes the developments in the fiscal situation, monetary policy, financial sector and the external sector while the final section discusses the drivers to growth and concludes the chapter.

Fiscal Challenges and Market-Preserving Federalism

India and China, whilst reforming their economies, face major fiscal challenges – India of surmounting its budgetary deficits and China of increasing its government revenues. Fiscal deficits of the central government in India in the latter half of the 1980s was in the range of 7-8% of gross domestic product (GDP) and the revenue deficit was about 2-3% of GDP. Fiscal consolidation, hence, was the major focus of the reform process introduced in 1991-92. The results of fiscal consolidation in India have been mixed with an improvement in the deficit figures during 1991-92 to 1996-97 while the late 1990s and early 2000s witnessed a reversal with continued deterioration of the revenue deficit. The second half of the 1990s also saw progressive worsening in the fiscal health of the States in India as a consequence of growing revenue expenditure, losses of state public sector enterprises, declining central transfers, inadequate user charges accompanied by a slow growth in revenues. Reform measures such as the Fiscal Responsibility and Budget Management Act 2003, and the Fiscal Responsibility and Budget Management Rules 2004, which seek to eliminate the revenue deficit by 2008-09 and reduce the gross fiscal deficit to 3% of GDP by March 2008 for the central government and incentives provided to States to undertake medium-term fiscal reforms accompanied by institutional measures such as rule-based fiscal policy (fiscal responsibility legislations and time-bound fiscal targets set by the Twelfth Finance Commission – elimination of revenue deficits by 2008-09 and a gross fiscal deficit target of 3% of GDP by 2009-10) at the States level offer hope for achieving successful fiscal consolidation. These reform measures seem to have had the desired effect as revised estimates of central government finances for 2005-06 indicate an improvement over their budget estimates viz. the gross fiscal deficit and revenue deficit as a percentage of GDP were at 4.1% (budgeted 4.3%) and 2.6% (budgeted 2.7%) respectively. For State finances, though, the revenue deficit was lower at 0.5% (budgeted 0.7%) the gross fiscal deficit was marginally higher at 3.2% (budgeted 3.1%) of GDP.[2]

Budgetary deficits in China, on the contrary, have been low. The deficit of the general government on an average for 1992-97 and 1997-2002 has been 0.5% and 1.9% of GDP respectively and the deficit in 2004 is 0.9% of GDP. These low figures could, however, be misleading as overall expenditure figures in China do not fully reflect actual total expenditure, as some part of expenditure is not recorded and provincial governments raise and spend funds off-budget. This is a consequence of unfunded expenditure mandates by the higher levels of government and also to hide revenues so as to become eligible for more resource transfers from higher level of governments. Further, over time the government has accumulated considerable implicit and contingent liabilities: For instance, non performing loans of financial institutions, a portion of which has already been recognised as government debt but the portion with asset management companies (after all saleable assets have been realised) may have to be recapitalised and will have to be reflected in the government's finances. Another source which could be reflected in government finances is illegally incurred local authority debt.[3]

China faced the problem of 'falling ratios' of government revenue to GDP and central government to general government revenue. The ratio of government revenue to GDP declined from 31.2% in 1978 to 11.2% in 1994. With a view to improving the revenue ratio the government in 1994 introduced fiscal reform which replaced the old discretion-based bargaining system of revenue sharing with a rule-based system of revenue sharing. The present system of fiscal contracting, a culmination of four major reforms starting in 1980, is called the tax assignment system (*fenshuizhi*) and focuses on (i) simplification and rationalization of the tax structure by reducing tax rates, tax categories and tax exemptions (ii) raising the revenue – GDP ratio (iii) raising the central to total revenue ratio and (iv) increasing transparency in the central – local government fiscal relations. This reform decomposed taxes into central, local and shared taxes. Shared taxes were to be split between the central and local governments according to a prescribed formula (e.g. VAT is shared as 75% for centre and 25% for provinces; income tax is shared as 60% for centre and 20% for provinces and the stamp tax is shared as 97% for the centre and 3 % for provinces). So as to ensure that the revenue of each province would not be lower than its 1993 level, it was decided that 30% of the increase in shared taxes would be transferred to the provinces as central compensation.

Consequent to this reform, the revenue position of the central government improved substantially and the ratio of government revenue to GDP increased to 15% in 2000 and to 19.3% in 2004 (figures computed by author from data in China Statistical Yearbook, various issues). However, this resulted in increased dependence of the provinces on the Centre. The 1994 reforms specify expenditure assignment between the central and provincial governments but were ambiguous on sub-provincial fiscal relations and there are no clear rules on transfer payments. Further, provincial governments were not authorised to adjust local taxes according to their needs and had no control over the tax rates or the base of their assigned taxes while expenditure responsibilities assigned were large resulting in large fiscal gaps at the provincial level. China's 1994 reform did not address the issue of extra budgetary funds. However, efforts to increase budgetary transparency has seen an increasing number of extra-budgetary items being brought into the budget and surcharges abolished for local authorities in rural areas. Consequently, there has been a reduction of extra-budgetary expenditures and revenues to 3.5% and 3.75% of GDP respectively in 2003.[4]

198

The modalities of expenditure and revenue assignment in India, on the other hand, are constitutionally defined between the Centre and States. The seventh schedule of the Constitution specifies the legislative, executive, judicial and fiscal domains of the Union and States through the Union, State and Concurrent lists. With the 73rd and 74th constitutional amendments in 1992, the Indian federation transformed itself into a three-tier structure. States were required to pass legislation appointing panchayati raj institutions (rural local bodies) and urban local bodies and sources of finance were identified for these bodies. India has multiple channels for inter-governmental resource transfers; namely, the Finance Commission, Planning Commission and centrally-sponsored schemes from different central ministries. Federal fiscal relations in India have resulted in considerable vertical fiscal imbalance because of the advantages the Centre enjoys in raising resources while considerable expenditure responsibilities are with the States.[5] For instance, in 2004-05 state governments could raise 63.61% of total current revenues as states' own revenues (approx 36.39% of their current revenues came from the Centre) while they could finance only 57.94% of their current expenditure from their own current revenues.

India and China, thus, have federal structures and it would be interesting to compare whether these federations satisfy the conditions of market-preserving federalism. The political foundations of market preserving federalism require that the government is strong enough to enforce legal rights and rules, to maintain the economy and credibly commit itself to honouring such rules. 'Reputation' can be considered as the key to ensure the credibility of commitments. However, reputation alone may be insufficient and may have to be reinforced by political institutions. Market-preserving federalism encompasses a set of conditions:

(F1) A hierarchy of governments with a delineated scope of authority exists so that each government is autonomous within its own sphere of authority.

199

(F2) The sub-national governments have primary authority over the economy within their jurisdictions.

(F3) The national government has the authority to police the common market and to ensure the mobility of goods and factors across sub-government jurisdictions.

(F4) Revenue sharing among governments is limited and borrowing by governments is constrained so that all governments face hard budget constraints.

(F5) The allocation of authority and responsibility has an insti-tutionalised degree of durability so that it cannot be altered by the national government either unilaterally or under pressures from sub-national governments.

Conditions (F1) to (F5) represent the ideal institutional arrangements for the prevalence of market-preserving federalism and the extent to which markets can be protected from encroachments by the political system. Condition (F1) defines federalism whilst compliance with conditions (F2) to (F5) is essential for market preserving federalism. Federalisms that violate F2 and F5 are characterised by an all-powerful Centre.[6]

India has been a de jure federal system since independence. The Indian federation has a three-tier structure and partly satisfies condition F1 of a minimal federal structure. As regards the autonomy of sub-national governments in their own jurisdictions (implicit in conditions F1 and F2) the Indian federation scores poorly. As mentioned above, the constitutional division of powers (fiscal included) between the Centre and the States are specified in the Union, State and Concurrent lists. The Centre can override the States on the concurrent list and residuary power is also assigned to the Centre. The outcome is a powerful central government and built-in vertical imbalances between the Centre and the States. Concerning condition F3, the common market condition, Article 301 of the Constitution provides for free trade and commerce throughout the country and thus ensures a common market in India. However, due to several restrictions imposed by policymakers, the advantages of a common market were never experienced in India.[7] States are engaged in exemption-proliferating tax competition which, apart from lowering States' own tax revenue, has also resulted in a multiplicity of tax rates and serious inefficiencies in States' tax systems. Rationalisation of indirect taxes with the implementation of the value added tax that would substitute sales tax can help generate one single market across India. Violation of F4 would imply that sub-national governments (States) do not face a hard budget constraint and hence have no financial incentive to be concerned about the effects of their fiscal actions. In India both central and state governments are working towards fiscal consolidation. Success in achieving the fiscal targets (delineated above) by both the Centre and the States will indicate the extent to which the Indian federation is able to satisfy condition F4. Thus, as concluded by Parikh and Weingast[8] and Rodden and Rose-Ackerman[9] India retains the hierarchy of federalism and has a long way to go before satisfying the main mechanisms that sustain market-preserving federalism.

China's political decentralisation has had an impact on central-local government relations, has enhanced the power of the local governments, and has created a new political system called *federalism – Chinese style*[10] which satisfies the conditions of market-preserving federalism albeit with important qualifications. About condition F2, China in the 1980s initiated decentralization of authority with increased control of local governments over their economies. Consequently, authority over several central government-controlled state-owned enterprises was delegated to local governments, and by 1985 central government-controlled state-owned enterprises accounted only for 20% of total industrial output. Decentralisation of authority in China was closely associated with the creation of special economic zones, coastal open cities, and development zones which enjoyed lower taxes and more authority over their economic development (e.g. authority to approve foreign investment) while other regions enjoyed much less authority. Policy reform was also delegated to local governments (e.g. price reform).

Fulfillment of condition F3 – the common market condition – was addressed by decentralisation in the 1980s, accompanied by increasing mobility of goods and factors across regions. However, the result has been an imperfect market as some regions have used their considerable political freedom to erect trade barriers. Condition F4: China, like India, introduced a system of revenue sharing between the Centre and the local governments in 1980 which was replaced by a new system in 1994 (detailed above). However, fiscal contracting in China is limited only to budgetary revenue and does not include the extra budgetary revenues of local governments which are retained entirely by local governments. Such fiscal decentralisation has provided substantial independence as well as fiscal autonomy to provincial and local governments and allows these governments to circumvent the hard budget constraint that applies to all levels of government as a result of falling government revenues and limited budgetary transfers under the fiscal decentralization scheme. Condition F5: Political freedom, individual rights, a system of private property rights, a law on contracts and a judicial system may have eluded China but decentralisation with the delegation of economic authority to local governments has created strong regional economic powers (e.g. Guangdong) and in a way may have provided an element of durability to economic reforms making reversal of economic reforms expensive.[11]

Monetary Policy
Monetary policy has played an important role in macroeconomic stabilisation in recent times and central banks form the core of modern market economies. The objectives of monetary policy in India are indicated in the regular bi-annual

policy statements of the Reserve Bank of India. Monetary policy in India has pursued the twin objectives of price stability and economic growth through the adequate provision of credit to the productive sectors of the economy. Although the emphasis between these two objectives has varied depending on the price – output situation, price stability has been the dominant objective of monetary policy since the initiation of the reform process in 1991.

Monetary policy in India in the 1990s was very different from that of the 1980s when it was subservient to the fisc. The development of the government securities market and de-linking of the automatic monetisation of the government's fiscal deficit since April 1997 has ensured that the Reserve Bank of India can follow an independent monetary policy. This is further strengthened by the FRBM Act 2003, which requires that from April 2006 the Reserve Bank of India cannot subscribe to government securities in the primary market.

Quantity variables dominated the transmission channel of monetary policy in the 1980s while in the 1990s the interest rate was the dominant channel of monetary policy transmission. The period mid-1980s to mid-1990s saw flexible monetary targeting. Since 1998-99 the Reserve Bank of India has switched to a broad-based multiple indicator approach. Further, there has been a concerted effort to shift from direct instruments to indirect instruments of monetary policy. Consequently, there is reduced reliance on reserve requirements and the Cash Reserve Ratio (CRR) has reduced from a peak of 15% in 1994-95 to 5% in 2004-05 and hopes to reduce further to its statutory minimum of 3% over a period of time while the Statutory Liquidity Ratio (SLR) has declined from 38.5% at the beginning of the 1990s to its statutory minimum of 25% by October 1997.

The Reserve Bank of India has put forth a proposal to the government to amend the Reserve Bank of India Act 1934, and the Banking Regulation Act 1949, to enable lowering of the CRR and the SLR to below the statutory limits if the monetary situation so requires. With reduced reliance on reserve requirements, liquidity management has been carried out through open market operations in the form of outright sale/purchase of government securities and daily repo and reverse repo operations. The bank rate and repo rate have emerged as direct interest rate signals. The liquidity adjustment facility introduced in June 2000 enabled the Reserve Bank of India to set short term interest rates. The shift in focus from the targeting of bank reserves to interest rates has emerged as the principal operating instrument of monetary policy. Subsequent to the large capital inflows in 2001-02, a market stabilisation scheme was introduced in April 2004 to absorb excess liquidity generated due to the accretion of foreign exchange assets, neutralise the impact of capital flows.

An additional instrument for liquidity management has been provided. The market stabilisation scheme mobilised Rs. 363.60 billion as of March 14, 2006. Several institutional and developmental measures were also introduced by the Reserve Bank of India, namely, setting up of a Technical Advisory Committee (akin to a Monetary Policy committee), rationalisation of the treasury bill market, introduction of primary dealers (who would play the role of the market maker) in the government securities market, introduction of auctions in the government securities market, making interest rates on government securities reflect market rates of interest and the introduction of the Real Time Gross Settlement system.

The success of monetary policy is evaluated with reference to the extent to which its objectives have been achieved. The Reserve Bank of India in recent years has been successful in controlling inflation which is currently hovering at 5%. The basic emphasis of monetary policy since the initiation of reforms has been to reduce market segmentation.[12]

China

Monetary policy objectives in China are revealed in the announcements of the People's Bank of China. Its objective is to 'maintain the stability of the value of the currency and thereby promote economic growth'. The instruments at the disposal of the People's Bank of China include the reserve requirements ratio, rediscounting, central bank base interest rate, central bank lending rate and open market operations and any other policy instruments specified by the State council.[13] The main instruments of China's monetary policy have been open market operations, the discount rate, and reserve requirements. For these instruments to be effective, the banks ought to be sensitive to the price of the Central Bank's funds and the money market rates.

Open market operations in China began as recently as October 1998 (initially with only one operation a week) when the People's Bank of China started cash trading of bonds which was replaced by bond-based repo transactions. In order to cope with the large foreign exchange inflows, the Central Bank started Ministry of Finance bond-based reverse repo operations in June 2002. However, by September 2002 the People's Bank of China had run out of bonds upon which to make repo transactions. Consequently, all repo contracts between 26 June and 24 September were converted into a new instrument, namely, People's Bank of China Bills and the first auction of these bills took place in March 2003. Trade in these bills accompanied by regular bill auctions have ensured the emergence of a benchmark for interest rates and has also improved liquidity. Since March 2004, 'floating rate' central bank rediscount lending was introduced i.e. the People's Bank of China could set the discount rate without seeking permission from the State Council. Further, floating rate rediscount lending will be introduced in a phased manner over three years to rural credit co-operatives.

Reserve requirements are used to stimulate credit growth and provide flexibility to banks in the management of their funds. This ratio was around 13% during 1988-98 and was reduced in 1998 to 8% and around 7.5% in 2004. In order to encourage lending by banks, the interest rate on required reserves was reduced from 9.18% in 1995 to 1.89% in 2003 and excess reserves earn an interest of 0.99%. A differentiated reserve ratio system was introduced in April 2004 wherein second tier banks have to hold 8% reserves (as against 7.5%) whilst rural and urban credit co-operative banks are exempted from this rule.[14]

India and the Financial Sector

Financial sector reforms have followed a gradual and cautious approach. The first phase of reforms aimed at creating an efficient, productive, and profitable financial sector while the emphasis in the second phase that began in the mid-1990s was on strengthening the financial system and introducing structural improvements.

Banking Sector

India has 85 commercial banks which account for 78% (total assets) of the financial sector, 3000 co-operative banks which account for 9% and 196 regional rural banks which account for 3% of total assets. Banking sector reforms followed a two-pronged approach: (i) enhancing competition and (ii) introduction of prudential regulations to match international best practices. Reforms in the banking sector have focused on measures that would enhance competition, increase the role of market forces, prudential and supervisory measures and institutional and legal measures. Significant of these measures are operational autonomy to public sector banks; reduction of public ownership by allowing banks to raise up to 49% of paid up capital from equity markets; transparent norms for entry of Indian private banks, foreign banks, joint venture banks and insurance companies; permission for foreign direct investment as well as portfolio investment; dismantling of the administered structure of interest rates, introduction of international best practices such as Basel I norms, setting up of debt recovery tribunals; establishment of Credit Information Bureau of India for sharing information on defaulters and other borrowers; promulgation of Securities and Reconstruction of Financial Assets and Enforcement of Security Interest (SARFAESI) Act

2002, to protect creditor rights; and introduction of CAMELS
supervisory rating system. The Basel I framework was
announced in 1988. Banks in India implemented Basel I from
1992-93 in a phased manner over a period of three years and
there has been a consequent improvement in the financial
health of the sector as can be seen in the improvements
achieved in capital adequacy and improved asset quality (Tables
1 and 2). The capital to risky assets ratio (CRAR) was initially set
at 8% but was increased to 9% in 1999-2000.[15] The overall
capital position of commercial banks has seen a substantial
improvement since 1996-97. The number of banks maintaining
a capital adequacy ratio of above 10% has increased from 64 in
1996-97 to 79 as of end March 2006. The capital adequacy ratio
of the banking system has also increased from 10.4% in 1996-97
to 12.8% as of end March 2006.

**Table 1 Distribution of Risk-Weighted Capital Adequacy of Scheduled
Commercial Banks**

Year	Between 9-10% (No. of Banks)	Above 10% (No. of Banks)	CRAR for all banks (Percent)
1996-97#	30	64	10.4
2000-01	11	84	11.4
2004-05	8	78	12.8
2005-06(P)	3	79	12.8

Source: Reserve Bank of India, Handbook of Statistics,2005-06;
Reserve Bank of India; Annual Report 2005-06
 # Between 8-10%; P – Provisional Figures

India, in 2004, moved to a 90 day non performing loan norm
from a 180 day norm. Despite the tightening of norms, non
performing loans as percentage of total advances and assets
have declined substantially from 15.7% as a proportion of total
advances in 1995-96 to 5.2% of total advances in 2004-05
(Table 2).[16]

207

Table 2 Non Performing Loans of Scheduled Commercial Banks (Percent)

Year	Gross Non Performing Loans/ Total Advances	Gross Non Performing Loans/ Total Assets
1996-97	15.7	7.0
2000-01	11.4	4.9
2004-05	5.2	2.6

Source: Reserve Bank of India, 2006

Compliance with Basel II

The policy approach to Basel II in India is to conform to '*the best international standards and harmonization with international best practices*'. Indian banks would initially adopt the Standardised Approach for credit risk and the Basic Indicator Approach for operational risk. Banks would move on to the advanced approach such as the internal ratings based approach after adequate skills are developed by both banks and supervisors. Implementation of Basel II would require additional capital requirements for banks in India. However, the present capital-to-risky-assets ratio of 12% in the system it is believed would provide the required cushion for banks. Banks have also started exploring various avenues to meet capital requirements and the Reserve Bank of India has issued guidelines enabling issuance of several instruments by banks viz. perpetual debt instruments, perpetual non-cumulative preference shares, redeemable cumulative preference shares, hybrid debt instruments to enable banks to raise capital. Banks were also advised to formulate and operationalise the Capital Adequacy Assessment Process as required under Pillar II and risk-based supervision has been introduced in 23 banks on a pilot basis. All commercial banks in India are expected to adopt Basel II norms with effect from March 31, 2007.[17] Although as indicated by the Governor of the Reserve Bank of India 'a marginal stretching beyond this date should not be ruled out in view of the latest indications on the state of preparedness'.[18]

Government Securities Market

Reforms in the government securities market in India, like reforms in the banking sector, have been institutional and have sought to increase so as to enable price discovery in respect of interest rates. Measures undertaken include replacement of the administered interest rates on government securities by an auction system for price discovery; introduction of primary dealers who would function as market makers in the government securities market; introduction of delivery versus payment settlement system with a view to ensure transparency; introduction of the 91-day Treasury Bill for managing liquidity and benchmarking; introduction of zero-coupon bonds, floating-rate bonds and capital-indexed bonds. Banks have been permitted to function as primary dealers since February 2006 and as since April 1 2006 the Reserve Bank of India cannot participate in primary auctions of government securities. With this step, the government securities market in India has transformed itself to a fully market-based system. Short sales in government securities have also been permitted in a calibrated fashion. Further, institutional measures are being initiated according to the recommendations of the 12th Finance Commission, wherein state governments would access the market directly (the central government would no longer raise resources on behalf of state governments). Hence, each State's fiscal health would determine the amount of resources it can raise from the market.[19]

Capital Market

The number of shareholders in India is estimated at 25 million. However, only something like two *lakh* persons actively trade in stocks. There have been significant improvements in the country's stock market trading infrastructure during the last few years and screen-based trading has replaced the traditional floor-based. Foreign institutional investors were allowed to invest in the Indian capital market securities from September 1992 and investments by foreign institutional investors in equity alone has increased substantially from Rs. 54.45 billion in 1993-94 to Rs. 486.50 billion in 2005-06. The National Stock Exchange (NSE), with nationwide stock trading and electronic display, clearing, and settlement facilities commenced operations from April 1993 and operates in the debt market, equity, and the derivatives segment.

Derivatives trading started in June 2000 with index options and futures and a system of rolling settlements has been introduced. The Securities and Exchange Board of India (SEBI) established in 1992 acts as the capital market regulator including mutual funds and is also empowered to register and regulate venture capital funds. SEBI has taken steps to improve greater corporate disclosures and improve corporate governance.

China and the Financial Sector

China's financial reform process began as early as 1979. The State Council, in 1984, decided that the People's Bank of China would perform the functions of a Central Bank (with a focus on monetary and foreign exchange policies). In 1994 four major banks were nationalised and transformed into state-owned commercial banks – the Industrial and Commercial Bank of China, the Bank of China, the Agricultural Bank of China, and the Construction Bank of China; three national policy-related banks were established – the Agricultural Development Bank of China, the State Development Bank and the China Import and Export Bank and private banks (e.g. China Minsheng Bank) were established. In 1995, the Commercial Bank Law was promulgated, creating the conditions for forming the commercial bank system and organisational structure, and providing a legal basis for changing specialised state banks to state-owned commercial banks.

Starting 1995, China re-organised its financial system and the four major commercial banks handed over tasks to national policy banks. The banking sector witnessed consolidation, saw bank branches being merged and closed. Simultaneously, rural and urban credit co-operatives were remodeled into co-operative banks. Since 1996 a group of joint-stock commercial banks have appeared and there has been a rapid increase in the number of financial institutions. In March 2003, the China Banking Regulatory Commission was established which would look at banking regulation and anti-money laundering.[20] Thus, like India, China's financial sector is dominated by state-owned banks. While the scale of the state-owned banks is enormous, the asset quality of these banks is unsatisfactory. State-owned banks have to lend to loss-making state-owned enterprises, generating huge non-performing loans. In 2000, authorities transferred nearly 1.3 trillion RMB (U.S. $150 billion) of state-owned commercial banks non-performing loans to the four asset management companies in an effort to improve asset quality. In mid-2001, non-performing loans remaining with state-owned commercial banks were nearly 27% of total loans while independent experts value it around 40%.

Following the transfer of non-performing loans to asset management companies, steps taken by banks themselves and injection of capital into the banking system saw non-performing loans as a ratio of total loans decline to 15.6 % in 2004 and the capital adequacy ratios of state owned commercial banks in China is around 6.8%. Banks in China are striving to reach the minimum 8% capital adequacy ratio prescribed by the Basel I norms. The inadequate capitalisation of Chinese banks is underscored by the fact that the Basel I norms of 8% are regarded as inadequate for emerging market economies and many of these economies have raised the capital ratio to 10% or more. Thus, the ability to control loan quality and better credit allocation can alone provide the solution to the problem of non-performing loans and enforce financial discipline.[21]

Compliance with Basel II
China has announced that its regime for capital requirements for its banks will continue to be that of the 1988 Basel Accord

(Basel I norms). A revised version of rules based on the Accord were announced in February 2004, to be fully implemented by January 2007. Hence, shifting to new Basel II norms soon after the implementation of this revised version would impose considerable costs on both banks and supervisors. Further, the high level of non performing loans of Chinese banks would make application of Basel II difficult. China does not expect its entire banking sector to implement Basel II norms until 2015.[22]

An important development in China's financial sector was the establishment of the stock market in the early 1990s. Consequently, the number of listed companies as well as the market capitalisation has increased substantially. The number of listed companies has increased from a mere 14 in 1991 to 1160 in 2001 to 1337 in 2004. The numbers doubled in 1992-93 after Deng Xiaoping's speech in Guandong. Stock market growth has been rapid but subject to several limitations on access and trading. Market capitalisation has also increased substantially from 3690.61(100 million yuan) in 2000 to 37055.57 (100 million yuan) in 2004. The Chinese financial system has made substantial progress in recent years. The domestic money market (CHIBOR) has expanded rapidly and there has been the emergence of consumer loans and housing finance. Though the financial supervisory and regulatory structure has been reorganised and rationalised consistent with international best practices, the government and other bond markets are small, fragmented, and illiquid and the number of instruments available to deal with liquidity fluctuations and manage risks are limited.[23]

To surmise, although the banking sector in both India and China are dominated by State-owned banks, the financial health of Indian banks has shown considerable improvement following the implementation of the Basel I norms and Indian banks are geared to transit to Basel II norms while the high level of non-performing loans continue to pose a major problem for the Chinese banking sector and could make adoption of Basel II norms difficult. Further, while the government and other bond markets in China are small, fragmented and illiquid, the government securities market in India has transformed into a fully market based system. However, though India's stock markets were established much before China's, the market capitalization of Chinese stock markets is much higher than India's.

External Sector

The extent of a country's integration with the world economy is captured by the share of exports and imports (merchandise trade) as a percentage of world trade and in the domestic economy by the share of exports and imports in the country's gross domestic product. Table 3 presents the foreign trade statistics and foreign direct inflows into India and China.

Table 3 Foreign Trade Statistics and Capital Flows: India and China

	Years	China	India
Exports of goods and services (% of GDP)			
	2001	23	13
	2003	30	15
	2004	34	19
Imports of goods and services (% of GDP)			
	2001	20	14
	2003	27	16
	2004	31	21
Share in World Merchandise Exports (%)			
	2001	4.3	0.7
	2003	5.8	0.7
	2004	6.5	0.8
Share in World Merchandise Imports (%)			
	2001	3.8	0.8
	2003	5.3	0.9
	2004	5.9	1.0
Share in World Export of Commercial Services (%)			
	1994	1.6	0.6
	2001	2.3	1.4
	2003	2.6	1.4
	2004	2.9	1.9

Share in World Imports of Commercial Services (%)

	1994	1.5	0.8
	2001	2.7	1.6
	2003	3.1	1.2
	2004	3.4	2.0
Foreign Direct Investment (U.S.$ billion)			
	2001	44.2	5.4
	2003	53.5	4.5
	2004	54.9	5.3

Source: (a) Shares of Exports and Imports as a percent of GDP, Foreign Direct Investment, World Bank – World Development Indicators, 2006 (b) Country Shares in World Trade, World Trade Organisation – International Trade Statistics, Tables I.5 and I.7 (various issues)

India and China are striving for greater integration with the world economy as can be seen from the growing share of exports and imports. China currently, however, is far ahead of India. China's exports as a percentage of GDP has always been nearly double that of India's. For instance, in 2004 China's exports were 34% of its GDP as compared to India's 19%. Also, China's imports as a percentage of GDP have always been around 1.4 times higher than India's. Likewise, China's share in world merchandise exports and imports has always been substantially higher than India's. China's share in world merchandise exports in 2004 was 6.5% (ranked 3rd) as compared to India's share of 0.8% (ranked 32nd) (Tables I.5 and I.7).[24]

In other words, China's share in world merchandise exports (imports) is more than eight times (five times) that of India in 2004. Although, India's share in the world exports of commercial services has increased by nearly three times from 0.6% in 1994 to 1.9% in 2004, China's share at 2.9% in 2004 is larger than India's. India's growing share in the world export of commercial services can be attributed to the growth of its software exports (IT and ITES-BPO) which have increased by almost thirty times from U.S.$ 0.754 billion in 1995-96 to U.S. $23.6 billion in 2005-

06. India in 2004 (with 17.7 billion) ranked second after Ireland (18.6 billion) in the export of computer and information services. Software accounted for 37.4% in of India's total services exports in 2004-05. Despite increasing competition, India continues to remain attractive due to its low cost of operations, skilled manpower and high quality of its product.[25]

Manufacturing goods have been the mainstay of China's exports and attribute to more than 90% of its exports. Exports of manufacturing goods have increased from U.S. $ 2397.6 (100 million yuan) in 2001 to U.S. $ 5527.7 (100 million yuan) in 2004.[26] Like India for software services, China continues to be an attractive destination for manufacturing due to its low labour costs.[27] An interesting aspect is the growing bilateral trade. The high cost of transport across the Himalayan border, the 1962 war and the subsequent political tension between India and China impeded economic and trade relations between the two countries.[28] Bilateral trade increased from a mere U.S. $0.0492 billion (49.2 million) in 1991 to 17.46 billion (17460.7 million) in 2006. China in 2005-06 emerged as the third major export destination for India and is its largest source of imports.[29]

Table 4 Bilateral Trade between India and China (U.S. $ million)

Year	Export	Import
1991	18.2	31.0
1996	332.7	812.0
2001	831.3	1502.2
2003	1975.5	2792.0
2004	2955.1	4053.2
2005	5615.9	7098.0
2006(Provisional)	6721.2	10739.5

Source: Reserve Bank of India, Handbook of Statistics 2005-06

India and China continue to be the most talked about destinations for foreign capital flows and attract both direct and

215

portfolio investments. Foreign direct investments into India, though increasing, are much smaller than China even after allowing for round tripping and differences in measurement. India in 2004 attracted only U.S. $ 5.3 billion as compared to China's U.S. $ 54.9 billion (Table 3). The Reserve Bank of India in its Annual Report 2005-06 has pointed to the emergence of India as a destination for foreign direct investment and has pointed to the AT Kearney[30] FDI Confidence Index Survey, India has improved its rank to the second most likely FDI destination after China in 2005 from fifteenth in 2002.[31] China's success in attracting huge capital inflows can be attributed to several factors such as a preferential policy orientation towards foreign direct investment, large regional market, excellent infrastructure, and low labour costs.[32] Xing[33] points out that the substantial flow of foreign direct investment into China could be also be attributed to the persistent devaluation of the yuan since the beginning of reforms till 1994. Foreign direct investment in China is export oriented and the devaluations reinforced China's comparative advantage in labour intensive industries, thus making China an attractive destination for increased capital flows.

Further, the creation of Special Economic Zones (where investors were exempt from regulations applicable otherwise in China, foreign ownership, relaxation in labour laws, excellent infrastructure) also played an important role in attracting foreign capital into China. India hopes to replicate the Chinese Special Economic Zone success and has recently passed the Special Economic Zone Act 2005 for the creation of such areas where, apart from provision of fiscal incentives, simplification of procedures for development, operation and maintenance, reduction in transaction cost by dispensing the requirement of provision of bank guarantee and the provision of excellent infrastructure with a view to improve export competitiveness and be net foreign exchange earners. However, the sensitive issue of changes in labour laws has been left to the discretion of the State governments in India and limits to foreign ownership continue in different sectors. Although the Act has been passed, the creation of Special Economic Zones is currently mired in debate (political and and social) and even the Reserve Bank India has indicated caution in the creation of these zones for the fears of loss of tax revenue.[34]

India Exchange Rate Policy

Reforms in the foreign exchange market were introduced with a view to broaden and deepen the market and allow for price discovery of the exchange rate. The exchange rate system evolved from a single currency fixed exchange rate system to determining the value of the rupee against a basket of currencies and later to a market-determined floating exchange rate regime in April 1993. The rupee, currently, is fully convertible on the current account while there is de facto full capital account convertibility for nonresidents and a calibrated liberalisation of transactions for residents. In an effort to develop the foreign exchange markets, several measures were undertaken viz. the development of the rupee – foreign currency swap market; the introduction of additional instruments such as foreign currency-rupee options; permitting authorized dealers to use cross-currency options, interest rate and currency swaps and forward rate agreements in international foreign exchange markets and considerable delegation of powers to authorised dealers whilst releasing foreign exchange for a variety of purposes. During the last decade, there has been a shift in the direction of India's trade to developing countries and emerging economies. To reflect this shift, the Reserve Bank of India in December 2005 revised its indices of the nominal effective and real effective exchange rate to include China and the euro zone. The six-country index now comprises the United States, the United Kingdom, the euro zone, Japan, China and Hong Kong. These six regions account for around 40% of India's total foreign trade in 2004-05.[35]

India Capital Account Convertibility

India revisited the subject of capital account convertibility in March 2006 and the Committee on Fuller Capital Account

Convertibility was setup. The committee has defined capital account convertibility as, "the freedom to convert local financial assets into foreign financial assets and vice-versa…Capital account convertibility can be, and is, coexistent with restrictions other than on external payments".[36] In other words, capital account convertibility would not necessarily mean zero capital regulation. The Committee has suggested a broad five-year three-phase roadmap spanning 2006-07 to 2010-11 to implement capital account convertibility in India. The actual implementation, though, would be determined by the authorities after an assessment of overall macroeconomic developments and other specific problems.[37]

China

A major shift in China's foreign exchange policy was its decision to end its currency's (renminbi) rigid peg to the dollar in July 2005 and move to a managed float against a basket of currencies (essentially comprised of the U.S. dollar, euro, yen and the South Korean won) which would trade within a narrow band of 0.3% against this basket of currencies.[38] Prior to this, since 1979, the Chinese government has implemented the foreign exchange fractional detainment scheme till 1994 after which it adopted the fixed exchange rate system where the yuan was pegged to the U.S. dollar. In 1996 the renminbi became convertible on the current account and foreign banks were allowed to operate renminbi transactions to a limited extent in Pudong in Shanghai. This facility was further extended to foreign banks in Shenzhen in 1998.[39]

Chinese Capital Account Convertibility

China has revealed that its current aim is to strengthen regulations governing cross border flow of capital and promote a more balanced international balance of payments. While China is pushing forward for capital account convertibility it has not set any timeframe to attain capital account convertibility.[40]

Drivers to Growth

India and China have in recent years been referred to as the 'back office' and 'workshop' of the world. The drivers to further growth in India would be its information technology and information technology-enabled services sector. Indeed, the World Economic Forum's Global Information Technology Report 2002-03 mentions that India's information technology industry is expected to grow at a compounded annual rate of 38% to reach U.S. $77 billion by 2008. Indian companies are making concerted efforts to retain their advantage by exploring untapped potential in IT consulting and system integration, hardware support, and installation and processing services. Further, by expanding their service offerings, enabling customers to deepen their offshore engagements, and moving from low-end business processes to higher value knowledge-based processes, for instance in accounting, legal services, insurance, architecture is having a positive impact. Biotechnology and life sciences outsourcing can also emerge as future drivers of growth for India. To transit to a 'knowledge economy', initiatives have developed around the three major pillars of the knowledge economy: education, innovation and information and communications technology. India possesses the key ingredient for this transformation: a large number of skilled English-speaking knowledge workers in sciences and a pool of qualified engineers.[41]

McKinsey research indicates that the next wave of global outsourcing will be in high-skilled manufacturing, areas where India has potential to grow for instance, automotive parts, speciality chemicals, electrical and electronic products. Engineering exports are emerging as an important segment of India's exports and have increased phenomenally from U.S. $ 1.2 billion in 1987-88 to U.S. $ 21.5 billion in 2005-06. However, for India to emerge as a major hub for offshore manufacturing, it needs to overcome major concerns of low domestic demand, lack of manufacturing clusters and poor infrastructure[42] India's favourable demographic profile over China could work to its advantage. The percentage of working population (15-59 years)

219

in India is projected to increase from 60% in 2005 to 61% in 2050 and its dependency ratio will decrease from 67% to 64% while for China the percentage of working population is projected to decline from 67.7% to 53.3% and the dependency ratio rise from 57% to 88% over the same period.

China can exploit its large talent of engineering graduates to compete in the global offshore information technology and information technology enabled services to emerge as a potent competitor. But to emerge as one, China needs to overcome its shortage of professionals in finance, accounting and business administration and focus on developing fluency in the English language.[43]

A bigger challenge for China lies in developing institutional structures for property rights, private sector and a judicial system. China ranks 95th and India ranks 53rd on the Economic Freedom of the World Index (an index developed by the Fraser Institute and measures the extent to which a country's policies and institutions support property rights, competition and personal choice).[44] India, on the other hand, needs to focus on physical infrastructure, improve the provision of public services and create a domestic market for goods and services. However, with growing bilateral trade and willingness to look beyond security concerns, India and China can co-operate and complement each other to create the concept of CHININDIA, perhaps an India whose time has come.

Notes

1 Srinivasan, T.N. 2006, "China, India and the World Economy", *Stanford Center for International Development Working Paper*, No.286.

2 Reserve Bank of India, 2006, Annual Report 2005-06.

3 OECD, 2005, Economic Surveys: China, OECD, 2005.

4 Ibid; Wang, S. 1997, "China's 1994 Fiscal Reform: An Initial Assessment", *Asian Survey*, Vol.37, No.9, pp.801-17. ; Shuanglin, L. 2002, "Tax Reforms and Government Revenues" in Wong, J. and L. Ding (ed.) *China's Economy into the New Century: Structural Issues and Problems*, Singapore University Press and World Scientific Publishing Company, Singapore.; Ming, Su and Zhao, Quanhou, 2004, China's Fiscal Decentralization Reform, http://www.econ.hit-u.ac.jp/~kokyo/APPPsympo04/paper.htm

5   Rao, G. 2005, "Changing Contours in Federal Fiscal Arrangements in India"
    in A. Bagchi (ed.) *Readings in Public Finance*, Oxford University Press, New
    Delhi

6   Montinola, G., Y. Qian and B.R. Weingast 1995, "Federalism Chinese Style:
    The Political Basis for Economic Success in China", *World Politics*, vol.48,
    no.1, pp. 50-81.
    National Bureau of Statistics, *China Statistical Yearbook* (various issues),
    http://www.stats.gov.cn/english

7   Bagchi, A. 2002, "Enforcing the Constitution's Common Market Mandate:
    Time to Invoke Article 307", *Economic and Political Weekly*, vol.57, June 15,
    2002.

8   Parikh, S. and Weingast, B.R. 1997, "A Comparative Theory of Federalism:
    India", *Virginia Law Review*, vol.83, no.7, pp.1593-1615.

9   Rodden, J. and Rose-Ackerman S. 1997, "Does Federalism Preserve
    Markets?", *Virginia Law Review*, vol.83, no.7, pp.1521-72.

10 Montinola, G. et al, 1995, op cit.

11 Ibid.

12 Mohan, R. 2006b, "Financial Sector Reforms and Monetary Policy: The
    Indian Experience", *Reserve Bank of India Bulletin*, July.

13 People's Bank of China http://www.pbc.gov.cn/english

14 Green, S. 2005, "Making Monetary Policy Work in China: A Report from the
    Money Market Frontline", *Stanford Centre for International Development
    Working Paper*, No. 245.

15 Mohan, R. 2006b, op cit.

16 Reserve Bank of India, 2006, op cit.

17 Gopinath, S. 2006, "Approach to Basel II", *Reserve Bank of India Bulletin*, June.

18 Reddy, Y.V. 2006, "Challenges and Implications of Basel II for Asia", *Reserve
    Bank of India Bulletin*, June.

19 Mohan, R. 2006a, "Recent Trends in the Indian Debt Market and Current
    Initiatives", *Reserve Bank of India Bulletin*, April

20 Yang, Ya-Hwei 2004, *Development and Problems in China's Financial System*,
    www.tsc.nccu.edu.tw/2004 conference

21 OECD 2003, "Economic Surveys: China", *OECD2003*; OECD 2005,
    "Economic Surveys: China", OECD, 2005.

22 Cornford, A. 2005, *The Global Implementation of Basel II: Prospects and
    Outstanding Problems*, www.g24.org/cornfor2.pdf

23 Yang, Y-H. 2004, op cit; Green, S. 2005, op cit.

24 International Trade Statistics, World Trade Organisation

25 Reserve Bank of India, 2006, op cit.

26 China Statistical Yearbook, 2005.

27 *China Daily*, China's Trade Surplus to exceed U.S. $140b, 6 November 2006,
    http://www.chinadaily.com.cn/china/2006-11/06/content_725402.htm

28 Srinivasan, T.N. 2004, "Economic Reforms and Global Integration" in Frankel, F.R. and H. Harding (ed.) *The India-China Relationship: Rivalry and Engagement*, Oxford University Press, New Delhi.

29 Reserve Bank of India, 2006, op cit.

30 2005

31 Reserve Bank of India, 2006, op cit.

32 Reserve Bank of India 2004, Report on Currency and Finance 2003-04.

33 Xing, Y. 2006, "Why is China so Attractive for FDI? The Role of Exchange Rates", *China Economic Review*, vol.17, pp.198-209.

34 *The Times of India*, RBI Echoes FM line on SEZs, 31 August 2006

35 Mohan, R. 2006b, op cit; Reserve Bank of India, 2006, op cit.

36 Reserve Bank of India, 2006b, *Report of the Committee on Fuller Capital Account Convertibility*.

37 Ibid.

38 Eiji, O Gawa 2005, *The Revaluation of the Yuan and China's Exchange Rate System Reforms*, http://www.rieti.go.jp/en/columns/a01_0178.html

39 Yang, Y-H. 2004, op cit.

40 Official announcement, Embassy of the People's Republic of China in the USA 12 April 2006

41 Dahlman, C. and A. Utz 2005, *India and the Knowledge Economy: Leveraging Strengths and Opportunities*, World Bank Institute, Washington D.C.

42 Luthra, S., R. Mangaleswaran and A. Pai 2005, "When to Make India a Manufacturing Base", *The Mckinsey Quarterly: Special Edition*.

43 Farrell, D. and Grant, A.J. 2005, 'China's Looming Talent Shortage', *The McKinsey Quarterly*, no.4, pp.70-79.

44 *Economist*, Overview: Emerging Market Indicators, 23 September – 29 September 2006

Further Reading

Bagchi, A. 2002, Enforcing the Constitution's Common Market Mandate: Time to Invoke Article 307, *Economic and Political Weekly*, vol.57, June 15, 2002.

Dahlman, C. and A. Utz 2005, *India and the Knowledge Economy: Leveraging Strengths and Opportunities*, World Bank Institute, Washington D.C.

Economist, Overview: Emerging Market Indicators, 23 September – 29 September 2006

Farrell, D. and Grant, A.J. 2005, China's Looming Talent Shortage, *The McKinsey Quarterly*, no.4

Gopinath, S. 2006, Approach to Basel II, *Reserve Bank of India Bulletin*, June.

Green, S. 2005, *Making Monetary Policy Work in china: A Report from the Money Market Frontline*, Stanford Centre for International Development Working Paper No. 245

Luthra, S., R. Mangaleswaran and A. Pai 2005, When to Make India a

Manufacturing Base, *The Mckinsey Quarterly: Special Edition*.

Mohan, R. 2006a, Recent Trends in the Indian Debt Market and Current Initiatives, *Reserve Bank of India Bulletin*, April

Mohan, R. 2006b, Financial Sector Reforms and Monetary Policy: The Indian Experience, *Reserve Bank of India Bulletin*, July.

Montinola, G., Y. Qian and B.R. Weingast 1995, Federalism Chinese Style: The Political Basis for Economic Success in China, *World Politics*, vol.48, no.1.

National Bureau of Statistics, China Statistical Yearbook (various issues), http://www.stats.gov.cn/english

OECD 2003, *Economic Surveys: China*, OECD 2003

OECD 2005, *Economic Surveys: China*, OECD, 2005

Parikh, S. and Weingast, B.R. 1997, A Comparative Theory of Federalism: India, *Virginia Law Review*, vol.83, no.7.

Rao, G. 2005, *Changing Contours in Federal Fiscal Arrangements in India* in A. Bagchi (ed.) *Readings in Public Finance*, Oxford University Press, New Delhi

Reddy, Y.V. 2006, Challenges and Implications of Basel II for Asia, *Reserve Bank of India Bulletin*, June.

Reserve Bank of India 2004, *Report on Currency and Finance 2003-04*.

Reserve Bank of India 2006, *Annual Report 2005-06*.

Reserve Bank of India 2006a, *Handbook of Statistics 2005-06*.

Reserve Bank of India 2006b, *Report of the Committee on Fuller Capital Account Convertibility*.

Rodden, J. and Rose-Ackerman S. 1997, "Does Federalism Preserve Markets?", *Virginia Law Review*, vol.83, no.7.

Shuanglin, L. 2002, *Tax Reforms and Government Revenues* in Wong, J. and L. Ding (ed.) *China's Economy into the New Century: Structural Issues and Problems*, Singapore University Press and World Scientific Publishing Company, Singapore.

Srinivasan, T.N. 2004, *Economic Reforms and Global Integration* in Frankel, F.R. and H. Harding (ed.) *The India-China Relationship: Rivalry and Engagement*, Oxford University Press, New Delhi.

Srinivasan, T.N. 2006, *China, India and the World Economy*, Stanford Center for International Development Working Paper No.286.

The Times of India, RBI Echoes FM line on SEZs, 31 August 2006

Wang, S. 1997, China's 1994 Fiscal Reform: An Initial Assessment, *Asian Survey*, vol.37, no.9.

World Bank 2006, World Development Indicators, 2006

World Trade Organisation, International Trade Statistics, various issues.

Xing, Y. 2006, "Why is China so Attractive for FDI? The Role of Exchange Rates", *China Economic Review*, vol.17.

Yang, Ya-Hwei 2004, *Development and Problems in China's Financial System*, www.tsc.nccu.edu.tw/2004 conference

Chapter 10

Challenges to the City in a Globalised World

Andreas Prindl

This chapter reviews the present role of the City of London as the world's leading international financial centre, the comparative advantages which brought it to this position and the possible challenges to the City in a globalised world. It starts with relating a personal experience: my Japanese parent firm selected London as its international base in the 1970s, and we set up a commercial banking operation here from scratch twenty years ago. What we found in so doing tells the story of the City of London perhaps better than pure statistics, although there are many of those in the analysis below.

Setting up a Foreign Bank in London
In 1984 I was asked by Nomura Securities of Japan to set up a new wholesale bank for them in London. They wished to enter the field of commercial wholesale banking, barred to them in

Tokyo by Japanese law and in New York by the Glass Steagall Act,[1] in order to develop new products and new customers abroad. Foremost in their mind was to learn new banking techniques, especially in the treasury area, and to combine these with their very large international securities transactions.

The Nomura group then had a small bank in Amsterdam, but it had not grown much in size or product range, being mostly an appendage to their Dutch securities business. Other European capitals where Nomura was represented, such as Frankfurt, Paris and Brussels, were in no sense international financial centres, and London was the obvious choice. Here Nomura had long established its European headquarters and directed the vast bulk of its international securities business. It already employed several hundred staff in the City.

After two years of negotiation, held back by problems of reciprocity between the Tokyo and London markets, the Bank of England approved our application to establish a new bank in late May 1986. (National Westminster concurrently received permission in Tokyo to establish a securities operation in Japan.) I told Head Office that it would likely take six months to find an entirely new staff, create operating and control systems, a marketing plan and all the other mechanisms needed. Tokyo set me a target to open on 3 November (which was actually only five month away) and indeed we then opened, with a grand reception at the Guildhall. One of the most prominent bankers in the City fell into the ceremonial carp pool erected for the evening in Guildhall, but that is another story.

In just five months we were able to hire some forty very competent staff in all areas: marketing, treasury dealing and control, credit, operations and internal audit. Everyone had already been trained in his or her skills and of course spoke fluent English, although they came from a number of countries. With the help of our UK accountants we set up the financial reporting and control systems quickly – Tokyo added some of their own, to better understand the new subsidiary and we instituted detailed operating standards throughout the pre-launch period, using techniques readily available in the market, known to and easily implemented by our new employees. Our local legal firm also helped me in a technical problem, potentially serious. I had set up the company at first with no staff or capital, as a limited company. Start-up costs were borne by this vehicle, which we then wished to turn into a PLC. But one couldn't then establish a PLC with negative capital. The British lawyers found an elegant solution for this problem.

When Nomura Bank International (NBI) opened that November, the staff came in, sat down at their desks and started working as if they had been there for years. No one needed training, just simple instruction as to the goals and policies of the bank and their specific responsibilities. Our product range began with corporate lending and simple deposit taking, but the main emphasis was on treasury: money market and foreign exchange, which Nomura did not undertake in Tokyo. The latter became the spearhead of our strategy, partly because corporate lending was difficult to build up and unremunerative. There were already sixty six other Japanese houses represented in London, and they offered very low lending rates to their house accounts. I had basically used JP Morgan's model for NBI, since I worked there for twenty years and saw how attractive and profitable its corporate business was. Ironically, JP Morgan itself was then turning towards investment banking and winding down its wholesale lending, as its corporate customers began to disintermediate and use the securities markets rather than bank borrowings. Such companies were also then reducing the often large number of banks with which they dealt. Thus NBI's treasury business built up quickly, while the loan book grew only modestly.

Our regulators at the Bank of England monitored us very carefully during the first years of operation. Nomura Bank International was an unusual entity; a new, potentially large bank owned by a Japanese securities house which had no knowledge of banking, but enormous financial power at home (also a reputation for very aggressive behaviour which at times fell outside regulatory limits). It was one of the main vehicles for recycling the large Balance of Payments surpluses Japan ran in that period. Our Head Office had no experience with our products or risk profiles, and was itself tightly controlled by the Ministry of Finance and Bank of Japan.

Therefore, everything NBI did was in most respects new for Nomura, and it was reasonable for the Bank of England to watch carefully how we controlled our lending and treasury risks. We were given moderate trading limits at first, but these were regularly reviewed and increased when we so requested. When we wished to add new products or expand off-balance sheet trading, our regulators were very positive about permitting us to do so, once they were convinced we could control the concomitant risks. Indeed, I well recall one case when the Bank of England said no to a request, then called us back a few days later saying it was permitted. When we inevitably broke limits, we were called on the carpet to explain why, but allowed to trade as before once we had explained which better controls we bad put in place to forestall this. I felt strongly that the Bank wanted us to succeed and did all they could reasonably do to facilitate.

The breadth and depth of London's financial markets immeasurably helped NBI's rapid growth. We could always secure new counterparties or expanded lines when our foreign exchange and derivative business grew. New, skilled dealers in those areas were easy to find, if sometimes expensive. And the expertise in legal and accounting matters which we regularly required was at our doorstep.

London's Comparative Advantages
The point of this little history of a new bank is to show in practice the enormous advantages London offered to participants in its market twenty years ago, as it does now, It is perhaps a little surprising that London has developed as a world class financial power. Great Britain is a medium sized country in GNP and population. Its economy has languished until

recently and still is not doing much better than the average of the EU. It has little excess capital to export, unlike the USA, several Far Eastern countries, or indeed itself in the 19th Century, and typically runs a deficit on its trade account. The UK has a few world class banks, especially HSBC, Royal Bank of Scotland, Barclays and Lloyds TSB, but other counties have more, and often bigger, domestic institutions. Britain has developed its financial markets, bringing in flows of finds and business from abroad which are employed or lent abroad, in a way quite disproportionate to its size. And its venerable merchant banks have long advised clients around the world, even if they are all now in the hands of foreign banks. Certainly its role as financier of America's infrastructure in the 1800s and even its administration of the British Empire were similar international experiences. What has especially fostered its present position is the investment by all the world's leading finance houses in large London bases, resulting in a type of financial and intellectual agglomeration not found on this scale anywhere else.

London's comparative advantages as a world financial centre can be listed as follows:

- A business-friendly environment. National and local government support business actively; the chief role of the Corporation of London and its Mayor is to encourage, publicise and support the City.
- Intelligent and flexible regulation. Lord Mayor David Brewer said in September 2006: "The way we do regulation is regarded as one of the key reasons for London's continued success".[2] Regulation here is principles based, rather than only rules based, allowing much more flexibility and individual treatment.
- A vast pool of financial skills. The United Kingdom employed 340,400 persons in wholesale finance in 2005, a third of the EU total. France employed 108,100 and Germany 207,000.
- A lack of foreign exchange restrictions and of unofficial

administrative controls or guidance, as is found elsewhere, such as in Japan.

- London's geographical position between Asia and America. (Admittedly, this is shared by all other European cities). The world's financial markets are global and never ending. At the end of Asia's trading day, London has started up; at the middle of London's trading day New York has begun trading, and near the end Asia is beginning again to deal with Europe.

- Other large related markets, especially insurance and metal and commodity exchanges, in the City.

- The vast array of advisory skills in law, accounting and risk management that are necessary for sound financial institutions.

- The use of English law in international contracts.

- The dominance of English in general in world trade and finance. (A further advantage may be the diversity of the British population, which means native speakers are readily available in any world language).

- The delights of living in London, for the scores of thousands of foreign bankers like me who have come here. Some simply call this 'city culture advantage', and compare London favourably to glum Frankfurt, complicated Tokyo or noisy New York.

Possible Drawbacks

That list of London's comparative advantages is well-known and the subject of speeches by all Lord Mayors. It is fair to point out some possible negative factors as well. These include high costs of personnel and expatriate housing. (Yet research by Mercer Human Resources Consulting shows that London is about the cheapest place in Western Europe to place expatriates from a tax regime point of view, much better than Paris or Milan, and ahead of Frankfurt[3]). Office rents are very high. Vehicle congestion in London is ever-present not helped much by the congestion charge, and transportation in general is poor. But these problems are found in other large cities as well.

Some Statistics

An international financial centre (IFC) can be defined as one where a significant proportion of financial transactions take place with non-residents. Financial services offered by an IFC may include taking of deposits from non-residents, raising funds for them through cross-border loans, bonds and equity issues, risk management techniques involving foreign exchange, derivatives and insurance, and advice on investment and business strategy, especially mergers and acquisitions. London at present is the world's leading financial centre in almost all major areas. It accounts for:

- 31% of all foreign exchange turnover. This is running at about $2.6 billion a day, and may reach $3 billion a day in 2007 and beyond, as foreign exchange has become an asset class by itself, with active participation by fund managers, pensions and hedge funds.
- 20% of cross-border lending.
- 36% of OTC derivatives trading.
- 48% of all foreign equity turnover.
- 50% of European investment banking deals.
- 60% of the world primary bond primary market and 70 % of the secondary market.
- More than 25% of insurance premiums written in the EU. Lloyd's annual capacity alone is presently £14 billion.

London has a critical mass of 500 foreign banks which maintain a presence in the City, some of them very large; virtually all non-European banks make London their European Headquarters. New York; Frankfurt and Paris average about 250 foreign banks, with much smaller staffs. Tokyo allows some 100 foreign banks to operate in Japan, but most concentrate on marketing for other parts of their group and haven't built up large assets.

Building London Bases

Trading statistics are impressive enough. Equally telling is the investment in London by the world's great financial houses, especially the purchase and integration of all the British merchant banks into foreign groups. Most large foreign banks use London as the hub and spoke model with the City at the centre. The highest skills are concentrated in London, other offices acting as sales promoters in local markets. Here are three examples:

Citibank is the largest American bank, with assets of $1 .6 trillion at 31 December 2005. 50% of its revenues are outside the USA, with much passing through its investment bank in London. This group, centred on the old merchant bank Schroders which it bought in 2000, ranks first in euro market debt finance, in issuance of international bonds and debt underwriting, and is second in global equity markets. 80% of its London revenues emanate from outside the UK.

Deutsche Bank, the largest German bank and owner of Allianz Insurance, has built its international trading and investment banking operations in London, rather than Frankfurt where it has its HQ in Germany's financial centre. It wishes to build its investment bank where the other players are, rather than in what is still a secondary centre.

J P Morgan Chase employs 11,000 people in its London European Headquarters, but only 411 in Germany, 417 in France and 171 in Italy.

Challenges to London's Pre-eminence

Can London maintain its pre-eminence as the world's most important financial centre in a globalised world? Can it continue to offer the skills base it now has? Indeed, will that physical skills base be necessary (in London) as electronic trading picks up in a globalised, instantaneous world? Will other centres develop the same array of advantages? Does the advent of the euro, in which Great Britain does not participate, in any way threaten its position? These issues are discussed below.

In terms of competition from other possible international centres, one can look at Frankfurt, Tokyo and New York / Chicago, as representing the most powerful financial centres and economies in the geographic region, and the places most likely to threaten London's position.

Frankfurt

Frankfurt's advantages are the traditionally strong German economy, a large financial infrastructure, a body of 207,000 banking staff and the presence of the European Bank. It has a tradition of excellent central banking by the old Bundesbank and careful regulation. Industry and banking are closely tied, with reciprocal shareholdings. However, Frankfurt is itself only one of several decentralised financial centres in Germany, together with Berlin, Hamburg and Munich. It does not have the agglomeration of skills available if they were all combined. Several German banks are building their bases for trading, underwriting and advisory services largely in London. 'Finanzplatz Frankfurt' has half the number of foreign banks, much smaller ancillary markets and fewer tax, accounting and legal advisers. Its skills base is still underdeveloped in comparison to London. Employment structures are inflexible. Frankfurt is also not seen as an attractive place to live. It may well remain the main centre for euro business transacted within the EMU per se, and will try hard to capture a major share of the rapidly growing equity and bond markets denominated in euros. Any threat to London will be longer-term.

Tokyo

Tokyo's international trade flows and resultant balance of payments surplus make it potentially a major player in international finance. We have already seen this in the 1990s, when Japan made 'samurai bonds' widely available to international borrowers as a way to recycle its trade surpluses. Japanese banks became very large (and continue to dominate world rankings due to steady consolidation after significant banking losses when the 1990s stockmarket and property bubble burst). They are, however, very tightly controlled by Ministry of Finance and Bank of Japan in their cross-border activities and cannot be said to have a free hand in creating international business. Nor are they renowned for innovation in the financial sphere. Anecdotal evidence points to cautious and traditional management in the Japanese commercial banks and emphasis on the domestic market; the two banks always seen as innovative and internationally orientated: Bank of Tokyo especially and Industrial Bank of Japan, no longer exist. An attempt was made in the 1980s to establish an offshore market in Tokyo, but this has not been as successful as its rivals in Hong Kong and Singapore. Only a modest step has been made towards the internationalisation of the yen. That would foster more use by international borrowers and investors of Tokyo, which in 2002 accounted for only 2.1% of total world exports of finance and insurance services. Great size does not make an international centre, if the authorities refuse to relax their grip and the domestic banks are looking inwards into their huge, recently long-troubled economy.

New York/Chicago
The American financial market is the largest in the world. Its wholesale finance activity had an output of 244 billion euros in 2005, out of a world total of 630 billion euros. But it is overwhelmingly domestic. The US accounts for 39% of world wholesale financial services; it has pulled ahead of the EU, which accounts for 28%, due to its larger, better integrated services market and stronger economic growth. But in terms of their shares of total world exports of finance and insurance services, the US holds 17.5% and the UK 23.7%. International financial activities in the US could easily change and grow: US regulatory bodies are supportive of American financial firms and certain markets, the New York Stock Exchange and the Chicago Mercantile Exchange (CME) for example, are already world-class players. An indication of sharper US competition in international financial markets was the announcement on 18

October 2006 that the CME and the Chicago Board of Trade were to merge, creating what they say will be the most extensive and diverse global exchange traded derivatives market.

The burden of regulation and reporting in the US, partly related to the Sarbanes-Oxley Act is often mentioned. Yet it can also be argued that America's high regulatory standards are a reason for the strength of its financial system. Foreign banks are very carefully scrutinised before being allowed to open; Russian banks have not been permitted there, unlike in London. A bigger issue may be the massive investment American banks have made in buildings, trading floors and staff in London. Should the US wish to create a larger international financial centre based on New York and/or Chicago, little would keep it from succeeding, but the initiative would have to come from the private sector; no significant government policy in that direction would be forthcoming. No-one promotes New York as the Corporation of London does for the City.

The Growth of the Euro

It was feared that when the Euro was created, and the European Bank placed in Frankfurt, that both developments would threaten the City of London. Britain does not participate in the euro.[4] But London is the leading centre for dollar business of all kinds, despite being a Sterling-based centre. Where a currency is used, or regulated, has little to do with where it is internationally traded.[5] 64% of all euro-zone foreign exchange trading is done in London. Four years after the euro was introduced, London-based banks handled mote than half of euro-denominated eurobond issuance and two thirds of secondary market trading. Longer-term, London will need to protect its role in euro-denominated issues and trading, and could be affected if a single financial regulator for Europe is created and the UK is still not in the EMU.

Deterioration of its own Advantages

What if London's own comparative advantages deteriorated? How might this happen? One of its greatest strengths is the favourable business climate and flexible regulation. These have flourished under a longstanding Labour government, and it is unlikely that a Tory regime would be less business-friendly or foster more restrictive, and costly regulation. The Liberal Democrat Party is also unlikely to change the overall climate, in the event that it gained power or was a factor in a coalition government.

One clear sign of the continued innovative and flexible regulatory system in the UK is the emphasis of the Financial Services Authority's (FSA) on ethical behaviour. In the area of business behaviour, the FSA attempts to determine the ethical principles of each company it regulates, and bases its scrutiny in a more benign, collaborative way if a regulated firm is demonstrably ethical.

Could London's skills base diminish? It's hard again to see how. Well paid, intellectually simulated, working in the heart of the world's markets, moderately taxed (and tax protected anyway if expatriates), its wholesale financial executives and traders have little reason to leave voluntarily. To paraphrase Dr Johnson, 'to tire of being a City banker is to tire of life'. For their employers to move them abroad in any volume would pre-suppose bigger and better opportunities elsewhere. These opportunities couldn't be purely domestic, since international skills are less fungible and transferable.

The section above concluded that no other financial centre would eclipse London in the near future, thus possibly drawing away its skill base. Some of the other advantages: its position between Asia and America, use of English overall and in contracts, won't change. The sister markets of Lloyds and other insurers, metals and commodities, are going to stay in London for the same reasons of efficiency, proximity, and market knowledge. And if all these markets stay, the ancillary advisers in law, accounting and the like will remain just as available.

Electronic Trading
Here there is a theoretical threat to London, indeed all physical centres, since if financial market personnel really can do their

job from a screen anywhere, there is little need to be in expensive city centres. Electronic systems mean that international financial transactions are instantaneous and can be undertaken from any location at infinitesimal cost. I remember our head foreign exchange trader in JP Morgan Tokyo, who did most of his trading, and created most of his profits, late at night from home. (We joked that he was in bed in his pyjamas at the time, and perhaps he was.) He rode the yen up, and the dollar down very successfully, alone. But one night he was badly caught out by the Plaza Hotel agreement, which bolstered the dollar, and lost much of the gains his one-way trading had brought. In a dealing room, with all the data and sense of market movements flowing from colleagues, friends in the market by telephone, or over lunch, or from the other electronic screens throughout the room, the amount of current information is vast; his losses wouldn't have happened if he had traded from our office.

I doubt that electronic trading, which in the case of foreign exchange has risen from 40% to 44% of the market in 2005, will diminish London's position much. Much of London's business is not trading per se, but advisory: pension fund management, bond and equity underwriting, merger and acquisition advice for example. None of these can be done from afar; all need the proximity of market participants and advisers. An interesting study by Richard O'Brien in 1992 concluded that eventually financial personnel could be dispersed to any location because screens would be enough for all kinds of markets.[6] He hasn't been proven right, nor is he likely to be. There is something indefinable about the importance of human interaction in a market like London, which passes on information and thus facilitates deals in the market, which can never be substituted for by electronics. Much qualitative information cannot be exchanged efficiently by electronic means, which are fine for data publication and straightforward dealing. But in the advisory areas of underwriting, mergers and acquisitions and the like, even body language and serendipity of face-to-face meetings are important Information received directly, not through the screen, is more trusted more confidential and more easily amplified.

Conclusion

I find no reason to believe that London will not maintain its position as the largest international financial centre for years to come. It is unlikely to lose the advantages which its great agglomeration of capital and skills has brought; indeed, such agglomerations tend to feed on themselves and grow further. This does not mean that Frankfurt will not develop in the same way, particularly as the 'domestic' centre for euro transactions. The largest financial market, the United States, could be much more important internationally, due to its size, efficiencies of scale and the continued world role of the dollar. Yet its main institutions have until now focused on building massive presences in London and it is difficult to foresee the repatriation of people and capital back to America which would bring this about in a way which would soon endanger the City of London.

Would we choose London again, twenty years later, to build Nomura Bank International? Certainly. And would we do that in 2017? All the indications say yes.

Notes

Most of the statistics come from *The Importance of Wholesale Financial Services to the EU Economy*, Centre for Economics and Business Research 2006; and the Corporation of London, and are not otherwise footnoted.

1   The Glass-Steagall Act 1933, was introduced in the US to cope with economic problems following the 1929 Wall Street crash and effectively kept banks out of the stockmarket. The 1999 the Gramm-Leach-Bliley Act, repealed Glass-Steagall.
2   Reported in *Financial Times*, 10/10/06.
3   Cited in *Financial News* Online, 2/5/05
4   Wisely in my opinion since the euro was created for political reasons and the European Monetary Union cannot meet the requirements of the disparate countries which use it.
5   *The Location of Financial Activity and the Euro*, HM Treasury 2003.
6   O'Brien, R. 1992, *Global financial Integration: The End of Geography*, Pinter Publishers.

Further Reading

Beaverstock, J. et al "Demystifying the Euro in European Financial Centre Relations: London and Frankfurt 2000-2001", *Journal of Contemporary European Studies*, August, 2005,

Butcher, S. "Tax climate gives London winning edge", *Financial News*, May, 2005.

Cassis, Y, 2006, *Capitals of Capital: A History of International Financial Centres, 1780-2005*. Cambridge University Press

Castells, M, 2000, *The Rise of the Network Society*, Blackwell.

CEBR: *The Importance of Wholesale Financial Services to the EU Economy 2006*. City of London, 2006.

Franke, D, "International financial centres: rivals or partner?" *die bank*, April, 2006.

O'Brien, R. 1992, *Global financial Integration: The End of Geography*, Pinter Publishers.

Schmidt, R and Grote, M, "Was ist und was braucht ein bedeutender Finanzplatz?" *Goethe University Frankfurt Working Paper Series in Finance and Accounting*, April 2005.

The Location of Financial Activity and the Euro, HM Treasury 2003.